The Princeton Review.

GED Basics

By the Staff of The Princeton Review

PrincetonReview.com

Random House, Inc. New York

The Princeton Review, Inc.
111 Speen Street, Suite 550
Framingham, MA 01701
E-mail: editorialsupport@review.com

ISBN: 978-0-375-42836-4

Editor: Calvin Cato
Production Editor: Michael Breslosky
Production Coordinator: Deborah A. Silvestrini

Manufactured in the United States of America on partially recycled paper.

10 9 8 7 6 5 4 3 2 1

Editorial

Robert Franek, Senior VP, Publisher
Laura Braswell, Senior Editor
Selena Coppock, Senior Editor
Calvin Cato, Editor
Meave Shelton, Editor

Production

Michael Pavese, Publishing Director
Kathy Carter, Project Editor
Michelle Krapf, Editor
Michael Mazzei, Editor
Michael Breslosky, Associate Editor
Stephanie Tantum, Associate Editor
Kristen Harding, Associate Editor
Vince Bonavoglia, Artist
Danielle Joyce, Graphic Designer

Random House Publishing Group

Tom Russell, Publisher
Nicole Benhabib, Publishing Director
Ellen L. Reed, Production Manager
Alison Stoltzfus, Managing Editor

Acknowledgments

The Princeton Review would like to thank Josh Nagel, Wendy Rosen,
Tom Steffen, Laura Braswell, and Heather Brady for their hard work
and contributions to this title.

Contents

Part I
Orientation

Chapter 1
Introduction

WHAT IS THE GED?

The General Educational Development test (GED) is actually five small subject tests that you can take in one day or over a series of days. Many people call the GED the high school equivalency test because when you pass the test, you earn a certificate that most colleges and employers recognize as equal to a high school diploma. With the exception of one short essay section, the test consists of only multiple-choice questions.

The GED is administered by the American Council on Education (ACE), a nonprofit company based in Washington, D.C. The ACE is a council representing the presidents and chancellors of degree-granting institutions. You can find out more information about the ACE at www.acenet.edu.

The GED was created in 1942 at the latter end of World War II. The United States Armed Forces requested the development of an exam to test the high-school academic skills of their personnel. Since then, the test takers have expanded to include a wide range of people. About 800,000 people take the GED each year, and nearly two-thirds qualify for a certificate. You can find more information about the GED and its history at www.gedtest.org. There are many reasons why people take the GED. Some test takers are homeschooled, while others take the test because of a career choice that doesn't allow for a traditional high school schedule. Either way, there is no shame in taking the GED. The GED equivalency certificate is invaluable in helping you achieve your goals.

Many people have taken the GED and gone on to have successful careers. Some famous GED test takers include:

Christopher Blizzard, Open Source Developer
Augusten Burroughs, Author
Ben Nighthorse Campbell, Senator
Michael Chang, Athlete/Professional Tennis Player
Bill Cosby, Actor/Comedian
Michael J. Fox, Actor
Jim Florio, Governor
Oscar de la Hoya, Athlete/Boxer
D. L. Hughley, Actor/Comedian
T. D. Jakes, Bishop of The Potter's House
Avril Lavigne, Singer/Songwriter
Fran Lebowitz, Author
Katharine McPhee, Singer/Songwriter
Ruth Ann Miner, Governor
Chris Rock, Actor/Comedian
Michelle Rodriguez, Actress
Jessica Simpson, Singer/Actress
Dave Thomas, Founder of Wendy's Restaurant
Mark Wahlberg, Actor

STRUCTURE OF THE GED

The GED is made up of five tests: Language Arts: Writing, Social Studies, Science, Language Arts: Reading, and Mathematics. Here is the overall breakdown of each test.

Language Arts: Writing

Part One: 50 Multiple-Choice Questions, 75 Minutes

Each question will consist of a sentence. Many of the sentences will have something wrong with them, and you must select the answer choice that fixes the sentence. You'll be expected to spot mistakes in:

Sentence Structure (use of clauses and phrases)	30%
Usage (grammar)	30%
Mechanics (spelling, punctuation, and capitalization)	25%
Organization	15%

Part Two: One Essay, 45 Minutes

For this section, you will be asked to write an essay about a particular topic such as "Cheaters never prosper. Do you agree or disagree?" The stance that you choose doesn't matter; your score is based on how well you express your opinion. Your essay should be well-organized, focused, and have good usage of grammar and sentence structure.

Social Studies

This exam contains a mix of short passages followed by a single question, and longer passages followed by three or four questions. Sixty percent of the questions will be based on graphic materials (that is—charts, diagrams, graphs, and cartoons). The good news is that no outside knowledge is tested; the answers to each question can be found in the passage or graphic provided. The following areas of social studies will be tested:

National History	25%
Government and Civics	25%
World History	15%
Economics	20%
Geography	15%

Science

The Science exam consists of a mixture of short passages followed by a single question, and longer passages followed by three or four questions. In many ways, this exam is similar to the Social Studies exam. Roughly fifty percent of the questions will be based on charts and graphic materials. You only need a general knowledge of principles. The answers to each question can be found somewhere in the passage or diagram provided. The questions address the following areas of science:

Life Science	45%
Physics and Chemistry	35%
Earth and Space	20%

Language Arts: Reading

For this section, you will be given a total of seven passages with accompanying questions. Three of the passages will be fictional passages from different time periods. You will also see one excerpt from a play, one poem, and two of the following passages: a review of a performance, an article about popular culture, or a business-related topic. After each one, you will be asked three to five questions designed to test your reading skills and your ability to analyze and apply what you've just read. The passages will be divided into the following sections:

Literary (fiction, play, poem)	80%
Nonfiction (review, workplace document, popular culture)	20%

Mathematics

Two Parts, 25 Questions Each

The Math exam consists of two parts, with emphasis placed on arithmetic problems that are similar to those you may have to do in your daily routine at home or at work. You will be allowed to use a calculator in the first part of the exam and not for the second part. About half of the questions will be based on diagrams or charts. Many of the questions will be multiple choice, but roughly ten questions will be short answer. The following areas of math will be assessed:

Number Operations/Number Sense	20%–30%
Measurement/Geometry	20%–30%
Data Analysis/Probability/Statistics	20%–30%
Algebra/Functions/Patterns	20%–30%

DO YOU HAVE TO TAKE THE TEST ALL AT ONCE?

The rules on this vary from state to state. Some states require you to take the entire set of tests in one day, while others are more flexible. To find out more information about the rules in your state, please refer to the web address on page 8.

MAKING THE GRADE

Each of the five GED tests is scored from 200 to 800. The Writing test is scored on a scale from 1 to 4. In order to pass the GED, you must get a score of at least 410 on each of the five tests, with an average score of 450. In layman's terms, you need to answer roughly half of the questions on each of the five tests correctly.

If you happen to fail one of the sections, there's no need to despair. You only need to take the sections that you didn't pass. So for example, if you passed the Language Arts, Writing, and Social Studies sections and didn't pass the Science and Math sections, you only have to take the Science and Math sections. Keep in mind that only your best overall scores are kept, so depending on your focus, you may want to retake the entire test again. Of course, when you retake the test, you will be given a different version of the test with different questions.

DO I NEED A PERFECT SCORE?

Keep in mind that you don't have to achieve a perfect score. However, there are a few states and colleges that award scholarships for people with very high GED scores. In general, there is no large incentive to get more than a passing grade, but you should strive to attain the best score possible.

IS THE GED TOUGH?

Well, yes and no. On the one hand, the GED is condensing years of high school learning in a seven and a half hour long test. And on average, 30 percent of all GED test takers do not receive a passing score. But at the same time, the GED is very standardized in what it tests—which makes it easier for you to predict what will be tested and study only what is necessary. Also, since the test itself can be completed in a day, there's no need to worry about your score being based on homework assignments and pop quizzes.

HOW DO I REGISTER FOR THE GED?

For information on how to register to take the GED test, call 800-62 MY GED (800-626-9433). If you want to contact the individual state programs directly, go online to www2.acenet.edu/resources/ged/center_locator.cfm

HOW IS THIS BOOK STRUCTURED?

In the chapters that follow, you will receive detailed overviews of all of the topics covered in the five subject tests. The Reading Comprehension and Writing chapters will give you an in-depth topic review of grammar, text analysis, and sentence structure. The Math, Science, and Social Studies sections will give you a strong foundation in those subjects. At the end of each chapter is a set of practice questions to help you apply the knowledge and skills that you gained. These questions are very similar to the questions that you will find on a real GED exam.

We are not going to go over anything except the most basic of test-taking strategies; this book is geared more toward refreshing your memory on the basics of your high school knowledge. When you think you are ready to take the GED itself, we highly recommend that you take a couple of practice tests under ideal testing conditions so you can get a feel of what the actual exam will be like. For full-length practice tests, please check out *5 GED Practice Tests* as well as our latest version of the *Cracking the GED* book. The tests in both books contain detailed answers and explanations to help you understand and avoid making the same mistakes on the real GED. Also, the ACE (the company that writes the GED) releases several half-length practice tests for you to take. We highly recommend that you try to obtain one. You can order official GED practice tests by calling 800-531-5015 or by checking out www.acenet.edu.

WHAT DO I NEED FOR THE EXAM?

Well, besides these strategies, you will need to bring your GED registration if you received it in the mail. If you didn't get it, don't worry. Call your local GED office (using the same phone number you called to get a registration packet) to make sure that you are scheduled to take the test. Below is a list of other items you need to bring:

- Several No. 2 pencils
- A blue or black ballpoint pen
- Two pieces of identification (a driver's license, social security card, birth certificate, green card, or passport are acceptable)

MORE TIPS FOR THE DAY OF THE TEST

A couple more tips: Be sure to dress comfortably. You are going to be sitting at a desk for several hours, and you don't want to be distracted by being too warm, too cold, or too itchy. If you don't have two pieces of identification, be sure to talk to your local examiner before the actual test date.

Try to have a solid meal (breakfast or lunch, depending on the time of day you are taking the exam), and be sure to bring a snack with you. As we mentioned before, the test is several hours, and you run the risk of "hitting the wall" and crashing if your blood sugar drops. Also, most examiners give breaks in between the sections of the test, so be sure to use that downtime wisely. Feel free to use the bathroom if you need to or walk around to get your circulation moving.

WHAT IS THE PRINCETON REVIEW?

The Princeton Review is a test-preparation company that has spent more than 20 years helping students achieve higher scores on standardized tests. We offer test-preparation courses in more than 500 locations in 12 different countries, as well as online. We also publish over 200 books ranging from test-preparation guides like the one you have in your hand, to books on getting into college, applying for financial aid, and getting on the right career track.

Our phenomenal success improving students' scores on standardized tests is due to a simple, innovative, and radically effective philosophy: Study the test, not what the test claims to test. This approach has led to the development of techniques for taking standardized tests based on the principles the test writers themselves use to write the tests.

The Princeton Review has found that its methods work not just for cracking the GED, but for any standardized test. We've already successfully applied our system to the GMAT, LSAT, MCAT, and GRE, to name just a few. Although in some ways the GED is a very different test from those mentioned above, in the end a standardized test is a standardized test. This book uses our time-tested principle: Crack the system based on how the test is written.

You are about to unlock a vast collection of powerful strategies that have one and only one purpose: to help you pass the GED exam. Our techniques work. We developed them after spending countless hours scrutinizing real tests. Our methods have been widely imitated, but no one else can achieve our rates of success. Read this book to find out how our techniques can help you crack the GED exam.

Chapter 2
General
Strategies

Although this book's focus is to give you the basics, we also want you to be familiar with the general strategies you need to ace the GED.

GUESSING

Pop quiz: Do you know how many points you can lose if leave an answer blank? The answer is zero! You read earlier in the book that the GED consists mainly of multiple-choice questions with five answer choices. Keep in mind that if you guess on these questions, you have a one-in-five chance of getting it right, and you are not penalized for making an incorrect answer. With odds like these, it would be silly not to guess on the exam.

Look at it this way: There are 230 multiple-choice questions on the GED (we're not counting the ten math short-answer problems or the essay). Let's say you are sleep-deprived and simply want to get the test over with so you pick answer choice (1) 230 times. Do you know how many answers you'd get right?—about 46. Crazy, right? Of course that's not the best strategy, but because there is no penalty, there's no harm in guessing if you aren't completely sure. So remember to answer every single question on the exam, even if you can't eliminate any of the answer choices.

PROCESS OF ELIMINATION

Let's take a look at the following question:

1. What is the capital of the United States of America?

   (1) Albany
   (2) Washington D.C.
   (3) 79
   (4) Dogs
   (5) Heat

Even if you aren't sure of the answer, you can safely eliminate three of the answer choices. Choice (3) isn't even a word; it's a number! In addition, choices (4) and (5) aren't the names of locations, so you can get rid of those as well. Now, you're left with two answer choices. Look at that: You increased your odds from one in five to one in two. That's a fifty-fifty chance of getting the question right. In case you're wondering, the correct answer is (2).

Process of Elimination (or POE) is a powerful tool that will help you make your guesses count. Wrong answers are easier to spot than correct answers for a variety of reasons. Sometimes the answers sound weird; other times, the answers don't make any sense. In very rare cases you can eliminate all the incorrect answer choices, but you can typically rule out at least two or three of the answers using this method. Let's look at another example:

---

2. Which of the following is an example of an animal?

(1) Tree
(2) Wing
(3) Grass
(4) Horse
(5) Glass

Using POE, you can safely eliminate (5), which isn't even an example of a living thing, much less an animal. Subsequently, you can also cross out (1) and (3), which are plants and not animals. (2) may throw you off, but keep in mind that a wing is only a part of an animal and not the full animal. The correct answer here is (4).

LETTING IT GO

Keep in mind that at the end of the day, all the multiple-choice questions are worth only one point. Since very hard questions are worth the same as easy questions, you don't want to get hung up on a question and derail your pacing. If you are ever stuck on a question, put a small mark on your answer sheet and move on. If absolute worse comes to worse, you can come back to that question when you are close to the end of your time and simply fill in an answer.

A WORD ON CALCULATORS

For the first math section of the exam, you are allowed to use a calculator, but there is a catch. You have to use the calculator provided by the GED Chief Examiner (fancy title, huh). The calculator they provide is the Casio FX-260, pictured below:

It is *very important* that you familiarize yourself with the Casio FX-260, since all calculators take some time to get used to and you don't want to be fumbling around while you are taking the exam. Normally, the examiner will show you a video about the calculator before the test begins, but you still don't want to take any chances. You can purchase the Casio FX-260 in a wide variety of stores; you can also buy it from ACE for less than ten dollars. Just call 1-800-531-5015.

THE WEIRDNESS OF CALCULATORS

The Casio FX-260 has three functions that can be pretty confusing. The first feature involves how to enter negative numbers (and if you aren't sure what negative numbers are, don't get nervous—we'll cover this in the Arithmetic chapter). To enter a negative number, you first have to enter the number, and then hit the "change sign" key located directly above the "7" key. The display now shows the negative number.

The second confusing feature involves parentheses (once again, don't get scared if you aren't sure about how parentheses work in math—we'll discuss this in the Arithmetic chapter). Parentheses in math usually mean an implied multiplication that you can't actually see on the page. You must remember to multiply to get the right answer. Here's an example: To enter the expression "9(8 + 4)," you would enter 9, then the multiplication key, then the left parentheses key, then 8, then the plus key, then the 4 key, then the right parentheses key. To complete the problem, press the equals key.

The last confusing feature involves square roots (we'll cover that topic too, in a later chapter). There is no dedicated square root key; instead it appears in a smaller font above the "x^2" key. So in order to find the square root of 4 (for example), first press 4, then press the shift key (located at the top left of the calculator), then press the "x^2" key. This will access the second function of the key and give you the square root (in this case 2). Keep in mind that you must press the shift key before the "x^2" key; if you did not press the shift key using 4 as an example, you would have simply squared the number (which would give you 16).

A NOTE ABOUT SCRATCH PAPER

Another part of the GED that may throw you off is that you are not allowed to write in the test booklets. On many other standardized paper-based tests, you are allowed to make marks in the book, by circling key items in the reading passages and making notes on diagrams. This isn't the case for this exam. This may sound a little silly, but using scratch paper can take a little bit of practice. Our recommendation is that you put your scratch paper directly beneath the problem you're working on to minimize distance. Also, label your work with the problem number so you don't confuse which calculations belong to which question you are currently working on.

DON'T CHEAT

This sounds like a glaringly obvious no-no, but it is worth noting. The old saying "Cheaters never prosper" is completely true here. ACE uses sophisticated methods to find out if anyone has cheated, and some testing companies use computers that will compare the answers of people who take the test in the same room. So please be sure to not let anyone copy your answers, and keep your eyes on your own paper. Besides, you want to feel like you've earned your passing grade, right?

HOW TO READ GRAPHICS

You will notice that the Math, Science, and Social Studies tests have questions that use graphics like charts, maps, coordinate line graphs, and bar and pie graphs. These graphs may seem scary or daunting but there are a couple of key factors that will help you to crack these questions. Let's take a look at a couple of examples.

BAR GRAPH

Take a look at the graph below:

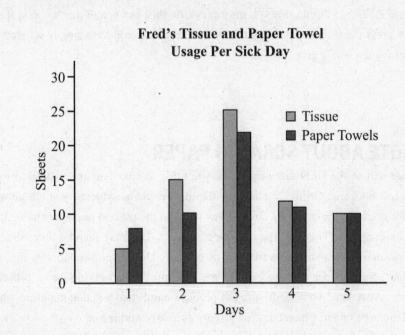

**Fred's Tissue and Paper Towel
Usage Per Sick Day**

Now it may be tempting to jump right into the graphic, but the first thing you should do is to read the title itself. Often the title will give you the information you need to interpret the graphic and let you know what you're looking at. This graph tells you the number of tissues and paper towels that Fred uses during a period of being sick for five days (that's a rough cold by the way).

Next, we look at the horizontal and vertical axes. The vertical axis (which runs up and down) lets us know the number of sheets of tissues and paper towels used. The horizontal axis (which runs along the bottom of the graph) tells us on which day the sheets were used. Now let's look at the question below.

1. Which day of the week did Fred use the least amount of tissues?

   (1) Day 1
   (2) Day 2
   (3) Day 3
   (4) Day 4
   (5) Day 5

This kind of question is called a comprehension question, because it asks you to locate the information on the graph. In this case, you are being asked which day Fred used the most tissues. Look at the graph and see which of the bars is the longest; be careful to ignore the bars that indicate paper towel usage. In this case, the answer is (1) Day 1.

Now let's look at the next question.

2. How many total sheets of tissues and paper towels did Fred use on Day 4?

   (1) 12
   (2) 20
   (3) 23
   (4) 25
   (5) 35

This question is an example of an application question. For questions like these, you are expected to use the information the graph provides in addition to your math skills to find the correct answer. In this case, you'll have to add the number of sheets used on Day 4. Since Fred used 12 tissues and 11 paper towels, we add these numbers together and get 23, or choice (3).

Let's move on to the next question.

3. According to the graph above, which day has the greatest difference between the number of tissues used compared to the number of paper towels used?

   (1) Day 1
   (2) Day 2
   (3) Day 3
   (4) Day 4
   (5) Day 5

This question is known as an analysis question, because you are expected to analyze the information in the graph and use it to solve the problem. For this instance, we can look at each day and count the difference between the number of tissues used versus the number of paper towels used. Day 1 had a difference of two sheets, Day 2 had a difference of five sheets, Day 3 had a difference of three sheets, Day 4 had a one sheet difference, and on Day 5 there was no difference in sheets. The correct answer is (2).

Now let's look at question 4.

4. Which of the statements below could best be supported by the graph?

(1) Fred contracted a rare form of strep throat.
(2) Fred used the most sheets of tissues and paper towels on Day 5.
(3) Fred uses more paper towels than tissues.
(4) Illness takes a toll on the human body.
(5) The largest difference between paper towel and tissue usage was on Day 2.

Finally this kind of question is considered an evaluation question. Although these questions appear rarely on the GED, you should be aware of them because they can be a little tricky. You are expected to interpret the data and choose the statement that is the best fit to classify what you have read. Choices (1) and (4) may be true but the graph does not discuss this information, so you can cross these out. Choices (2) and (3) can be dismissed outright, since both statements contradict the information shown in the graph. Choice (3) is the best fit here.

CHART

Let's look at the chart below:

Hair Color	Number of Hairs on Average at Age 40 (in Thousands)	Number of Hairs Lost Per Year (in Thousands)
Blondes	200	4
Brunettes	350	1
Redheads	90	1
Purpleheads	140	0

As with graphs, the first thing that you want to pay attention to when reading a chart is the title. This chart compares the numbers of hairs on a person's head by color. The color categories are blondes, brunettes, redheads, and purpleheads. Although the existence of purpleheads may rattle you, ignore any odd implications and keep interpreting the rest of the information you see on the chart. The first column tells you the number of hairs on average that people at age 40 have, and the second column tells you the number of hairs on average that blondes, brunettes, redheads, and purpleheads lose per year.

1. According to this chart, what is the average number (in thousands) of hairs that a blonde will have at age 45?

   (1) 140
   (2) 180
   (3) 190
   (4) 196
   (5) 200

For this application question, you're going to have to do some slightly complicated math. First, take a look at the chart. You'll see that at age 40, blondes start with 200,000 hairs. Since the answer is going to be in thousands, let's simplify this to 200. Next, we know that blondes lose four thousand hairs per year (again, we'll simplify this number to 4). Since we know that 45 is five years away from 40, we have to multiply 4 by 5, which gives us 20. Finally, we subtract: 200 − 20 = 180. The correct answer is (2).

2.   Which of the statements is best supported by the information in the chart above?

(1)   Brunettes and redheads share similar genes
(2)   Redheads and purpleheads collectively have more hair at age 40 than brunettes
(3)   Blondes have more fun
(4)   Purpleheads are the least in danger of going bald
(5)   Redheads will most likely go bald by age 50

This is another example of an evaluation question. By looking at the chart, you can see that purpleheads do not lose any hair per year. Thus, it is safe to assume that purpleheads are the least in danger of going bald. Choices (2) and (5) go against the data in the graph, choice (1) is not supported by any evidence in the chart itself, and choice (3) is a well-known catchphrase that has nothing to do with the question at hand. Choice (4) is the best answer.

PIE CHARTS

The most important thing to know about the pie chart is that all the pieces of the pie added together equals 100 percent (if the pie is divided into percentages) or one (if the pie is divided into fractions). Because of this, if you are ever missing information about one piece of the pie, you can figure it out by adding the other pieces together and subtracting that total from 100 (or 1 if the pie is split into fractions). Let's take a look at the pie chart on the following page:

Most Entertaining People

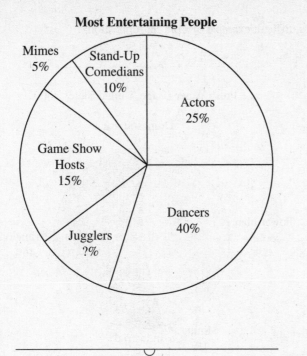

1. What percentage of the pie chart consists of jugglers?

   (1)   1%
   (2)   5%
   (3)   10%
   (4)   20%
   (5)   25%

As we said in the paragraph above, we simply add up the percentages of the other pieces of the pie and subtract them from 100: 100 − 95 = 5. Thus, choice (2) is the best answer. This is an example of a measurement, or number operations, question.

Here's a more difficult example of a pie chart question:

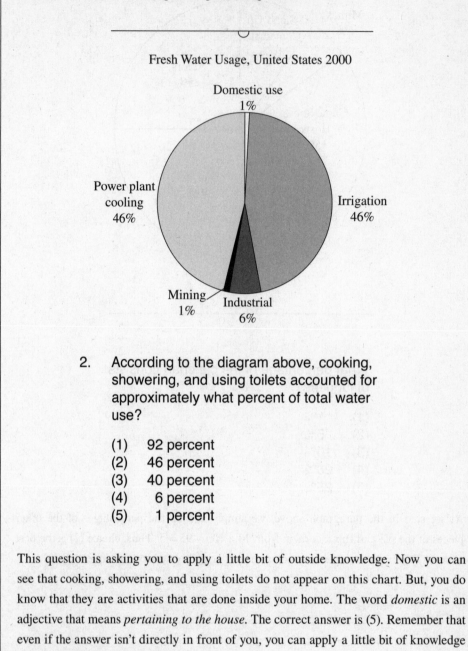

Fresh Water Usage, United States 2000

Domestic use
1%

Irrigation
46%

Industrial
6%

Mining
1%

Power plant
cooling
46%

2. According to the diagram above, cooking,
    showering, and using toilets accounted for
    approximately what percent of total water
    use?

    (1)   92 percent
    (2)   46 percent
    (3)   40 percent
    (4)   6 percent
    (5)   1 percent

This question is asking you to apply a little bit of outside knowledge. Now you can
see that cooking, showering, and using toilets do not appear on this chart. But, you do
know that they are activities that are done inside your home. The word *domestic* is an
adjective that means *pertaining to the house*. The correct answer is (5). Remember that
even if the answer isn't directly in front of you, you can apply a little bit of knowledge
in other skill sets to help you solve a question.

MAPS

The maps that you'll find on the GED are pretty straightforward and better yet, you don't have to be a geography bee champion to understand them. You won't be expected to memorize the names of capital cities. The question below should help you get more comfortable with reading maps.

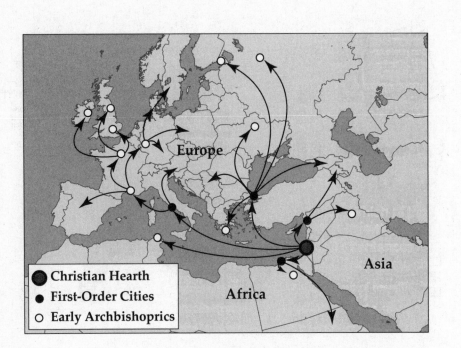

1. According to the map, in which continent did Christianity take the strongest hold?

    (1) Africa
    (2) Asia
    (3) Australia
    (4) Europe
    (5) South America

First of all, don't panic if you don't recognize what archbishoprics are (for the record, they are areas governed by an archbishop, who is a church authority figure) or what the Christian Hearth is. Your main focus is to observe the spread of Christianity through Europe, Asia, and Africa. For this question, you can use Process of Elimination right off the bat here. This map only has three continents labeled, so you can automatically get rid of choices (3) and (5). As you can tell from the map, a majority of arrows, first-order cities, and early archbishoprics are based in Europe. So your best answer is (4).

Let's take a look at another map, one that references a pre-Civil War United States. Don't be thrown off by the topic. The key here is to be able to analyze the data in front of you.

The United States After the Passing of the Kansas-Nebraska Act, 1854

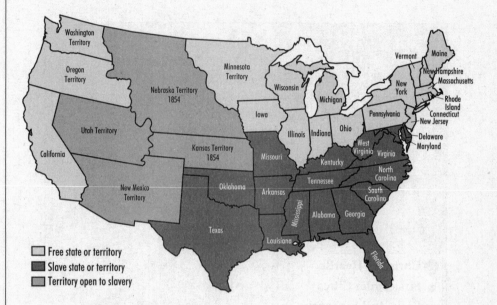

1. Which of the following states is the most northern of the free states?

(1) Iowa
(2) New Jersey
(3) Pennsylvania
(4) Connecticut
(5) Maine

This is a simple comprehension question. On all maps the most northern locations can be found lying closer to the top of the page, whereas southern locations are situated closer to the bottom. A glance at the map will tell you that the right answer here is choice (5), Maine.

2. According to the map, citizens from which of the following states would most likely disagree about the institution of slavery?

(1) New York and Vermont
(2) Georgia and South Carolina
(3) Iowa and Illinois
(4) Texas and Ohio
(5) Kentucky and Tennessee

Here is a trickier application question that asks you to use the shading key to find the correct answer. As you can see the map is divided in three categories: free states and territories; slave states; and territories that are open to slavery. In this case, the correct answer is going to have a state that is considered a free state and a state that is a slave state. Thus the correct answer here is (4).

3. A farmer who wants to move out West to start a new life but is very anti-slavery would move to which of the following territories?

(1) Kansas Territory
(2) Minnesota Territory
(3) New Mexico Territory
(4) Utah Territory
(5) Nebraska Territory

This is another example of an application question where you have to take a close look at what the question is asking. Surely if the farmer is very anti-slavery, he (or she) would not want to take the chance to move to a territory that is open to slavery. By looking at the map and seeing which shaded territories represent which political alliances, you can see that the only territory that the farmer would move to is the Minnesota Territory. Your best fit answer is (2).

INTERPRETING SOCIAL STUDIES AND SCIENCE PASSAGES

Later on in the book, we will discuss how to tackle standard reading passages, but we want to give you a quick brush-up on how to treat social studies and science-based passages in the book.

DOCUMENTS

Take a look at the following list of the United States Bill of Rights, the first ten amendments of the United States Constitution that granted numerous powers and protections to citizens of the U.S.

United States Bill of Rights

Amendment	Description
First	Freedom of speech, assembly, and the press; guarantees the right to petition
Second	Right to keep and bear firearms
Third	Protection from having to house soldiers
Fourth	Protection from illegal searches and seizures of personal property
Fifth	Protection against any abuse of government authority
Sixth	Right to a trial by a jury of one's peers and the right to access a lawyer
Seventh	Right to a civil trial by jury
Eighth	Protection against cruel and unusual punishment and high bails
Ninth	Guarantees every citizen rights that are not specifically spelled out in the Constitution
Tenth	Powers not granted to the federal government are reserved to the States or the people

1. Which of the following amendments allows for a trial by jury?

   (1) First and Second Amendments
   (2) Third and Sixth Amendments
   (3) Sixth and Seventh Amendments
   (4) Eighth and Ninth Amendments
   (5) Ninth and Tenth Amendments

This is a comprehension question, and you are being asked to identify which amendments discuss a trial by jury. The correct answer here is (3). Don't be fooled by (2); although the Sixth Amendment does mention a trial by jury, the Third Amendment does not.

---

2. Patricia prints a story in the *National Times Press* about the Doom Corporation headquarters being relocated to the Hall of Justice and the controversy surrounding the decision. In response, the Doom Corporation forces the *National Times Press* to fire her. Patricia and the *National Times Press* plan to file a lawsuit. In this lawsuit, which amendment could Patricia cite as being violated?

   (1) First Amendment
   (2) Second Amendment
   (3) Eighth Amendment
   (4) Ninth Amendment
   (5) Tenth Amendment

For this application question, you are expected to interpret the data that you read in the Bill of Rights and apply it to this particular case. Here you're first clue is that we are discussing the *National Times Press*. The use of the word *press* here should tip you off to the First Amendment, which guarantees freedom of the press. Thus, the correct answer is (1). And let's hope she wins the case against the ominous Doom Corporation.

Next is an example of a science article about sewage treatment plants. Be warned that these articles may not cover the most riveting of topics. Sometimes an article may be about lasers and other times the articles may be about the reproductive cycles of spiders (which could be cool if you're into studying bugs or icky if you have arachnophobia).

In the United States, sewage pipes deliver wastewater to a sewage treatment plant to be cleaned. The water is first filtered through screens (in what's called a physical treatment) to remove debris such as stones, sticks, rags, toys and other objects that were flushed down the toilet. The remaining water is passed into a settling tank, where suspended solids settle out as sludge. This treatment is known as primary treatment and it removes about 60 percent of suspended solids and 30 percent of organic waste.

After this, the wastewater undergoes a secondary treatment in order to continue to remove biodegradable waste and organic matter. This treatment can be done using trickling filters, in which bacteria digest waste as it seeps over bacteria-covered rock beds. At the end of secondary treatment, 97 percent of the suspended solids; 95–97 percent of the organic waste; 70 percent of the toxic metals, organic chemicals, and phosphates; 50 percent of the nitrogen; and 5 percent of the dissolved salts have been removed from the wastewater.

1. The goal of the second stage of a sewage treatment plant is to

    (1) remove the large solid material
    (2) aerate the water
    (3) make muddy water clear
    (4) remove DDTs from the water
    (5) lower the amount of organic material in the water

Uh-oh, science overload! Now you may not have entirely understood this article (and trust us, it may be a bit of a doozy), but the gist of what this article is telling you is the ways in which wastewater is cleaned. Moreover, it tells you that wastewater is cleaned via two treatment processes. If you look in the second paragraph, the article states that the secondary treatment removes biodegradable waste and organic matter. Furthermore, the end of the article says that 95 to 97 percent of the organic waste is removed after both the primary and the secondary treatment, compared to the mere 30 percent removed by primary treatment. The clear answer here is (5).

Now that we've covered the basics, take a look at the other sections of the book. We'll cover how to read poetry, drama, fiction, and non-fiction texts in the next chapter. In addition, you'll receive a condensed course in social studies, math, and the sciences.

Part II
GED Subject
Review

Chapter 3
Writing

INTRODUCTION

There are two parts to the Language Arts, Writing section on the GED. In Part I you will answer 25 multiple-choice questions, and in Part II you will write an essay based on a question, or prompt. We'll talk about Part II more later.

The 25 questions in Part I focus on your ability to revise, or correct, small reading passages. These passages are usually business-type letters or informational/how-to documents. In each of the 25 questions, you will be asked to improve part of the passage. It is like you are an editor, and you are being asked to fix errors and make the writing better.

Here are the four main categories of questions for Part I, as defined by ACE (the people who write the test):

- Organization—identifying topic sentences/main idea, dividing text into paragraphs, moving sentences around, combining and dividing paragraphs
- Sentence Structure—getting rid of sentence fragments, punctuating or separating run-on sentences
- Usage—using the right word for the meaning of the sentence; being able to pick the right word from words that sound alike but are spelled differently
- Mechanics—using the correct subject-verb agreement, pronoun, and verb tense

Part II consists of the essay, but many of the skills you need for Part I are helpful in writing a good, high-scoring essay. We'll highlight those skills as we review Part I.

What do each of these question types involve?

ORGANIZATION QUESTIONS

Organization questions on the GED generally ask about a passage or paragraph in general, focusing on the "flow" or the "effectiveness" of the passage or paragraph. A question is probably an organization question if it does NOT focus on a specific sentence or word in the passage.

The Topic Sentence

To best attack organization questions, you need to understand what a topic sentence is. The topic sentence introduces the **main idea** of a paragraph or passage. One of the most important concepts to understand on both Parts I and II of the Language Arts section is the main idea or **topic sentence**. You should be able to identify and write a topic sentence.

Every passage and every paragraph has a topic sentence. It is usually the first sentence because it introduces the rest of the paragraph. It is the one sentence that could be a "title" for the paragraph or passage. Every other sentence would fit under that title and support the main idea of the topic sentence.

On the GED, each paragraph will be referred to by a letter and each sentence in a paragraph will be numbered. Take a look at paragraph A below.

(A)

(1) In 2030 B.C., cucumber seeds were transported from India and planted in the Tigris Valley in the present-day Middle East. (2) It is here that we find the first documented evidence of cucumbers being preserved in a salty brine—"pickled"—and eaten in this form. (3) Pickles have been around for thousands of year, their uses ranging from consumption to health and beauty applications. (4) Aristotle spoke about the medicinal benefits of cured cucumbers (what we know as pickles). (5) Legend has it that Cleopatra attributed her extreme beauty at least in part to pickles, and Julius Caesar believed pickles enhanced vitality, and cucumbers even pop up in the Bible at least twice.

Which sentence could be a title that would describe all the other sentences, making it the topic sentence? Sentences 4 and 5 talk about specific uses of pickles, so these sentences aren't good candidates for the topic sentence.

Look at sentences 1, 2, and 3. Which is the most general of the sentences, and includes ideas from all the other sentences? Sentence 1 is only about transporting pickles, so that doesn't work as the topic sentence. Sentence 2 is about the proof that pickles were made. That doesn't cover the rest of the sentences. We have only sentence 3 left, which talks about how long pickles have been around and how many different uses they have. It is a perfect topic sentence.

Essay Skill

Being able to identify the topic sentence will help you in writing your own topic sentence later in Part II.

Essay Skill

All of the sentences in a paragraph should support the main idea.

How Will This Look on the GED?

A typical question about identifying a topic sentence may look like this:

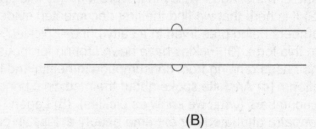

1. Which of the revisions below would most improve the organization of paragraph A?

   (1) move sentence 1 to the end of paragraph A
   (2) begin paragraph A with the new sentence, "Americans have long loved pickles."
   (3) move sentence 3 before sentence 2
   (4) move sentence 3 to the beginning of paragraph A
   (5) combine sentences 6 and 7

The best answer is (4); move sentence 3 to the beginning of the paragraph. Now the topic sentence is in the beginning of the paragraph, where it belongs.

(B)

(6) Christopher Columbus was growing cucumbers on the island of Haiti after he came to the New World. (7) Amerigo Vespucci made sure his ships were packed full of scurvy-preventing pickles. (8) Evidence of pickles and cucumbers in North America dates back several hundred years. (9) By 1820 America had its first pickle-producing plant, built by Nicholas Appert. (10) Americans have been enjoying pickles ever since.

2. Which revision would improve the flow of paragraph B?

   (1) delete sentence 10
   (2) put sentence 10 at the beginning of the paragraph
   (3) put sentence 8 at the beginning of the paragraph
   (4) change full in sentence 7 to fully
   (5) add Therefore to the beginning of sentence 10

Quick Note

Organization questions usually have words or phrases like "organization, improve the flow, improve the effectiveness, effective revision." The questions ask about a paragraph or the entire passage.

This question asks about "flow," so you know you are most likely dealing with organization. The flow of the paragraph refers to the logical progression. In other words, does the first sentence introduce the main idea (making it the topic sentence)? Do the rest of the sentences all support the main idea? That means the rest of the sentences give examples of what the topic sentence is talking about, or they further explain what the topic sentence is talking about or maybe they do both. Each sentence after the topic sentence should clearly relate to the topic sentence.

On the GED, paragraphs that flow correctly will have:

- A topic sentence first
- Supporting sentences following
- No unrelated sentences
- No sentences out of order

This question asks about flow, so you have to check each of the points above.

A quick scan of the answer choices tells you that there are two choices that move a sentence to the beginning of the paragraph. Since the topic sentence should be at the beginning of the paragraph, question 2 above might be about the topic sentence. Let's look at those two choices first.

Answer choice (2) suggests putting sentence 10 at the beginning of the paragraph. Sentence 10 ends with the phrase "ever since." Ever since when? Maybe it's a continuation of paragraph A. Let's see how that would read:

Here's the last sentence from paragraph A:

> (5) Legend has it that Cleopatra attributed her extreme beauty at least in part to pickles, and Julius Caesar believed pickles enhanced vitality, and cucumbers even pop up in the Bible at least twice.

Now sentence 10 from paragraph B:

> (10) Americans have been enjoying pickles ever since.

There is no mention of Americans anywhere in paragraph A, and the last sentence talks about people who are definitely not American enjoying pickles. It doesn't make sense to start the next paragraph with sentence 5.

What about choice (3), which puts sentence 8 at the beginning of the paragraph?

Let's see how the paragraph would look with sentence 8 at the beginning:

(8) Evidence of pickles and cucumbers in North America dates back several hundred years. (6) Christopher Columbus was growing cucumbers on the island of Haiti after he came to the New World. (7) Amerigo Vespucci made sure his ships were packed full of scurvy-preventing pickles. (9) By 1820 America had its first pickle-producing plant, built by Nicholas Appert. (10) Americans have been enjoying pickles ever since.

Sentence 8 says there is evidence that pickles have been in America for hundreds of years. Could this be a kind of title for the paragraph? Do the rest of the sentences in the paragraph support this title, or main idea? Yes, they do. Answer choice (3) is the best answer.

Take a quick look at the other answer choices, so you can see why choice (3) is the best answer. There is no reason to delete sentence 10, as answer choice (1) suggests. If we changed full to fully in sentence 7, it would read "ships were packed fully of scurvy-preventing pickles." "Fully of" is not correct, so answer (4) is not good. Adding Therefore to sentence 10 would imply that Americans enjoy pickles because people brought them over and make them. That's not correct. It's more likely that it's the other way around—people brought pickles to America because Americans like them. Answer choice (3) is the best answer.

Combining and Dividing Paragraphs

The GED will also ask you to make decisions about how to combine and divide paragraphs. Knowing how to find the topic sentence will also come in handy here.

Look at the passage below.

(A)

(1) On August 7, 1794, President George Washington sent a militia of thirteen thousand men to stop an uprising of angry farmers in western Pennsylvania. (2) The commander in charge was General "Light-Horse Harry" Lee. (3) Washington himself headed up the troops.

(B)

(4) The trouble had started in 1791, when the national government placed a heavy tax upon whiskey. (5) This tax effectively erased any profits Pennsylvania farmers could earn from their crops. (6) So farmers began to harass the tax collectors. (7) Their protests continued for the next three years, escalating into riots, barn burnings, attacks on government agents.

(C)

(8) There were wider implications of Washington's 1794 action against the farmers. (9) This was the first time the Militia Act of 1792 was put into practice. (10) The law had been passed in order to "execute the laws of the union, (and) suppress insurrections," and this gave the national government the right to use out-of-state troops to put an end to an uprising in another state.

(D)

(11) When Washington ordered the suppression of the disgruntled farmers, he was asserting the authority of the new federal government over the states. (12) It was a display of national power.

1. Which of the following revisions would improve the passage?

    (1) move paragraph D to the beginning of the passage
    (2) combine paragraphs A and B
    (3) combine paragraphs C and D
    (4) delete paragraph D
    (5) delete sentence 10

Essay Skill

The main idea of your essay should be introduced in the first paragraph.

If you see a question about improving the passage, it's likely to be about the organization of the passage. One of the first points to check for in a well-organized passage is that the main idea is introduced in the first paragraph.

The **main idea** of a passage is *what the passage is mostly about.* It's similar to the way a topic sentence introduces the main idea of a paragraph—the main idea of a passage would make a good title for the passage. The main idea should be introduced in the first or last few sentences of the first paragraph. The rest of the passage should give you more information or an explanation of the main idea.

The best way to find the main idea is to ask yourself "What is this passage about?" Try to answer the question in one sentence.

In this case, we can say: "This passage is about how the early United States government treated farmers who were angry about taxes."

When you see questions about moving paragraphs around to improve a passage, make sure you understand the main idea of the passage first.

Let's go through each answer choice for question 1.

Answer choice (1) suggests moving paragraph D to the beginning. This would make sense if the main idea of the passage were introduced in paragraph D. The main idea is what the government did about farmers who were protesting against taxes. In paragraph D, sentence 11 starts with "When Washington ordered the suppression of the disgruntled farmers," but we have no introduction to what is being discussed. When did this happen and why? That's explained in paragraphs A and B, so we'll leave paragraph D where it is.

Should we combine paragraphs A and B, as answer choice (2) suggests? Does paragraph B start a new idea? It does, so this paragraph can stand on its own; there is no reason to combine paragraphs A and B.

Should we combine paragraphs C and D, as answer choice (3) suggests? Paragraph C is about the wider implications (effects) of Washington's action. Paragraph D is still talking about an implication of what Washington did, so combining these two paragraphs is a good idea. Answer choice (3) may be the best answer.

Quickly review answer choices (4) and (5). There is no reason to delete paragraph D because it contains supporting sentences for the main idea of paragraph C, as we just found out. There is no reason to delete sentence 10 because it also supports the main idea of paragraph C.

The best answer is answer choice (3), combining paragraphs C and D.

---○---

Here is another organizational situation in which you have to decide whether or not to divide a passage.

---○---

(A)

(1) Most children these days don't see an eye doctor until they are of school age. (2) Well, it may surprise you to learn that eye doctors recommend that a child's first eye exam be at the age of six months old! (3) Eye-care health practices begun early in life can maximize eye-care health throughout a child's lifetime. (4) Dr. Yuri Yevnekov of the University of Dorchester Optometric Center explains: "Only when their child exhibits an obvious difficulty do parents normally take their children to the doctor. (5) But there are some not-so-evident eye problems that, when not caught and treated early on, can become bigger problems later on." (6) In addition to an early exam, eye specialists recommend a variety of activities and vision-strengthening toys to reinforce and improve healthy vision during the first year of your baby's life. (7) It is recommended that in the first 5 months babies have access to bright rattles and squeaky rubber toys. (8) A mobile in the baby's crib can help develop eye strength, too. (9) As the baby gets older you can add colorful toys in the bath and stuffed animals. (10) Toys that can be pulled apart and stacked also serve to facilitate eye development.

1. Which of the following revisions would most improve this passage?

   (1) move sentence 6 to the end of paragraph A
   (2) divide the paragraph after sentence 5
   (3) divide the paragraph after sentence 6
   (4) change a variety of in sentence 6 to many
   (5) no revision is necessary

This is a very long paragraph, so it may be a good idea to split it up. Notice, too, that two of the answer choices talk about dividing the paragraph, so it's a good idea to consider these choices first. When a question is about dividing or combining, focus on the topic sentence(s) or main idea of the passage. What is the main idea of the passage? It is that eye-care health should be started when a child is an infant. The first five sentences are all related to this idea.

However, in sentence 6, the paragraph starts to discuss activities and toys to promote eye health. Sentences 7 through 10 are all about the different activities and toys that can be used. Sentence 6 starts a new main idea and should be the start of a new paragraph. Answer choice (2) is the best answer.

Essay Skill

Make sure you start a new paragraph when you start a new idea.

Moving and Deleting Sentences

You may also be asked to rearrange sentences within a paragraph. For example, one sentence might be out of place in a paragraph because it introduces the topic, but it is not the first sentence. Take a look at the following paragraph.

(1) Americans tend to pour hot boiling water over tea leaves when brewing a cup of tea. (2) In contrast, the British are horrified by the idea of using boiling water. (3) They insist that the water be just approaching the boiling point because boiling water scalds the tea, giving it a sour flavor. (4) The British also say that the tea leaves should be immersed into the water better than pouring the water over the tea. (5) Most Americans actually prefer drinking coffee. (6) Though they speak the same language, Americans and the British have different ideas about how to brew a cup of tea.

1. Which revision would improve the flow of the passage above?

    (1) put sentence 5 after sentence 1
    (2) delete sentence 3
    (3) put sentence 6 before sentence 1
    (4) change scalds in sentence 5 to burns
    (5) add For example to the beginning of sentence 3

As always, for an organization question you should find the topic sentence first.

Is there one sentence here that summarizes the general idea of this paragraph? The paragraph talks all about the differences in the way the British and Americans make tea, so a good topic sentence will include something on both the British and Americans. Most of the sentences are about either the British way of making tea or the American way of making tea, so none of the first five sentences summarizes the whole paragraph.

Only sentence 6 talks about both Americans and the British. It explains what the rest of the paragraph talks about, so it's a good choice for a topic sentence. In this case, answer choice (3) suggests putting sentence 6 before sentence 1, and that looks like a good idea. This way there is a clear topic sentence that introduces what the paragraph will be about. The best answer is answer choice (3).

Here is another question for this passage:

––––––––––––––––––––––––––––––

2. What is the most effective way of organizing the paragraph above?

(1) delete sentence 1
(2) swap sentences 1 and 6
(3) put sentence 1 after sentence 5
(4) delete sentence 5
(5) the paragraph is the most effective the way it is now

A good place to start in answering this question is with answer (2) because it mentions sentence 6, which we've already determined to be the topic sentence. Would it make sense to swap sentences 1 and 6? No, because sentence 2 starts "In contrast," which is referring to the fact that Americans boil water for tea from sentence 1. If we moved sentence 1, sentence 2 would not be contrasting anything.

For the same reason, it wouldn't make sense to delete sentence 1, which is answer (1), nor would it make sense to put sentence 1 after sentence 5, which is answer (3).

Now we only have to consider answers (4) and (5). How about deleting sentence 5, as answer (4) suggests? The whole paragraph is about tea, how the Brits make tea, how the Americans make tea, and this sentence is about coffee. Would the flow of the paragraph be better if we deleted it? Yes, it would, because this sentence doesn't really belong here. When you are considering deleting a sentence, see if it falls under the general idea of the topic sentence. The topic sentence is all about tea, and sentence 5 is about coffee, so it's a good idea to get rid of it. The best answer is answer choice (4).

––––––––––––––––––––––––––––––

Essay Skill

Your first sentence is your topic sentence. It introduces a paragraph or states the main idea of the essay.

You may see a passage that is more informational or instructional. The same rules about flow and organization apply to this type of passage.

How to Use Your Fast-O-Matic Moisture Meter

(1) The Fast-O-Matic Moisture Meter is a great tool for you, the casual gardener, to determine how often and how much you need to water your houseplants. (2) It comes with a special ready-to-mount storage rack that you can easily hook over a wall or fence or attach to a wood surface. (3) Its dimensions are 12" × 9.5" by 2" and weighs no more than 3.2 pounds.

Testing for Moisture

Step 1—It comes ready to use and requires no batteries.

Step 2—Insert the probe into your flowerpot halfway between the plant and the edge of the pot, making sure to keep the probe upright. The deeper the pot, the deeper you should sink the probe into the soil.

Step 3—Take note of your meter reading, averaging between readings if necessary.

Step 4—As you insert the probe, the needle on the moisture meter may oscillate. This is because the soil is not uniformly moisturized. In order to avoid a false reading, probe the soil at least three times at different positions in the pot.

Step 5—Carefully remove the probe from the soil. Do not yank.

Step 6—DO NOT leave the probe in contact with moist soil for an extended period of time. It is designed for intermittent test readings.

1. What is the most effective way of
   organizing the information above?

   (1) no revision is necessary
   (2) move Step 1 up into the introductory
       paragraph
   (3) delete Step 1
   (4) delete Do not yank. in Step 5
   (5) move Step 3 to before Step 2

Don't select "no revision is necessary" (answer choice 1) until you've considered the other answer choices. Should we move Step 1 into the introductory paragraph, as answer choice (2) suggests? Well, is it introductory information or is it a step in testing for moisture? Let's look at Step 1 again:

Step 1—It comes ready to use and requires no batteries.

It doesn't really tell us to do anything, does it? This means it is introductory information and should be in the introductory paragraph with the other information about how much the moisture meter weighs and how big it is.

Let's consider the other answer choices just to be sure. We know we do not want to delete Step 1, so answer choice (3) isn't correct. There is no reason to delete Do not yank. It seems like helpful information to add to Step 5. It wouldn't make sense to move Step 3 before Step 2. You have to insert the probe before you take the reading. The best answer is (2).

———————○———————

Adding Sentences

Sometimes the GED asks you to get creative and add sentences to a passage. These types of questions are about finding sentences that support the main theme of the passage.

Let's take another look at the paragraph about British and American tea-drinking habits.

(1) Americans tend to pour hot boiling water over tea leaves when brewing a cup of tea. (2) In contrast, the British are horrified by the idea of using boiling water. (3) They insist that the water be just approaching the boiling point because boiling water scalds the tea, giving it a sour flavor. (4) The British also say that the tea leaves should be immersed into the water better than pouring the water over the tea. (5) Most Americans actually prefer drinking coffee. (6) Though they speak the same language, Americans and the British have different ideas about how to brew a cup of tea.

3. What would most likely be the first sentence of a paragraph that followed this one?

    (1) The British are also more particular about the appropriate time of day to drink tea.
    (2) The British drink tea with scones or sandwiches at teatime.
    (3) American coffee drinkers usually don't drink tea at all.
    (4) Boiling water for tea also has many health benefits of which most people are not aware.
    (5) According to a recent survey, Americans who drink coffee can drink as much as four or five cups a day.

Essay Skill

Make a logical transition from one point to the next.

For a question like this one that asks about continuing the passage or paragraph, you want to find something that carries forward the idea of the last sentence in the previous paragraph. Just as in conversation, in writing you don't just jump from one idea to another without some kind of continuity.

Since the passage talks about the tea-drinking habits of the British and Americans, the next paragraph should pick up on this idea. Which sentence says something about the way these two groups drink tea? Answers (3) and (5) are about coffee, so they are not good choices. Answer (4) goes back to a particular detail in the previous paragraph, so this would really belong in the first paragraph.

Answers (1) and (2) both talk about British tea-drinking habits. Since the first paragraph makes comparisons, answer (1) makes more sense because it still seems to be comparing. You can tell there is still a comparison being made because of the use of the words "more particular." Answer choice (1) is the best answer.

Consider this letter from a salesperson for Corporate Story Publications.

(A)

Dear Mr. Jiminez:

(1) It was a pleasure meeting you briefly at last week's Import/Export Americas event. (2) It's amazing how small the world does seem sometimes considering that we both earned our undergraduate degrees at Onondaga State. (3) I suppose we were destined to eventually meet face-to-face.

(4) I was fascinated by your synopsis of the history of South American Furnishing over the past 40 years. (5) Clearly, your company has a rich corporate heritage and tradition. (6) Your company has leaders with great foresight and imagination who keep South America Furnishing competitive as you continue to lead in the industry.

(7) As I was mentioning to you, Corporate Story Publications is a specialty publisher that focuses on corporate publications including annual reports, corporate profiles and corporate histories. (8) We have been in business for over 15 years and during that time have grown from a two-person start-up, to a serious corporate publisher with over 100 employees. (9) We have been contracted by over a dozen Fortune 500 companies to produce both annual and special occasion publications on their behalf.

1. Which of the following sentences would most likely follow sentence 9?

   (1) Your company would pay anywhere from $2,300 to $10,500 for our great annual reports and profiles.

   (2) I met a lot of other people who went to Onondaga at the event and some of them knew you, too.

   (3) South America Furnishing is obviously a cutting-edge company that needs someone to write its history and stuff.

   (4) I would like to set up a meeting with you and show you some of the corporate work we've done for companies similar to yours.

   (5) If you guys think you'd like to publish some corporate reports, I think that'd be a great idea for your company.

Answer choice (1) leaps ahead too quickly. The salesperson has not even proposed the idea of working for South American Furnishing; it wouldn't make logical sense to quote a price right away. Answer choice (2) goes back to the beginning of the letter and doesn't belong after sentence 9. This doesn't make the letter "move ahead" to the point, which is that the author wants to get Mr. Jiminez as a client. He's a salesman, remember. Answer choice (3) uses "and stuff," which is too casual for a business letter. Answer choice (4) is appropriate. Remember, the author of the letter is a salesperson so a logical next sentence would lead to meeting with a potential client again. Sentence (5) is too casual, using "you guys" and the contraction "that'd." Answer choice (4) is the best answer.

Here is another business document. Consider the flow of the paragraphs in the passage as you read.

(A)

(1) Abel's Records Management & Data Storage (Abel's) is a full-service, computerized records management company providing secure storage and indexing of paper records, digital media, and other business-critical information.

(B)

(2) Abel's personalized service includes retention schedules, data conversion and ORC, and records relocation. (3) Our customer's records are safe in our 30,000 square foot facility. (4) Our comprehensive security system features exterior and interior cameras for 24-hour monitoring of the premises. (5) We provide specially designed boxes and other supplies which make handling records easier.

(C)

(6) In today's business environment, quick and easy access to critical information gives our client companies a competitive advantage. (7) Client companies are able to provide exceptional customer service and cut order fulfillment time, sometimes by half.

1. Which of the following sentences would most likely follow sentence 6?

   (1) Karim Abel, owner of Abel's, has over twenty years of experience in the field.
   (2) Our medical records storage and indexing services are used nationwide by medical professionals and insurance companies.
   (3) Our state-of-the-art technology, unprecedented security and quick-response service help client companies increase response time while keeping costs under control.
   (4) Competitive advantage is indispensable in today's cutthroat world.
   (5) Abel's systems can be used to manage and simplify regulatory compliance, which is obligatory in the current environment of ever-increasing regulatory intervention.

We're talking about paragraph C, so we have to figure out the main idea of that paragraph. The two sentences in paragraph C are about competitive advantage and customer service, so we should look for a sentence that is within this theme. The sentence in answer choice (1) takes us back to the owner's history, which is irrelevant here. Answer choice (2) focuses on medical records, which doesn't seem to fit anywhere in this passage. Answer choice (3) is about "helping client companies" and "keeping costs under control." That goes with the theme of customer service and competitive advantage, so that's a good answer.

Let's just check out the rest of the answers to make sure we've got the best one. (4) is a generic statement about competitive advantage, which is okay, but since (3) specifically addresses Abel's capabilities, it's a better choice. (5) introduces a new topic, regulatory compliance, which does not belong in paragraph C. Answer choice (3) is the best answer.

ORGANIZATION DRILL

(A)

(1) With a staff of 42 full-time employees, our workforce includes eight individuals who use automatic or manual wheelchairs, two individuals who are blind or visually impaired, and two individuals who use service animals. (2) Kahan Industries has reviewed and updated its emergency evacuation plan in order to effectively address the specific needs and preferences of individual employees and its office location. (3) Our office is located on the 3rd through 6th floors of a building in downtown St. Louis. (4) We have been in business for over 50 years and are leaders in the industry.

(B)

(5) To review and revise our evacuation plan, our agency first organized a small volunteer emergency evacuation committee. (6) Subsequently, the committee met with building management, local fire department personnel, and a manufacturer of evacuation chairs, as well as other agencies and groups with evacuation plans involving persons with disabilities.

(C)

(7) Many individuals and federal agencies have requested a copy of our evacuation plan, and, therefore, we are posting our plan on our website. (8) However, because our plan is specifically designed for our workforce, building and location, we thought that it might be of value to also identify and provide discussion of some of the critical issues and questions that we faced in updating our plan.

1.	Which of the following sentences would most likely follow sentence 5?

	(1)	We have designated two locations for employees to meet after evacuating the building.
	(2)	Our offices are equipped with five two-way radios.
	(3)	The committee began by meeting with staff to discuss evacuation issues in general.
	(4)	The committee is composed of all floor wardens, a fire safety specialist and a secretary.
	(5)	The first item on the committee's agenda will be identifying all emergency exits.

2.	Which of the following would most improve the organization of paragraph A?

	(1)	move sentence 3 to the beginning of the paragraph
	(2)	move sentence 2 to the beginning of the paragraph
	(3)	move sentence 2 after sentence 4
	(4)	end paragraph A with a new sentence, "Our competitive edge has been maintained by…"
	(5)	end paragraph A with a new sentence, "No other company in our industry has a better safety record than ours."

3.	What is the most effective way of organizing paragraph A?

	(1)	delete sentence 1
	(2)	change <u>With a staff of 42 employees</u> to <u>Kahan Industries has 42 employees</u>
	(3)	delete sentence 3
	(4)	delete sentence 4
	(5)	move sentence 4 to before sentence 1

(A)

(1) Child Housing is home to two national programs, sponsored by the National Housing Project, designed to build neighborhood strength to fight crime and violence. (2) One is the United Safe Neighborhood organization (USN). (3) USN members deliver direct services to a range of residents and organize block watches, community festivals, and neighborhood clean-ups.

(B)

(4) The second program is Your Home Here. (5) Accomplishments such as establishing 26 block watches and beautifying a community park all within its first year make this program a model for national emulation.

(C)

(6) Child Housing is partnering with Renew and New Horizons to construct 45 three- and four-bedroom apartments close to local schools and a city recreation center.
(7) Each has an attached garage and modern appliances including a gas range, frost-free refrigerator and air conditioning.

(D)

(8) Named the nation's best affordable multifamily housing development, these 45 units were 100 percent leased before completion — proving the demand for affordable housing far exceeds the supply. (9) One of the reasons for this is the lack of affordable housing for people earning under $40,000 annually. (10) Open floor plans allow parents to cook, run laundry, and help with homework all at the same time. (11) Working single parents earning $15,000 to $26,460 year are the targeted tenants.

(E)

(11) Child Housing Nonprofit Services (Child Housing) provides funding and technical assistance to community development corporations (CDCs) for neighborhood social services, new housing construction and old building renovations. (12) The CDCs are Giving Homes, Calvin's Housing, 20th Street Housing, Care Home Units, and Affordable Housing Properties.

4. Which of the following revisions would most improve the flow of paragraphs C and D?

    (1) divide paragraph D after sentence 9
    (2) move sentence 8 before sentence 6
    (3) move sentence 10 after sentence 6
    (4) delete sentence 7
    (5) delete sentence 6

5. Which revision would improve the flow of the passage?

    (1) move paragraph E to the beginning of the passage
    (2) move paragraph A to the end of the passage
    (3) delete paragraph B
    (4) move paragraph D before paragraph C
    (5) delete paragraph D

6. Which is the most effective revision of the passage?

    (1) add a paragraph to the beginning introducing the National Housing Project
    (2) add a paragraph to the end focusing on the floor plans of the apartments
    (3) combine paragraphs C and D
    (4) combine paragraphs D and E
    (5) delete paragraph E

ANSWERS AND EXPLANATIONS

Organization Drill

1. **(3)** Look at the next sentence 6, which starts "Subsequently, the committee..." The sentence before that should talk about something the committee did first. Be careful, sentence 5 is about what the *agency* did, not the committee. The only answer that is about what the committee did first is answer choice (3).

2. **(2)** This question has to do with the topic sentence ("improve the organization" is a clue). Sentence 3 is not a topic sentence, so it shouldn't come first, as suggested in answer choice (1). The best topic sentence here is sentence 2, where the main idea of an emergency evacuation plan is introduced, so answer choice (2) looks good. The sentence in answer choice (4) is irrelevant to the main idea, and the sentence in answer choice (5) is not necessary and not really on the topic of the evacuation plan.

3. **(4)** The most effective way of organizing paragraph A is to delete sentence 4, as answer choice (4) suggests, which has nothing to do with the main idea, the evacuation plan. Changing the wording of sentence 1, as suggested in answer choice (2), would make it grammatically incorrect. Sentences 3 and 4 are relevant and should be left in.

4. **(3)** Dividing paragraph D after sentence 9 is tempting because sentence 10 doesn't belong in this paragraph, but sentences 10 and 11 by themselves do not make a good paragraph. However, moving sentence 10 after sentence 6, in paragraph C, makes sense because it would be near sentences 6 and 7, which describe the apartments physically.

5. **(1)** Paragraph E introduces Child Housing Nonprofit services and the other organizations that are working to help communities, so it belongs in the beginning of the passage. The other paragraphs are all relevant and all in a good order.

6. **(3)** Combining paragraphs C and D makes sense because all the sentences in these paragraphs discuss the 45 apartments being built by Child Housing and its partners. The passage is not about the National Housing project, so choice (1) isn't correct, and there is no need for an extra paragraph about the floor plans.

SENTENCE STRUCTURE

Questions about sentence structure focus on specific sentences (as opposed to whole passages or paragraphs). You have to be familiar with grammar rules for these questions. You will be fixing sentence fragments, combining and dividing sentences, and correcting errors with commas and other punctuation. You will also organize sentences, using word order and punctuation, to correctly express more than one idea in a single sentence.

Sentence Fragments

Sentence fragments are incorrect or incomplete sentences. Why? Because they do not have a subject and a verb. They are incomplete.

> *Going to the market on Sunday where the vegetables are always fresh.*

This sentence has a lot of words, there are descriptions of things, and you know *what's* happening, BUT...*who* or *what* is going to the market? What is the subject?

This is not a complete sentence. It is a fragment, so it's incorrect.

To fix it, you have to add a subject:

> ***Grace*** *is going to the market on Sunday where the vegetables are always fresh.*

Or you could change the subject to yourself:

> ***I'm*** *going to the market on Sunday where the vegetables are always fresh.*

Or you could go a completely different route:

> ***My dog Spot*** *is going to the market on Sunday where the vegetables are always fresh.*

You know how dogs love fresh eggplant.

A correct sentence doesn't have to be long. It could be simply:

> *I run.*

This has a subject (I) and a verb (run), so it's not a fragment. No matter what the length, every sentence must have a subject and verb.

Quick Note

Every sentence must have a subject (noun) and a verb.

This could get a little tricky when a word looks like it's a verb, but it's actually a noun in disguise. This is done by adding the ending "-ing" to a verb.

"Run" is a verb. "Running" may be a noun.

This is a complete sentence: *The bulls run.*
It has a noun/subject and a verb.

This is a fragment: *The running of the bulls.*
Why? Because "the running of the bulls" is an event. It is a noun/subject.

This is a complete sentence: *I taste the wine.*
It has a noun/subject and a verb.

This is a fragment: *The wine tasting.*
Why? Because "the wine tasting" is an event. It is a noun/subject.

1. Sentence 1: Jane lighting the campfire before it got too dark to find dry wood.

    Which correction should be made to sentence 1?

    (1) insert a comma after <u>campfire</u>
    (2) delete the word <u>before</u>
    (3) change <u>lighting</u> to <u>lit</u>
    (4) replace <u>the</u> with <u>a</u>
    (5) change <u>too</u> to <u>to</u>

Let's take a look at answer choice 1. There is no reason to put a comma after campfire. If we put a comma in the sentence

  Jane lighting the campfire, before it got too dark to find wood.

That doesn't fix the fact that this is all one big subject with no verb. Later, we will talk more about when it is correct to use a comma. What about answer choice 2? The word "before" in this sentence is correct. Look at how the sentence would be without "before."

  Jane lighting the campfire it got too dark to find dry wood.

This doesn't fix the fact that this is a fragment, and it makes no sense. The necessary change here is to change <u>lighting</u> to <u>lit</u> as follows:

Jane lit the campfire before it got too dark to find dry wood.

Let's review the -ing thing using this sentence. "Jane lighting the campfire" is an event. It is a noun. There is no verb in this sentence even though it looks like there is one, "lighting." The word "lighting" is a noun here.

As a matter of fact, the whole thing is one big subject. Look at what happens when we add something to the end:

Jane lighting the campfire before it got too dark to find dry wood was a good idea.

Do you see how that whole first part, from "Jane" to "wood" is the subject? That whole part could be replaced by the word "it."

It was a good idea.

What was a good idea?

Jane lighting the campfire before it got too dark.

But if you replace "lighting" with "lit," the sentence reads:

Jane lit the campfire before it got too dark to find dry wood.

Now we have a subject and a verb. It is a complete, correct sentence.

———————◯———————

Misplaced Modifiers

Don't worry; finding misplaced modifiers sounds a lot harder than it is. You don't have to know what they're called; you just have to recognize when there's a problem and be able to fix it.

It is simply making sure that the subject of the sentence *stays* the subject of the sentence.

Just check this out:

Walking down the street, a car jumped the curb right in front of me.

Sounds okay at first, right? But if you read it closely, you'll see that it's incorrect. The first part of this sentence is called the *modifier*. Why? Because it modifies, or describes, the subject of the sentence. And what's the subject of this sentence? It's kind of a hidden subject, meaning it's *you* or *I*.

What's a hidden subject? Here's a brief refresher on the hidden subject thing. When you have a sentence like the one above, the understood subject is *I*. In other words, "(I was) walking down the street…" Just as when you tell someone to do something, the subject of the sentence is *you*. If Mom says, "Take out the garbage." she really means "(You) take out the garbage."

So, the subject of the sentence about the car jumping the curb is *I*. The first part describes what *I* was doing. In order to be correct, the second part of the sentence must also describe *I*, but it doesn't. It describes the car. The way the sentence is written now, it sounds like the *car* was walking down the street. So we have to fix this. There are a couple of ways you could do this. You could use a connecting word:

I was walking down the street, and a car jumped the curb right in front of me.

Or you could change the second part:

Walking down the street, I saw a car jump the curb right in front of me.

If the sentence begins with a modifier, meaning it's describing a subject, the second part after the comma must start with that subject. Look at these:

Spiraling out of control, shoes now cost twice as much as they used to.

Shoes are not spiraling out of control; the cost of shoes is. So to fix it:

Spiraling out of control, the cost of shoes has doubled.

How about this one?

Wearing too much make-up, my dog stared at me as if I were a stranger.

Who is wearing too much make-up? *I* am. *I* is the subject, so *I* must come after the comma.

Wearing too much make-up, I noticed my dog staring at me as if I were a stranger.

Conjunctions

For some GED questions you need to know how to correctly combine independent clauses into one sentence.

What's an independent clause?—you may ask.

The words aren't that important, and you don't have to remember what they're called, but you must understand the idea. An independent clause is a bunch of words that could be a sentence all by itself. In other words, there is a noun and a verb, and the words make sense alone.

What's a noun again? It's a person, place, or thing. The subject of a sentence is a noun. Nouns include words such as:

I
You
He
Senator
Book
Car
Rabbit
Meatloaf
Carburetor
Sock
Toe
Life
Space

A verb is an action word. It is what the noun is doing. For example:

The senator likes rabbit patterns on his socks.

The verb in this sentence is *likes*. It is what the noun, *senator*, is doing. What's the senator doing? He's liking.

The noun that is *doing something* is the subject of the sentence. In other words, the senator is the only noun that is doing something in this sentence. The socks aren't doing anything, so they are not the subject. The rabbit patterns aren't doing anything, so they are not the subject.

Every sentence or independent clause has a noun and a verb. It has some person, place, or thing that is doing something.

So, let's get back to combining two independent clauses. One of the ways to do this is to use a conjunction. Remember those? Conjunctions are words such as: *and, but, or, so, for, nor,* and *yet.*

These words aren't difficult, but let's just review what they mean and how they're used.

Word	What It Means	How to Use It
for	because, due to	gives a reason/explanation
and	in addition, also, plus	join objects (like in a list) or clauses
nor	not, neither	joins objects or clauses after a negative word or idea
but	except, however, in an unexpected way	compare and contrast objects or clauses
or	an option or choice	gives alternative options or choices
yet	however, but	contrast objects or clauses
so	as a result	the second thing is a result of the first thing

An easy way to remember these conjunctions is with the acronym FANBOYS

F—for
A—and
N—nor
B—but
O—or
Y—yet
S—so

If you see one of the FANBOYS words in a sentence, check to see how it's used. If it is joining two independent clauses, make sure there is a comma before the conjunction.

A good way to approach a question with one of the FANBOYS in the sentence or in the answer choices is to think about how the two parts of the sentence relate to each other.

Try this one:

I showed up for the interview Tuesday, it was moved to the following Wednesday.

These are two independent clauses. Each part of the sentence has a noun, or subject, and a verb. The first clause, before the comma is *I showed up for the interview Tuesday.* The subject is *I* and the verb is *showed up.* It is an independent clause. The second part, after the comma, is *it was moved to the following Wednesday.* The subject is *it* and the verb is *was moved.* It is an independent clause.

The sentence is incorrect as it is, because you cannot have two independent clauses separated by just a comma. We need the FANBOYS.

To decide which of the FANBOYS to use, think about how the two sentences relate to each other. The first idea is "I showed up for the interview Tuesday," and the second part is "it was moved to the following Wednesday." The way these two parts relate to each other is that the two ideas are kind of opposites, so a word such as "but" would work: I thought it was Tuesday, but (in an unexpected way) it was moved to Wednesday.

If there is an answer choice with "but" in it, you should look at that one first. Let's see how "but" works:

I showed up for the interview Tuesday, but it was moved to the following Wednesday.

We could also use "yet":

I showed up for the interview Tuesday, yet it was moved to the following Wednesday.

Either one could be a correct answer choice.

You may also get a run-on sentence with two separate independent clauses that are combined incorrectly:

Our company sponsors a gym membership program they've found that a healthy employee is a productive employee.

Essay Skill

Use FANBOYS correctly to combine two independent clauses in one sentence.

The two independent clauses are:

1. *Our company sponsors a gym membership program*
2. *they've found that a healthy employee is a productive employee.*

They each have a noun and a verb. Which of the FANBOYS could we use to put these two ideas together correctly? Well, how are these two ideas related? One is the cause of the other. The company sponsors gym memberships because they want healthier, more productive employees. For this one we can use "for":

Our company sponsors a gym membership program, for they've found that a healthy employee is a productive employee.

Try this once more:

All of the trains out of town are delayed I will get to the cabin very late.

This is a run-on sentence with two separate clauses that are combined incorrectly. The two independent clauses are:

1. *All of the trains out of town are delayed*
2. *I will get to the cabin very late*

How do these two clauses relate to each other? Let's look at FANBOYS. In this case, the second clause is the result of the first clause.

We can use *so* to connect the clauses:

All of the trains out of town are delayed, so I will get to the cabin very late.

We could also reverse the order of the clauses and use *for*:

I will get to the cabin very late, for all of the trains out of town are delayed.

Quick Note

All of the FANBOYS conjunctions must be used with a comma right before the conjunction.

Fragment, Misplaced Modifier, and Conjunction Drill

1. Not understanding the directions <u>that she was given, the streets of Paris were like a maze</u>.

   Which is the best way to write the underlined portion of this sentence? If the original is the best way, choose option (1).

   (1) that she was given, the streets of Paris were like a maze.
   (2) that she was given, she was lost in the maze of streets in Paris.
   (3) that she was given, the streets of Paris got her lost in their maze.
   (4) the maze of streets of Paris made her lost.
   (5) the streets of Paris for her were an incomprehensible maze.

2. Sentence 2: The shoes in the window were on sale for thirty dollars I had twenty-five dollars with me.

   Which correction should be made to sentence 2?

   (1) insert a comma and <u>yet</u> after <u>dollars</u>
   (2) insert a comma after <u>dollars</u>
   (3) change <u>were</u> to <u>was</u>
   (4) insert a comma and <u>for</u> after <u>dollars</u>
   (5) insert <u>and</u> after <u>dollars</u>

3. Sentence 3: Kip fixing the light switch in the front room before he went to work.

   Which correction should be made to sentence 3?

   (1) change <u>fixing</u> to <u>fixed</u>
   (2) change <u>fixing</u> to will <u>fix</u>
   (3) delete <u>switch</u>
   (4) change <u>went</u> to <u>going</u>
   (5) delete <u>before</u>

4. Sentence 4: The recent hike in gas prices discouraging long family vacations.

   Which correction should be made to sentence 4?

   (1) change hike to increase
   (2) insert a comma after prices
   (3) change long family vacations to a long family vacation
   (4) change discouraging to discouraged
   (5) change discouraging to stopping

5. Simon was not given any advantages in life, he became successful.

   Which correction should be made to sentence 5?

   (1) delete the comma after life
   (2) change he to Simon
   (3) insert and after life
   (4) insert for after life
   (5) insert yet after life

6. Wondering why there was a bird in the classroom, it flew up against the windows as the students giggled.

   Which is the best way to write the underlined portion of this sentence? If the original is the best way, choose option (1).

   (1) in the classroom, it flew up against the windows as the students giggled.
   (2) in the classroom, the bird flew up against the windows as the students giggled.
   (3) in the classroom, the students giggled as it flew up against the windows.
   (4) the students giggle in the classroom as it flew up against the windows.
   (5) flying up against the windows in the classroom as the students giggled.

Combining and Dividing Sentences

On some GED questions, you will have to make decisions about whether to split a sentence up or combine two sentences using a comma with a conjunction or certain other types of punctuation.

In order to be able to conquer questions that ask you to combine and divide sentences, you have to know a little about punctuation. Let's start with the **comma**. Take a look at the sentence below.

(1) Legend has it that Cleopatra attributed her extreme beauty at least in part to pickles, Julius Caesar believed pickles enhanced vitality.

Remember: This sentence is incorrect as it is because independent clauses cannot be separated by a comma by itself. What's the solution? Well, we can divide this sentence into two sentences. We make each independent clause a sentence:

Legend has it that Cleopatra attributed her extreme beauty at least in part to pickles. Julius Caesar believed pickles enhanced vitality.

This makes each part a separate sentence, and it is a correct choice.

Another way to fix the sentence is to replace the comma with a semicolon (;) as it is below.

Legend has it that Cleopatra attributed her extreme beauty at least in part to pickles; Julius Caesar believed pickles enhanced vitality.

You may also use a conjunction with a comma, as we saw earlier:

Legend has it that Cleopatra attributed her extreme beauty at least in part to pickles, and Julius Caesar believed pickles enhanced vitality.

When two clauses generally have the same idea, like the two above that talk about two people who liked pickles, the word "and" is a good conjunction to use.

You may also be asked to combine sentences. Look at the two sentences below.

Celia loved to eat sushi. Her boyfriend Jim hated all kinds of fish.

How would you combine these two sentences?

Think about how they relate to each other. Celia loves sushi and Jim does not like fish of any kind. They are opposing ideas. Which FANBOYS word is good to use for opposing ideas? Let's try the word *but*.

Celia loved to eat sushi, but her boyfriend Jim hated all kinds of fish.

Yet would work, too:

Celia loved to eat sushi, yet her boyfriend Jim hated all kinds of fish.

The Semicolon

There is also a way to combine sentences that doesn't involve any conjunctions. You can use the semicolon to separate two independent clauses without any conjunction. This is most common when the two ideas are similar.

Legend has it that Cleopatra attributed her extreme beauty at least in part to pickles; Julius Caesar believed pickles enhanced vitality.

In this case, the sentence is about two people who thought pickles were beneficial. Here are two more examples of semicolons.

The cheetah is the fastest animal on the planet; it is capable of running up to 120 kilometers per hour.

Remember, since we have two independent clauses, you may also divide this sentence into two sentences:

The cheetah is the fastest animal on the planet. It is capable of running up to 120 kilometers per hour.

Run-On Sentences

This is another kind of incorrect independent clause issue you may remember from third grade (or not—it doesn't matter). A run-on sentence is one in which two or more ideas are stuffed together into one sentence incorrectly without the use of a semicolon or comma with a conjunction.

Take a look at the following sentence:

I was always the tallest girl in the class all the boys were shorter.

You have two complete independent clauses here that are just sitting next to each other in a sentence with no comma, conjunction, or semicolon. This is incorrect. We can fix this by adding a semicolon:

I was always the tallest girl in the class; all the boys were shorter.

Or by adding a comma with a FANBOYS conjunction:

I was always the tallest girl in the class, and all the boys were shorter.

Or by dividing it into two sentences:

I was always the tallest girl in the class. All the boys were shorter.

Try these:

We have to ship this order express if we don't the customer won't accept it.

I am paid every two weeks my rent is due at the end of each month.

I possess excellent word processing and spreadsheet skills I don't have as much Internet experience.

For any of these sentences, you can use a period to divide the clauses into two sentences. You may also use a semicolon to separate the independent clauses. You may also use commas with conjunctions. The first sentence might use *for* while the second sentence could use *and*. The last sentence is especially appropriate for using *but*.

More Ways to Combine Sentences

Certain questions on the GED will test your ability to correctly combine two sentences using other connecting words such as:

because, since, so that—used to show cause and effect
although, though, even though—used to contrast or oppose ideas
where, wherever—indicates the location of whatever is going on in the sentence
after, before, until, while, when, whenever—indicates time
if, unless—to indicate a condition or doubt
as if, as though—indicates similarity

You may see these sentences in a passage:

(1) Researchers don't have all the answers. (2) There is some intriguing information on the topic.

How would you combine these sentences using one of the words or phrases in the list above?

These sentences have contrasting ideas. Researchers don't have all the answers, but there is still intriguing information. So you want a word or phrase that can contrast these two ideas. *Although, though,* and *even though* are possibilities.

These connecting words will either go in front of the first clause or the second clause. Let's try it in front of the first clause:

Even though researchers don't have all the answers, there is some intriguing information on the topic.

Although researchers don't have all the answers, there is some intriguing information on the topic.

Though researchers don't have all the answers, there is some intriguing information on the topic.

They all work pretty well. Remember these words when you have a question that asks you to combine two sentences. Try this one:

---

1. (1) Zack will get a large annual sales bonus. (2) Zack exceeds sales expectations.

   The most effective combination of sentences 1 and 2 would include which of the following groups of words?

   (1) Since Zack will get a large annual sales bonus
   (2) So that Zack exceeds sales expectations
   (3) If Zack exceeds sales expectations
   (4) So that he won't get a large annual bonus
   (5) Unless he won't get a large annual bonus

The general idea in this sentence is that Zack won't get a large bonus if he doesn't exceed sales expectations. If you're thinking, "Well, this won't happen *if* that doesn't happen" or "This will happen *if* that happens," that's a conditional situation. One thing will or won't happen *on the condition* that some other thing will or won't happen.

For a conditional situation, the words *if* or *unless* are used. Which action depends on the other action? In this sentence, Zack's bonus depends on his sales. That means that the sentence "Zack will get a large annual sales bonus" is the dependent clause. It *depends* on some condition. "Zack exceeds sales expectations" is the independent clause. It is the condition that the other clause depends on. You do not have to know what they're called; just know that one part depends on the other in a conditional sentence.

The word *if* or *unless* is placed in front of the independent clause "Zack exceeds sales expectations" as follows:

If Zack exceeds sales expectations, Zack will get a large annual bonus.

That sounds good.

Just to show you what happens if you put the *if* or *unless* in front of the dependent clause:

If Zack gets a large bonus, Zack will exceed sales expectations.

This is a little weird and doesn't really make sense. You usually get a bonus *after* you exceed sales expectations. Remember: In a conditional sentence always place the *if* or *unless* in front of the independent clause.

---

2. (2) The economy still hasn't recovered from the last crisis. (3) The unemployment rate is more depressed than it's been in years.

    The most effective combination of sentences 2 and 3 would include which of the following groups of words?

    (1) Unless unemployment rates are more depressed
    (2) So that unemployment rates are more depressed
    (3) Although unemployment rates are more depressed
    (4) Though the economy still hasn't recovered
    (5) Because the economy still hasn't recovered

What is the relationship here? Unemployment rates are dependent upon the economy. That means that sentence 3 is dependent upon sentence 2, so we should try the connecting words in front of sentence 2. That means we're considering answers (4) and (5).

Answer (4): Though the economy still hasn't recovered, the unemployment rate is more depressed than it's been in years.

"Though" contrasts these two ideas, but these two ideas are actually similar: The economy is depressed and unemployment is down.

So, "Because" is probably a better choice. Let's check it out:

Because the economy still hasn't recovered, the unemployment rate is more depressed than it's been in years.

Voila—that works!

SENTENCE COMBINATION AND DIVISION SUMMARY

There are several ways to combine independent clauses or sentences. They are:

1. comma with a conjunction (FANBOYS)
2. semicolon
3. other connecting words such as *because, while, although, etc.*

You can also divide a sentence with incorrectly combined independent clauses by creating two sentences, each with an independent clause.

SENTENCE COMBINATION AND DIVISION DRILL

1. Sentence 1: The college's plans for expansion included a new science building and a new dormitory if the funding drive is successful, there will be enough money for both.

   Which correction should be made to sentence 1?

   (1) insert a period after <u>dormitory</u> and after <u>successful</u>
   (2) delete the comma after <u>successful</u>
   (3) change the comma after <u>successful</u> to a semicolon
   (4) insert a semicolon after <u>dormitory</u>
   (5) delete <u>for both</u>

2. Sentence 2: Roskilde's main museum is devoted to those early inhabitants, the Vikings once wandered throughout Europe and may have traveled all the way to North America as well.

   Which correction should be made to sentence 2?

   (1) delete the comma after <u>inhabitants</u>
   (2) insert a period after <u>inhabitants</u>
   (3) insert a comma after <u>Europe</u>
   (4) change <u>is</u> to <u>was</u>
   (5) delete <u>as well</u>

3. Sentence 3: My most memorable vacation as a child was a trip I took to the Grand Canyon with my grandfather, I was only eleven at the time.

   Which correction should be made to Sentence 3?

   (1) insert a period after <u>Canyon</u>
   (2) insert commas around <u>as a child</u>
   (3) insert a period after <u>grandfather</u>
   (4) remove the comma after <u>grandfather</u>
   (5) change <u>was</u> to <u>were</u>

4. Sentence 4: The probe sent back startling images of Saturn's surface, including photographs of a giant hurricane system more than 500 <u>miles across, the mission is</u> not over.

   Which is the best way to write the underlined portion of sentence 4? If you think the original is the best way, choose option (1).

   (1) miles across, the mission
   (2) miles across, nor the mission
   (3) miles across, because the mission
   (4) miles across, for the mission
   (5) miles across, yet the mission

5. Sentence 5: Karlene was surprised <u>by the promotion she didn't think</u> she had earned it yet.

   Which is the best way to write the underlined portion of sentence 5? If you think the original is the best way, choose option (1).

   (1) by the promotion she didn't think
   (2) by the promotion, she didn't think
   (3) by the promotion and she didn't think
   (4) by the promotion nor she didn't think
   (5) by the promotion, for she didn't think

6. Smith hadn't had any other job except the one he held at the Farnsworth Corporation <u>all his life, nor did he know</u> any other way to earn money.

   Which is the best way to write the underlined portion of sentence 6? If you think the original is the best way, choose option (1).

   (1) all his life, nor did he know
   (2) all his life and he didn't know
   (3) all his life but he didn't know
   (4) all his life; yet did he know
   (5) all his life, for he didn't know

ANSWERS AND EXPLANATIONS

Fragment, Misplaced Modifier, and Conjunction Drill

1. **(2)** "Not understanding the directions that she was given" is a modifier. It is describing a person, "she," who is the subject. The clause after the comma must start with the subject, "she." Answer choice 2 is the only one that does this.

2. **(1)** This is a run-on sentence, and the two clauses must be joined with the proper conjunction. Answer choice 1 uses the correct conjunction *yet* because the two independent clauses are opposing ideas.

3. **(1)** As it is, this is a fragment because there is no verb. "Kip fixing…" is a noun. Watch out for those "-ing" endings. Answer choice 1 is correct. Answer choice 2 is close, but it is not correct because the action should be in the past and "will fix" is in the future. We know we need the past tense in this sentence because "before he went to work" is in the past.

4. **(4)** This is another "-ing" ending to watch out for. The use of the word "discouraging" makes this one long subject—that is, it's a fragment. So, changing *discouraging* to *discouraged* fixes the problem. Answer choice 4 is the best answer.

5. **(5)** The two parts of this sentence are kind of opposite. He didn't have advantages, but he became successful anyway. Inserting "yet" is the best choice, so answer choice 5 is the best answer.

6. **(3)** The first part of the sentence talks about someone or something "wondering." Who's wondering? It's not the bird. It's the students, so the words after the comma should be "the students." Answer choice 3 is the best. Answer choice 4 starts with "the students," too, but be careful here because it doesn't fit in the sentence as it is. It moves the words "in the classroom," so it doesn't make sense. Be sure to read the sentence completely as you test each answer choice.

Sentence Combination and Division Drill

1. **(4)** The two independent clauses are "The college's plans for expansion… dormitory" and "if the funding drive…both." Some kind of division needs to be inserted after dormitory. A semicolon after dormitory correctly divides the sentence into two independent clauses. Answer choice 4 is the best answer.

2. **(2)** The two independent clauses are "Roskilde's main museum….inhabitants" and "The Vikings once wandered…" A period after *inhabitants* correctly divides this into two sentences. Answer choice 2 is the best answer.

3. **(3)** The two independent clauses are "My most memorable…grandfather" and "I was only eleven…" Making these two separate sentences by putting a period after *grandfather* is the appropriate correction. Answer choice 3 is the best answer.

4. **(5)** Inserting "yet" here properly contrasts the two ideas and correctly joins the two independent clauses. They got back startling images, but they are still not done with the mission. None of the other conjunctions or connecting words is correct here. Answer choice 5 is the best answer.

5. **(5)** There is a cause/effect going on here. Karlene was surprised because she didn't think she'd earned the promotion, so we need something that means "because." "For" works well here. FANBOYS to the rescue. Answer choice 5 is the best answer choice.

6. **(1)** This sentence is correct as it is with the use of the connecting word "nor" because two negative ideas are being joined. One is that Smith hadn't had any other job, and the other is that he didn't know any other way to make money. Answer choice 1 is the best answer.

Essay Skill

Knowing some basic grammar rules will help you write better sentences for the essay section.

USAGE

This is where all the grammar really kicks in on the GED. You'll be correcting sentences with errors in subject-verb agreement, verb tense, and pronouns. Many of the issues in this section will help you with other kinds of questions such as those dealing with sentence structure.

Subject-Verb Agreement

We discussed subjects (nouns) and verbs in the sentence structure section, but here's a review.

The subject of a sentence is the person, place, or thing that is doing something in the sentence.

The Sports Palace on Barrow Street is one of the largest structures in her hometown.

What is the subject of this sentence? The subject will always be a noun (person, place, or thing), so let's identify the nouns: *Sports Palace, Barrow Street, structures,* and *hometown.*

Which is the subject? It's the Sports Palace. It is the only noun that is doing anything. If you're not sure which noun is the subject, ask yourself what each noun is doing.

What is <u>Barrow Street</u> doing? Not much. It's just a street, and the sentence doesn't describe anything that it's doing.

What is <u>structures</u> doing? Nothing—it's just part of the description of the Sports Palace.

What about <u>hometown</u>? Hometown isn't doing anything.

The <u>Sports Palace</u> is doing something. What's it doing? It's being one of the largest structures in my hometown. The <u>Sports Palace</u> is the subject.

What's the verb? Is. Just "is." That's all we need.

The subject-verb agreement is correct here. In a sentence, the verb must agree in number with the subject. A singular subject must have a singular verb. A plural subject must have a plural verb. The <u>Sports Palace</u> is singular and <u>is</u> is singular, so there is agreement. This sentence is correct the way it is.

Here's how the GED may present this to you.

Sentence 10: The Sports Palace, one of my hometown's largest structures, are where the basketball team practices.

The GED will often put the subject pretty far away from the verb to make a question more challenging. In this case, they stuck "one of my hometown's largest structures" in between The Sports Palace and are so that it's easy to lose track of the subject and verb. They also put structures right next to are so that are looks correct.

Once you find the subject and verb, keep your focus on them. In sentence 10 above, the subject is The Sports Palace, which is singular (there's just one of 'em). The verb should be the singular "is." So we have to fix that:

The Sports Palace, one of my hometown's largest structures, is where the basketball team practices.

Try this one:

Sentence 11: The diversity of life on the seven continents of the world, with its complexity and varied characteristics, constantly surprise scientists.

What is the subject? The nouns are: *diversity of life, seven continents, complexity,* and *scientists.*

Which is the subject? It's *the diversity of life*. What does the diversity of life do? In this sentence as it is written, it "surprise." You wouldn't say "the diversity surprise" because diversity is a singular noun, so it needs the singular form of the verb. If you have trouble figuring out what the correct singular form of the noun is, think of replacing it with a pronoun.

What's a **pronoun**? It's a word that takes the place of a specific noun. It stands in for a person, place, thing, or idea. Here is a table of pronouns.

Noun	Pronoun
Jim	He
Mary	She
Building	It
Friends	They
Shoes	They

We would use "it" to replace "diversity."

So now let's put the pronoun together with the verb. Which is correct?

it surprise or *it surprises?*

Make a whole sentence if you're not sure.

It surprise me or *it surprises me?*

"Surprises" is the correct word.

So, we have <u>the diversity of life surprises</u>. We have to fix sentence 11 by changing <u>surprise</u> to <u>surprises</u>:

The diversity of life on the seven continents of the world, with its complexity and varied characteristics, constantly surprises scientists.

Try these noun-verb agreement sentences:

————————————◯————————————

1. *Tom and I, after eating a big breakfast, am going to the beach.*

What pronoun would you replace the subject with? The subject is: *Tom and I.* It could be replaced with "we."

We am going to the beach or *We are going to the beach?*

We are going to the beach is correct.

Correct: *Tom and I, after eating a big breakfast, are going to the beach.*

————————————◯————————————
————————————◯————————————

2. *The search for extraterrestrial beings, viewed as a waste of time by most scientists, were popular in the 1960s.*

What pronoun would you replace the subject with? The subject is *the search for extraterrestrial beings.* It is not the <u>beings</u>; it's the <u>search</u>, so the subject is singular. It could be replaced with "it."

It were popular or *It was popular?*

It was popular is correct.

Correct: *The search for extraterrestrial beings, viewed as a waste of time by most scientists, was popular in the 1960s.*

Compound Subjects

The subject of a sentence may be a **compound subject**, which means that two people or things are joined as one subject with the word "and."

For example:

Lennon and McCartney
Cain and Abel
Pride and joy
Ebony and ivory
You and I

Each of the nouns in a compound subject may be singular, but together they make a plural subject.

Lennon and McCartney were part of the Beatles.
Cain and Abel were brothers.
Pride and joy are feelings.
Ebony and ivory live together in perfect harmony.
You and I are studying for the GED.

What's wrong with this sentence?

Incorrect: *Paul and his sister Marie is going to be late for the movies.*

The subject is <u>Paul and Marie</u>. It is a compound plural subject. That means we need a plural verb:

Correct: *Paul and his sister Marie are going to be late for the movies.*

Incorrect: *The flight from Istanbul to Athens, and the oral exam Sandrine will have to face when she gets home, is causing her stress.*

Correct: *The flight from Istanbul to Athens, and the oral exam Sandrine will have to face when she gets home, are causing her stress.*

What's the subject? It's the compound subject <u>the flight</u> and <u>the oral exam,</u> so it is a plural subject.

When "Or" Connects Two Subjects

If two singular nouns are connected by "or" rather than "and," they do not make a compound subject. That's because "or" means that it's going to be one or the other.

Let's go back to Paul and Marie.

Correct: *Paul or Marie is going to be late for the theatre.*

Why is this correct? Because one of them is going to be late, not both. Pretend there is one seat available on the bus to the theatre, and either Paul or Marie is going to be able to take it. Because only one of them can get on the bus, either Paul is going to be late or Marie is going to be late. The word "or," when used with two singular subjects, creates a singular compound subject.

Incorrect: *Soda or coffee are available with your meal.*

Correct: *Soda or coffee is available with your meal.*

You only get one of them. One of them *is* available.

You are not going to be asked *what* a compound subject is on the GED. You just have to be able to recognize when a subject is singular or plural and use the correct form of the verb.

Quick Note

Two singular nouns joined by "and" form a plural subject.

Two singular nouns joined by "or" make a singular subject.

There are some nouns that seem like they should be plural, but they are generally singular. You just have to know these. The most common nouns to fall under this category that appear on the GED are:

- The Netherlands (or the name of any city, state or country)
- the government—one unit made up of many people
- the company—one unit made up of many people
- the family—one unit made up of many people
- the audience—one unit made up of many people
- politics (why? because it's a science—think "political science")
- measles (why? because it's a disease)
- the number
- the amount

Each of these subjects takes the singular form of the verb:

The Netherlands is…

The number of people at my party was…

The measles is…

The amount of money in my account is…

SUBJECT-VERB AGREEMENT DRILL

1. Sentence 1: The United States are about one-half the size of Russia and slightly larger than China.

    Which correction should be made to sentence 1?

    (1) insert a comma before <u>and</u>
    (2) change <u>are</u> to <u>is</u>
    (3) change <u>United States</u> to <u>U.S.</u>
    (4) insert <u>is</u> before <u>slightly</u>
    (5) change <u>are</u> to <u>were</u>

2. Sentence 2: The audience, in anticipation of the rock star's long-awaited comeback appearance, wait with bated breath for the warm-up act to finish.

    Which correction should be made to sentence 2?

    (1) change <u>appearance</u> to <u>appear</u>
    (2) insert a comma after <u>breath</u>
    (3) change <u>for</u> to <u>on</u>
    (4) insert <u>in the theater</u> after <u>breath</u>
    (5) change <u>wait</u> to <u>waits</u>

3. Sentence 3: Samuel and his sister Suzanne is going to be very popular this summer with their friends because they have a new swimming pool.

    Which correction should be made to sentence 3?

    (1) change <u>they have</u> to <u>he has</u>
    (2) delete <u>his sister</u>
    (3) delete <u>Suzanne</u>
    (4) change <u>because</u> to <u>for</u>
    (5) change <u>is</u> to <u>are</u>

4. The bouquet that the bride carried down
the aisle were made of wildflowers
gathered by her younger sisters.

Which correction should be made to
sentence 4?

(1) change <u>were</u> to <u>was</u>
(2) change <u>down</u> to <u>through</u>
(3) delete <u>of</u>
(4) change <u>younger</u> to <u>young</u>
(5) delete <u>that</u>

5. The fact that customers are taking more
than their share of complementary hors
d'oeuvres are somewhat disturbing to the
bar manager.

Which correction should be made to
sentence 5?

(1) change <u>their</u> to <u>they're</u>
(2) delete <u>The fact that</u>
(3) change <u>are taking</u> to <u>do take</u>
(4) change <u>are somewhat</u> to <u>is
somewhat</u>
(5) delete <u>bar</u>

6. The president of the association and the
representative of the worker's union is
attending the meeting in Washington, D.C.
next Wednesday.

Which correction should be made to
sentence 6?

(1) change <u>attending</u> to <u>attend</u>
(2) change <u>is</u> to <u>are</u>
(3) insert a comma after <u>union</u>
(4) insert a comma after <u>D.C.</u>
(5) insert a comma after <u>association</u>

ANSWERS AND EXPLANATIONS

Subject-Verb Agreement Drill

1. **(2)** The subject is *The United States,* which is one of those special singular subjects. Remember, all names of cities, states and countries are singular. That means we need a singular verb, so we change *are* to *is*. Answer choice (2) is the best answer.

2. **(5)** The subject is *the audience,* which is one of those special singular subjects. That means we need a singular verb, so we change *wait* to *waits*. If you have trouble thinking of the correct verb form, replace the noun with a pronoun. Replace *the audience* with *it*. Now your choice is: *it wait* or *it waits*. *It waits* is correct. The best answer is (5).

3. **(5)** *Samuel* and *his sister* is a compound subject, so it is plural. The verb must be in the plural form, so we change *is* to *are*. Answer choice (5) is the best answer.

4. **(1)** The subject is *the bouquet*. It is singular, so the verb should be singular. We change *were* to *was*. Answer choice (1) is the best answer.

5. **(4)** The subject is a long one—*the fact that customers are taking more…etc.* The subject is basically *the fact,* which is singular. We need a singular verb, so we change *are somewhat* to *is somewhat*. Answer choice (4) is the best.

6. **(2)** *The president of the association and the representative of the worker's union* is one big compound subject so it is plural. We need a plural verb, so we change *is* to *are*. Answer choice (2) is the best.

PRONOUNS

We discussed how pronouns help us figure out subject-verb agreement. There are other ways pronouns are used and tested on the GED. First, let's get a good handle on what pronouns are. The table below shows common pronouns. You don't need to memorize them; just be aware of whether a pronoun is singular or plural.

Singular	Plural	Can Be Singular or Plural
I, me	we, us	none
he, him	they, them	any
she, her	both	you
it	some	who
each	these	which
another	those	that
either		theirs
neither		
one		
other		
such		
mine		
yours		
his, hers		
ours		
this		
that		

You know these words. You probably know how to use them all correctly, too, but you don't give much thought to how they work in a sentence. Time to give them some thought!

First, you have to make sure that the pronoun agrees in number with what it's referring to. This is similar to subject-verb agreement, which we just discussed. Take a look at this sentence:

Candace planted roses in her windowsill box, and it bloomed in the early spring.

Where is the pronoun? If you're not sure, scan the list above and see which word in the sentence is on the list. The pronoun is it. Remember: A pronoun replaces a noun. The sentence says *it bloomed*. What bloomed? The roses bloomed. The word *roses* is plural, so the pronoun should be plural: *they bloomed*.

Correct: *Candace planted roses in her windowsill box, and they bloomed in the early spring.*

You have to be sure, too, that the pronoun is clearly referring to a noun, that there can be no doubt what the pronoun is replacing. Look at this sentence:

The Yankees and the Angels played so many extra innings in the tie-breaking game that they just went home to sleep after they won.

What is the pronoun here? Check the list if you need a reminder. The pronoun is *they*. It's a plural noun.

Which noun does the pronoun refer to? There are a few plural nouns in this sentence: *Yankees, Angels,* and *innings.*

We know the innings didn't go home to sleep. Did the Yankees? Did the Angels? We don't know. This pronoun is ambiguous, meaning we don't know what it's referring to. We have to fix that. The best way to do that here is to insert the correct noun, whether it's the Yankees or the Angels:

The Yankees and the Angels played so many extra innings in the tie-breaking game that the Yankees just went home to sleep after they won.

Now it's clear.

Try this one:

Sigmund and his brother went to visit their friend Cole in the hospital and parked his car in the adjacent lot.

What's the pronoun? Check the list if you're not sure.

It's *his*. Whose? We don't know. Is it Sigmund's car? His brother's car? Cole's car? Maybe Cole needed someone to park his car; you never know. He is in the hospital, after all.

The point is, we don't know. We have to make it clear, so we stick one of the guy's names in to make it clear whose car we're talking about:

Sigmund and his brother went to visit their friend Cole in the hospital and parked Sigmund's car in the adjacent lot.

Here's how a pronoun question would look on the GED:

1. Sentence 1: The city government <u>has said that they are starting to crack down</u> on people who don't pay their parking tickets.

    Which is the best way to write the underlined portion of this sentence? If the original is best, choose option (1).

    (1) has said that they are starting to crack down
    (2) have said that they are starting to crack down
    (3) said they are cracking down
    (4) said it is starting to crack down
    (5) have said it is starting to crack down

You notice here that we have three answer choices with *they* and two answer choices with *it. Government* is one of those group nouns that is singular, so the pronoun must be singular. The pronoun is *they.* That's plural. To correct this we need a singular pronoun: *it,* so it's between (4) and (5). Answer choice (5) would make the sentence read, *The government have said,* so the subject-verb agreement is incorrect. Answer choice (4) is the best answer.

The GED will often just change a pronoun in the middle of a sentence or a passage. Watch out for these kinds of errors. For example:

 One is only capable of doing the job for which you have been trained.

The pronouns in this sentence just changed from *one* to *you.* This exact type of shift, from *one* to *you* or *he* or some other pronoun besides *one,* is a favorite of the GED. It is incorrect. Both of the pronouns must be the same.

Incorrect: *When he decides to finally elect a major, one will be able to focus more.*

Correct: *When he decides to finally elect a major, he will be able to focus more.*

Also correct: *When one decides to finally elect a major, one will be able to focus more.*

The pronoun just has to be consistent.

Incorrect: *You may arrive at the station late if one's departing train is delayed.*

Correct: *You may arrive at the station late if your departing train is delayed.*

Also correct: *One may arrive at the station late if one's departing train is delayed.*

This is just a weird little thing the GED likes to test that you should know about. Whenever you see "one" used in a sentence, look for this error and make sure the pronouns are consistent throughout the sentence.

———————○———————

You may also see this consistency thing in a passage. See the instruction-type passage below.

———————○———————

Instructions: (1) The Negative Number printed on the back of your photographs corresponds with the Negative Number found at the edge of each strip of film. (2) Mark the box beneath the desired Negative Number to indicate the quantity of reprints or enlargements we want for that photo. (3) Specify whether an enlargement or reprint is desired by writing "E" (for enlargement) or "R" (for reprint) next to the quantity desired.

Which correction should be made to sentence 2?

(1)   insert a comma after <u>Number</u>
(2)   change <u>quantity</u> to <u>quantities</u>
(3)   change <u>we</u> to <u>you</u>
(4)   insert a comma after <u>reprints</u>
(5)   change <u>that</u> to <u>a</u>

There is no reason to insert a comma after <u>Number</u>, nor is there any reason to change <u>quantity</u> to <u>quantities</u>.

Should we change <u>we</u> to <u>you</u>? Sentence 1 refers to "your photographs," so the pronoun to use should be consistent with that. Making the change to <u>you</u> is correct to keep the consistency, so answer choice (3) is the best answer.

———————○———————

Tense

The GED will also test consistency of verb tense in a passage or sentence. Verb tense just means using the past tense, the present tense, and the future tense correctly. You don't have to know what it's called; you just have to know how to use it.

First of all, what is verb tense, exactly? Verb tense is using the correct form of the verb for the timing of the action. Here are some basic examples as a refresher:

You use the present tense when you're talking about the present.

I am sitting at my desk typing on my laptop.

This sentence is in the present tense. It is happening right now.

You use the past tense when you're talking about the past.

I sat at my desk typing on my laptop yesterday.

This sentence is in the past tense. It already happened.

You use the future tense when you're talking about the future.

I will sit at my desk typing on my laptop later.

This sentence is in the future tense. It hasn't happened yet, but it's gonna.

Here is a quick review of the basic tenses of the verb *to be,* which shows up pretty often on the GED: *I am* is in the present; *I was* is in the past; *I will be* is in the future. *You are* is in the present; *you were* is in the past; *you will be* is in the future.

If a sentence starts in the present, it should stay in the present.

I am sitting at my desk typing on my laptop, and music played in the background.

At first this may sound okay, but the first verb, *sitting,* is in the present tense, and the second verb, *played,* is in the past tense.

We can fix this by changing *am sitting* to *sat* as seen in the following:

I sat at my desk typing on my laptop, and music played in the background.

or changing *played* to *is playing* if you want it all in the present tense:

I am sitting at my desk typing on my laptop, and music is playing in the background.

The GED also tests tense consistency in a passage. You have to make sure all the verbs are in the same tense. Look at the passage below:

---

(1) Artwork done on paper is extremely fragile and difficult to preserve. (2) If you want to keep your piece of paper art for an extended period of time, it's important that you frame and treat it properly. (3) If you matted and framed it right, you can hang a piece of paper art on your wall and enjoy it undamaged for many years to come.

1. Sentence 3: <u>If you matted and framed it right, you can hang</u> a piece of paper art on your wall and enjoy it undamaged for many years to come.

    Which of the following is the best way to write the underlined portion of this sentence? If you think the original is the best way, choose option (1).

    (1) If you matted and framed it right, you can hang
    (2) If matted and framed right, you can hang
    (3) If you matted and framed it right, you hung
    (4) If you mat and frame it right, you can hang
    (5) If you mat and frame it right, can hang

You can tell that this question is about verb tense because there are different verb tenses in the answer choices. Let's figure out what tense the rest of the passage is in.

The first few verbs are in the present tense: *is extremely fragile, you want, you frame*.

So all the verbs should be in the present tense. <u>Matted</u> should be changed to *mat* and <u>framed</u> should be changed to <u>frame</u>. Both answer choice (4) and (5) have the correct verb tense; what's the difference? In choice (5) the word *you* is deleted, and that makes no sense because then the sentence would read: *If you mat and frame it right, can hang a piece of paper art on your wall…*

The best choice is (4), which has the verbs in the present tense.

───────────────○───────────────

Try this one:

───────────────○───────────────

Tips for Using the Watering Guide

Keep these tips in mind when using the watering guide. Remember: The watering guide only offers suggestions for watering. Exercise judgment by becoming familiar with your plant's unique needs.

1. Size of flowerpot: Soil in small pots dries out faster than soil in large pots. Check the soil in your small pots frequently—they may need to be watered more often than indicated in the watering guide.
2. Type of flowerpot: Baked clay is more porous than plastic. Therefore, the soil in a clay-potted plant becomes drier more quickly than the soil in a plastic-potted plant.
3. Type of light: Plants placed in direct sunlight become drier faster than plants in shade or partial sunlight.
4. Location of flowerpot: Proximity to a heater or radiator affects plant soil. The closer the soil is to the heat source, the faster the soil dries out.
5. Overwatering: This does not refer to the amount of water poured onto a plant at a given time. It refers to how frequently you water your plants. If you water your plants too frequently, they experienced root rot, which ultimately kills plants.

Quick Note

Always put a choice back into the paragraph or sentence, and read it through to see if it makes sense.

1. Tip 5: Overwatering: This does not refer to the amount of water poured onto a plant at a given time. It refers to how frequently you water your plants. <u>If you water your plants too frequently, they experienced root rot, which ultimately kills plants.</u>

    Which is the best way to write the underlined portion of Tip 5? If you think the original is the best way, choose option (1).

    (1) If you water your plants too frequently, they experienced root rot, which ultimately kills plants.
    (2) If you watered your plants too frequently, they experienced root rot, which ultimately kills plants.
    (3) If you water your plants too frequently, they experience root rot, which ultimately kills plants.
    (4) Watering your plants too frequently, they are experiencing root rot, which ultimately kills plants.
    (5) Water your plants too frequently experiences root rot, which ultimately kills plants.

Remember: Tense must be consistent through the whole passage. All the verbs, except for one in Tip 5, are in the present tense. Here are some of the verbs: *dries, is, becomes,* and *water.*

These are all in the present tense, but the verb *experienced* in Tip 5 is in the past tense. We must change it to the present tense to make it consistent with the rest of the passage. The subject of the sentence in Tip 5 is *they.* The correct verb in the present tense is *experience,* so the sentence becomes:

If you water your plants too frequently, they experience root rot, which ultimately kills plants.

Answer choice (3) is the best answer.

PRONOUN AND TENSE DRILL

1. My father, who I hear snoring loudly every night, <u>always slept in</u> his long johns.

   Which is the best way to write the underlined portion of this sentence? If you think the original is the best way, choose option (1).

   (1) always slept in
   (2) always sleeps in
   (3) will always sleep in
   (4) did always sleep in
   (5) always slept with

2. We were resting after our hike when just outside the door to the cabin <u>we heard the howling of wolves—a sound that make our hair stand on end</u>.

   Which is the best way to write the underlined portion of this sentence? If you think the original is the best way, choose option (1).

   (1) we heard the howling of wolves—a sound that make our hair stand on end.
   (2) we hear the howling of wolves—a sound that made our hair stand on end.
   (3) we heard the howling of wolves—a sound that made our hair stand on end.
   (4) we hear the howling of wolves—a sound that make our hair stand on end.
   (5) the howling of wolves we heard—a sound that make our hair stand on end.

3. When Sid <u>broke the vase, it ran</u> to tell his aunt Sally.

    Which is the best way to write the underlined portion of this sentence? If you think the original is the best way, choose option (1).

    (1) broke the vase, it ran
    (2) broke the vase, ran
    (3) broked the vase, Sid ran
    (4) broke the vase, he ran
    (5) broke the vase, she ran

4. The bride and groom drove away in their car <u>while they ran behind, shouting and laughing</u>.

    Which is the best way to write the underlined portion of this sentence? If you think the original is the best way, choose option (1).

    (1) while they ran behind, shouting and laughing.
    (2) while they run behind, shouting and laughing.
    (3) while the children ran behind, shouting and laughing.
    (4) while she ran behind, shouting and laughing.
    (5) and it ran behind, shouting and laughing.

5. The Avida project began in the late 1990s, when Chris Adami, a physicist, sought to create computer programs that <u>performed simple addition problems and reproduce inside a digital environment</u>.

    Which is the best way to write the underlined portion of this sentence? If you think the original is the best way, choose option (1).

    (1) performed simple addition problems and reproduce inside a digital environment.
    (2) performs simple addition problems and reproduces inside a digital environment.
    (3) did simple addition problems and reproducing inside a digital environment.
    (4) performed simple addition problems and reproduced inside a digital environment.
    (5) will perform simple addition problems and will reproduce inside a digital environment.

6. The spacecraft's successful entry, in 2004, into orbit around the world represented the culmination of a vision <u>that take more than 20 years to realize</u>.

    (1) that take more than 20 years to realize.
    (2) who take more than 20 years to realize.
    (3) it takes more than 20 years to realize.
    (4) took more than 20 years to realize.
    (5) that took more than 20 years to realize.

ANSWERS AND EXPLANATIONS

Pronoun and Tense Drill

1. **(2)** You can tell this is a verb tense question because all of the answer choices are different forms of the verb "to sleep." So, we have to check out the tense of the other verbs. "I hear snoring" is in the present tense, so "sleep" should be in the present tense: My father (always) sleeps. The best answer is (2).

2. **(3)** The first part of the sentence says "We were resting." It is in the past tense. The rest of the verbs in the sentence should also be in the past tense. It should be "we heard" and "a sound that made," so answer choice (3) is the best choice. You may think that answer choice (2) sounds good in a story-telling kind of way. The GED is testing for consistency of verb tense; they are not too creative. Stick with keeping all of the verbs in a sentence in the same tense for the GED.

3. **(4)** This is a pronoun question. You can tell because in the answer choices all the pronouns are different, except for answer choice (3), which uses Sid, but there is no reason to say "Sid" again, and the verb "broked" is incorrect. So, we ask ourselves "what ran to tell Aunt Sally?" Sid did = *he did*. Answer choice (4) is the best answer.

4. **(3)** Another pronoun question. Who was running behind the car? If we leave it "they," then it seems that the bride and groom were running behind the car, which doesn't make sense. We need another subject to be running— the children. Answer choice (3) is the best answer.

5. **(4)** To figure out what this question is about, look at the answer choices. They all have different forms of "perform" and "reproduce." It's a verb tense question. The question is about the 1990s when Chris Adami sought to create stuff. It's all in the past tense. Only answer choice (4) has both "performed" and "reproduced" in the past tense.

6. **(5)** This is all about the verb "take." We are talking about 2004, and the first verb is in the past tense—"represented." We want to keep the past tense, which in this case is "took." We need "that took," so answer choice (5) is the best answer. If you're not sure why "that" is needed, read the whole sentence aloud with and without it, and you'll probably see why it's needed.

ESSAY

In Part II of the GED, you write an essay based on a prompt. That means that you are given a couple of sentences about a topic. For instance:

Though certain technologies have served to damage our environment, the freedom to make and build technology is as important as any other freedom in a free society.

Then the GED asks:

Do you agree or disagree with this statement? Write an essay of about 250 words presenting your view and supporting it with specific examples from your own experience or your observations of others.

This is the basic format. They give you something to think about and you give your opinion of it in about 250 words. How much is 250 words? Well, consider that the prompt is about 25 words. If you write ten sentences that are as long as the prompt, you have your 250 words.

Who Reads These Essays?

Each person who grades your essay has only about two minutes to review it. They are not going to get into a deep analysis of what you say, how well each sentence is constructed, whether you used the best, longest words to make your point, and what it all means to humankind. They look for a few major things:

1. Is the essay well-organized?
2. Does your introductory paragraph clearly state your opinion and mention how you will back your opinion up?
3. Does each body paragraph have a clear topic sentence followed by supporting information?
4. Do you have a logical conclusion paragraph that kind of sums up what you said?

A good way to organize your 250 words is into five paragraphs. These paragraphs can be organized as follows:

The First Paragraph

State your opinion (agree/disagree); mention the several ideas that support your opinion.

Your opinion is that you agree or disagree with the statement. It also could be that there is support for both sides of the argument. There are no right or wrong answers. The highest-scoring essays will have a clearly expressed opinion followed by several examples or observations. The most important thing for you to do is to organize your essay well. Your opinion doesn't matter.

In the section about organization in Part I, we discussed topic and supporting sentences and the main idea. You'll need the same tools when you write the essay.

The first sentence is your topic sentence that expresses the main idea. It can be a paraphrase of the question.

Remember: Clearly state your opinion. Let's say we think that the freedom to make technology is as important as any other freedom. Your first sentence could be:

Though certain technologies have served to damage our environment, the freedom to make and build technology is as important as any other freedom in a free society.

Or:

Despite potential damage to the environment, the freedom to make and build technology is as important as any other freedom in a free society.

But there are some interesting ways to beef this up and make it so that you are doing more than just repeating what is written in the prompt. You could say:

Whether the freedom to make and build technology should be unlimited is a controversial subject. The benefits of technological innovations overcome the potential environmental damages caused by these innovations.

In the introductory sentences above, we stated the main idea of the essay. First we stated our opinion, and then we addressed the opposing view. It is always good to address the opposing view.

Now we brainstorm to think of ideas that support the main idea. We have to think: Why do we say that? What makes us think this?

Some ideas that support our main idea:

Technological inventions help improve our quality of life.
The freedom to be creative is important to human happiness.

Technological advances can actually help minimize negative environmental impact.

Individuals should be able to do anything that doesn't harm others.

Three or four ideas are sufficient. As part of the first paragraph, you want to touch upon these ideas to sort of give a "preview" of what the reader will see in the rest of the essay.

Whether the freedom to make and build technology should be unlimited is a controversial subject. The benefits of technological innovations overcome the potential environmental damages caused by these innovations. In fact, certain technological inventions can help minimize environmental damage and improve our quality of life. Also, the freedom to be creative is important to human happiness and we should be able to pursue any projects that don't harm others.

Now we have an introductory paragraph that:

1.   states our opinion
2.   addresses the opposite view
3.   introduces all our supporting ideas

The Second, Third, and Fourth Paragraphs

Now we want to write a couple of sentences about each of the ideas we brought up in the introductory paragraph.

Let's say we want to talk about technologies that help minimize environmental damage in the next paragraph. We can start paragraph 2 of this essay with introductory phrases such as:

One reason this freedom is so important...
There are several technologies that help protect the environment...
Ways in which technology can help minimize environmental damage...

In this paragraph we can talk about things like:

"Green technologies" like recycling and those light bulbs that use less energy
technologies that help dispose of harmful waste or chemicals that make waste less harmful
Hybrid cars that use less fuel

These do not have to be things that you know a lot about. They could be (and usually are) just things that you've heard about from reading the newspaper or hearing the news. Of course, you could be a green technology maven and use all your expertise too.

We can start paragraph 3 by introducing the idea of creativity being a freedom.

The freedom to pursue technological innovation is also important because...
The freedom to invent new technologies is important to human well-being...

Paragraph 4 can be about our rights to do what we want, as long as it doesn't hurt anybody. Here you can talk about one of the basic premises of the Constitution—which is exactly that: Do whatever you want as long as it doesn't harm anyone else.

The Final Paragraph

Paragraph 5 will sum it all up. Your first sentence is basically a repetition or paraphrase (repeating it in other words) of your topic sentence from the 1st paragraph:

For all these reasons, I believe that the pursuit of technological developments is a basic freedom for people. Many technologies that are created and built not only don't hurt the environment, but help preserve and protect it. If we don't allow people the freedom to build and create new technologies, we are slowing human progress down and stifling a basic human need—to be creative.

That's it. Follow this basic template for all your essay practice, and you will become good at this. It is important to practice writing essays because it helps you come up with good examples and experiences for your supporting paragraphs. You'd be surprised how much you can "recycle" supporting information.

For example, let's take a look at another prompt:

The Internet has been praised as a boon to human communication, giving us the ability to exchange ideas with millions of people on the planet. However, the Internet is effectively creating an anti-social world, where we are losing our ability to converse face-to-face.

The GED will ask you to agree or disagree with this statement, so make sure you understand what the statement says. The whole thing boils down to:

The Internet is bad. It makes us anti-social.

Do you agree or disagree? Or do you think there are two sides to the story? Let's explore saying that we think there are points to be made on both sides of the story.

So our first paragraph would start with a topic sentence.

Though the Internet has greatly helped human communication, making it possible to communicate with people all over the world, there is the argument that it is making us anti-social.

We think there are two sides to this story, so we say so.

Whether the Internet is a boon or a bust for humanity is a great debate. It's true that the Internet is a great communications tool. It has enabled small home-based businesses to thrive and has greatly helped business communications in general. However, there are some people for whom it's become a replacement for actual human interaction and has, indeed, made some of us anti-social.

We've already got 50 words. This isn't necessary, but it usually turns out that you write about 50 words per paragraph for 5 paragraphs. That gets you to your 250 words.

You can almost see the 3 body paragraphs forming here. That's what you want to do; you want to let the reader know what's coming up in the next few paragraphs.

1st paragraph—small home-based businesses helped by the Internet
2nd paragraph—business communications in general helped by the Internet
3rd paragraph—some people sit home and don't do anything else

For the first paragraph, maybe you know someone who has a small, thriving Internet business. Or maybe you've purchased things on the Internet from small businesses or you have a small Internet business. Or you can pretend you know someone who has a small Internet business. You can talk about how the business you know about:

- Has low costs
- Is open 24 hours
- Enables the owner to work whenever he/she can
- Has customers all over the world

You get the picture. Just these 4 points alone will take up at least 50 words.

In the second and third paragraphs you can talk about business communications:

- Salespeople can talk to customers without the expense or hassle of travel
- Businesses can coordinate shipping at any time of day or night
- Company meetings can be held over the Internet

Now, in the fourth paragraph, talk about the people who sit home being anti-social. You can make things up here, cite an article you read about someone that never goes out, talk about young people not getting out and interacting which makes for adults with no confidence, and so on.

Finally, in the fifth paragraph, sum it all up. Repeat your main point:

In the final analysis, it is debatable whether the Internet, in the end, is good or bad for humanity.

Then recap what you've talked about:

It is undeniably beneficial for people who want to start small businesses from home at a low cost. All kinds of businesses benefit from being able to communicate with customers, suppliers and colleagues all over the world at any time. On the other hand, there are people who depend on the Internet for all their communication and are somewhat anti-social, so there are some drawbacks.

And you've got another 250-word essay.

The more you practice this 5-paragraph template, the better you will get at organizing your ideas. Also, you will develop a reservoir of facts and ideas that you can use to answer the essay question on the GED.

The Non-Opinion Essay

Not all the essay questions on the GED will ask for your opinion.

Movies and books are often thought of as sources of pure entertainment, but many of these artistic works teach us important life lessons.

Identify a movie or book that conveys an important life lesson. Write a composition of about 250 words explaining why you feel this artistic work is not just pure entertainment but rather imparts a life lesson. Provide reasons and examples to support your view.

There is no agreement or disagreement here; you just write about a book or movie that you feel teaches a life lesson. We don't see this type of question too much on the GED, but you can still use the template to create a good essay.

First Paragraph

In your first paragraph, identify the movie or book. For example:

I think that the film Shawshank Redemption, as well as being a very entertaining film about a banker's time in prison, offers the viewer an important life lesson. The lesson this film teaches us is to make the most of our situation, to remain positive, and to appreciate small tokens of goodwill. The hero in this movie, Andy Dufresne, befriends his fellow inmates and uses his skills as a banker to help inmates and make good connections that help him to eventually escape.

You may not have seen this movie or remember it too much, but here are some details from the film that help form the body paragraphs:

- Andy befriends Red, who gets him posters and a rock hammer
- Andy helps the guards with their taxes
- Andy helps the warden launder money (not a great thing to do, but it gets him a private cell—he's making the most of it!)
- Andy is protected by his friends after being assaulted
- Andy uses his goodwill to get a job and help expand the prison library

The second paragraph can be about Andy making the most of his situation. He makes friends, he gets a rock hammer, and he continues to pursue his rock collection hobby. All these things make him happy even though he's in prison.

The third paragraph can be about how Andy helps people, despite being in what some would describe as a helpless situation. He helps the prison guards with their taxes, and he helps the warden with his money laundering, getting a private cell in exchange.

The fourth paragraph can talk about his escape. It turns out that Andy has been slowly digging a tunnel with his little rock hammer. Here you can add some life lessons about determination and persistence too.

The fifth paragraph can sum it all up:

Even in what most people would call the worst possible situation, the hero of the film perseveres and still tries to make friends and help people. Through his continued determination and patience, he is able to escape his prison. This film teaches us about the importance of staying positive, despite the situation, and persevering even when all seems lost.

Now think about a movie you've seen or a book you've read that has life lessons. Most books and movies do.

Outline your essay. Jot down notes about what would go in each of the five paragraphs. Don't just start writing—get your notes down first so you can just refer back to them as you construct your essay, just as we've been doing here.

_____

_____

_____

_____

_____

_____

_____

_____

_____

_____

_____

_____

_____

_____

Supporting Sentences

Once you get your notes down about what you want to say, try not to use words such as "good" or "bad" repeatedly. It's better to use words that are a little more descriptive than just "good" or "bad."

Here are some ideas for words you can use:

Good	Bad
Beneficial	Detrimental
Positive	Negative
Helpful	Harmful
Encouraging	Discouraging
Useful	Useless
Important	Unimportant or of no importance
Boon	Bust

Of course it depends on what you're writing about, but try to fit some of these words in, rather than just using "good" or "bad." Using them once or twice is fine, by the way, but just try to use a variety of words. Also, tell the GED people why something is good or bad. Don't just write:

Government-run schools are good.

You could say:

Government-run schools are beneficial for society because they are free to everyone.

Don't just say:

The movie was encouraging.

Say:

The movie encouraged me to keep trying to reach my goals, even if sometimes the situation seems helpless.

Don't just say:

It's really bad to use cell phones.

Say:

It's rude to have a full conversation on a cell phone when you're on a bus or sub-way car or other enclosed area where everyone can hear you.

Using the following prompts, practice writing your own essays. Research things that you know you'd like to use as supporting evidence but don't know enough about. In other words, if you think a certain book or historical event would be good support for your idea, look it up and find out about it. This way you'll have this information for other essays when you practice and for the real GED essay.

1. The advent of cell phones and smart phones has made it possible for people to be reached at any time of day or night. Studies say that this increases stress levels and compromises quality of life for many businesspeople who are "always working," without any time off for their personal lives.

    Do you agree or disagree with this statement? Write an essay of about 250 words presenting your view and supporting it with specific examples from your own experience or your observations of others.

    Paragraph 1—introduction and supporting ideas:

    _____

    _____

    _____

    _____

    _____

    _____

    _____

    _____

Paragraph 2—supporting idea #1:

_____

_____

_____

_____

_____

_____

_____

Paragraph 3—supporting idea #2:

_____

_____

_____

_____

_____

_____

_____

Paragraph 4—supporting idea #3:

_____

_____

_____

_____

_____

_____

_____

Paragraph 5—conclusion:

_____

_____

_____

_____

_____

_____

_____

2. Some health professionals argue that childhood obesity can be combatted by taking away children's electronic games and access to the Internet so they are forced to get outside and move around.

Do you agree or disagree with this statement? Write an essay of about 250 words presenting your view and supporting it with specific examples from your own experience or your observations of others.

Paragraph 1—introduction and supporting ideas:

_____

_____

_____

_____

_____

Paragraph 2—supporting idea #1:

_____

_____

_____

_____

_____

Paragraph 3—supporting idea #2:

_____

_____

_____

_____

_____

Paragraph 4—supporting idea #3:

_____

_____

_____

_____

_____

Paragraph 5—conclusion:

_____

_____

_____

_____

_____

3. In some states taxes are used to
    help cover the costs of transportation,
    textbooks and special needs for private
    school students. Private schools should
    not be funded with public tax dollars.

    Do you agree or disagree with this
    statement? Write an essay of about
    250 words presenting your view and
    supporting it with specific examples from
    your own experience or your observations
    of others.

Paragraph 1—introduction and supporting ideas:

_____

_____

_____

_____

_____

Paragraph 2—supporting idea #1:

_____

_____

_____

_____

_____

Paragraph 3—supporting idea #2:

_____

_____

_____

_____

_____

Paragraph 4—supporting idea #3:

_____

_____

_____

_____

_____

Paragraph 5—conclusion:

_____

_____

_____

_____

_____

Extra ideas for getting good supporting information:

A great place to go for good supporting information, the stuff that's going to fill paragraphs 2, 3, and 4 for your essay, is the newspaper or other news media. This is where you'll find great ideas for current issues and debates. You'll find that many of the current issues and debates have been going on for a while. Debates about the use of taxes, great leaders, social trends, and how technology affects our lives have been going on for years, and these themes are likely to come up on the essay.

Another terrific source is classic literature. You don't have to go read _War and Peace_; you can just go to a website like Cliff's Notes and get summaries of the stories. After a while you'll sense general themes such as:

- Man (or woman, of course) against evil force
- Man against his own inner evil
- Rebel against society
- Rebel against a government
- Man overcoming great fear
- Love overcoming all
- Family ties overcoming all
- Loyalty (to whatever) overcoming all
- Persistence pays off

These sound familiar because you see them over and over again in films, movies, books, and even in the news. Become familiar with some of the great literature works that use these themes. They almost all do use these themes, so it's not a difficult task.

Here is a sampler of some of the major literary writers that can be great sources for supporting ideas in your GED essay:

Mark Twain

Ernest Hemingway

Toni Morrison

F. Scott Fitzgerald

William Faulkner

Gabriel Garcia Marquez

Henry David Thoreau

Tennessee Williams

Katherine Anne Porter

You get the idea. Go look these people up online or elsewhere and find summaries of their greatest works. Become familiar with them and you've got great fodder for your essay.

ESSAY IN SUMMARY

Here is a summary of your most useful tools for conquering the GED essay:

- Use a 5-paragraph essay template
- Read the newspaper
- Become familiar with at least 3–4 story plots from "great" literature
- Create index cards with supporting points for the general themes
- Practice, practice, practice

If you practice writing these essays as often as possible leading up to your test, you will become a pro at writing the 5-paragraph essay.

WRITING DRILL

Questions 1 through 7 refer to the following passage.

(A)

(1) When the sunlight strikes raindrops in the air, they act as a prism and forms a rainbow. (2) The rainbow is a division of white light into many beautiful colors. (3) These take the shape of a long round arch, with its path high above, and its two ends apparently beyond the horizon.

(4) There are, according to legend, a boiling pot of gold at one end. (5) People look, but you never find it. (6) When a man looks for something beyond his reach, his friends say one is looking for the pot of gold at the end of the rainbow.

(B)

(7) Others have tried to explain the phenomenon physically. (8) Aristotle thought that the rainbow was caused by reflection of the sun's rays by the rain. (9) Since then physicists have found that it is not reflection, while it is a refraction by the raindrops that causes the rainbows.

(C)

(10) Throughout the centuries people have explained the rainbow in various ways. (11) As a miracle without physical explanation. (12) To the Hebrews it was a token that there would be no more universal floods. (13) The Greeks used to imagine that it was a sign from the gods to foretell war or heavy rain. (14) The Norsemen considered the rainbow as a bridge over which the gods passed from earth to his home in the sky.

1. When the sunlight strikes raindrops in the air, they act as a prism and forms a rainbow.

   Which correction should be made to sentence 1?

   (1) change <u>sunlight</u> to <u>Sunlight</u>
   (2) delete the comma after <u>air</u>
   (3) insert a period after <u>air</u> and change <u>they</u> to <u>They</u>
   (4) change <u>forms</u> to <u>form</u>
   (5) no correction is necessary

2. Sentence 4: There are, according to legend a boiling pot of gold at one end.

   Which correction should be made to sentence 4?

   (1) change <u>There are</u> to <u>There is</u>
   (2) delete the comma after <u>are</u>
   (3) insert a comma after <u>gold</u>
   (4) change <u>one</u> to <u>its</u>
   (5) no correction is necessary

3. Sentence 5: People <u>look, but you</u> never find it.

   Which of the following is the best way to write the underlined portion of sentence 5? If you think that the original is the best way, choose option (1).

   (1) look, but you
   (2) look but you
   (3) look but they
   (4) look, but they
   (5) look because they

4. Sentence 6: When a man looks for <u>something beyond his reach, his friends say one is looking</u> for the pot of gold at the end of the rainbow.

Which of the following is the best way to write the underlined portion of sentence 6? If you think the original is the best way, choose option (1).

(1) something beyond his reach, his friends say one is looking
(2) something beyond his reach; his friends say one is looking
(3) something beyond his reach, his friends say he is looking
(4) something beyond their reach, his friends say he is looking
(5) something beyond their reach, they he is looking

5. Sentence 9: Since then physicists have found that it is not reflection, while it is a refraction by the raindrops that causes the rainbows.

Which of the revisions below would most improve the flow of sentence 9?

(1) change the comma after <u>reflection</u> to a period
(2) delete the comma after <u>reflection</u>
(3) change <u>while it is</u> to <u>but</u>
(4) change <u>while</u> to <u>and</u>
(5) change <u>causes</u> to <u>cause</u>

6. Which of the revisions below would most improve the flow of paragraph C?

(1) insert "Some accepted it as" at the beginning of sentence 11
(2) replace the period after sentence 10 with a comma
(3) insert a comma after sentence 13 to connect it to sentence 14
(4) change <u>gods</u> to <u>Gods</u> in sentence 14
(5) end paragraph C with a new sentence, "Rainbows have always been pleasing to the eye."

7. Which of the revisions below would most improve the organization of the passage?

(1) begin paragraph A with a new sentence, "Many people have tried to explain the origins of the rainbow."
(2) move sentence 6 to the end of paragraph C
(3) move paragraph C before paragraph B
(4) move sentence 8 before sentence 7
(5) end paragraph C with a new sentence, "Only Aristotle tried to explain the origins of the rainbow."

Advertising Your Business

Questions 8 through 15 refer to the following passage.

(A)

(1) We all depend more or less upon the public for our support. (2) We all trade with the public—lawyers, doctors, retail store clerks, artists, actors, airline company presidents, and computer technicians. (3) Those who deal with the public must be careful that their goods are valuable, genuine and will give satisfaction. (4) When you have a product or service that you know will please you're customers, let them know that you have it through advertising.

(B)

(5) In a country like this, where nearly everybody gets the news, whether it's through reading the newspapers, watching TV or reading online, it is unwise to keep quiet about your product or service. (6) Hundreds and thousands of people, if not millions, may read your advertisement, while you are attending to your routine business.

(C)

(7) Many, perhaps, see your ads while you are asleep. (8) The whole philosophy of life is, first "sow," then "reap." (9) The way the farmer does it, planting his potatoes and corn, sowing his grain, and then going about something else. (10) He never reaps first and sows afterwards. (11) This principle applies to all kinds of business, and to nothing more eminently than advertising.

(D)

(12) To make the most impact, it is important to advertise regularly placing one ad in a Newspaper is usually not effective. (13) It is commonly known in the advertising world that the reader of an ad does not see the first mention of an ordinary advertisement. (14) It usually takes a consumer at least seven views of an advertisement before he is ready to purchase. (15) "Cross-pollinating," by using television, print and Internet advertising, is also recommended to increase a potential customer's exposure to your product.

8. Sentence 1: We all depend more or less upon the public for our support.

   Which correction should be made to sentence 1?

   (1) add, "In the advertising world," to the beginning of the sentence
   (2) insert a comma after <u>less</u> and after <u>public</u>
   (3) change <u>public</u> to <u>Public</u>
   (4) insert a comma after <u>depend</u> and after <u>less</u>
   (5) insert a semicolon after <u>less</u>

9. Sentence 3: Those who deal with the public must be careful that <u>their goods are valuable, genuine and will give satisfaction</u>.

Which of the following is the best way to write the underlined portion of this sentence? If you think the original is the best way, choose option (1).

(1) their goods are valuable, genuine and will give satisfaction
(2) they're goods are valuable, genuine and will give satisfaction
(3) there goods are valuable, genuine and will give satisfaction
(4) their goods are valuable, genuine, and will give satisfaction
(5) there goods are valuable, genuine, and will give satisfaction

10. Sentence 4: When you have a product or service that you know will please you're customers, let them know that you have it through advertising.

Which correction should be made to sentence 4?

(1) insert a comma before product and after service
(2) replace <u>you're</u> with <u>your</u>
(3) delete the comma after customers
(4) insert <u>and</u> after <u>customers,</u>
(5) replace <u>it</u> with <u>them</u>

11. Sentence 5: In a country like this, where nearly everybody gets the news, <u>whether it's through reading the newspapers, watching TV or reading online, it is unwise</u> to keep quiet about your product or service.

Which of the following is the best way to write the underlined portion of sentence 5? If you think the original is the best way, choose option (1).

(1) whether it's through reading the newspapers, watching TV or reading online, it is unwise
(2) whether its through reading the newspapers, watching TV or reading online, it is unwise
(3) whether it's through reading the newspapers, watching TV, or reading online, it is unwise
(4) whether its through reading the newspapers, watching TV, or reading online, it is unwise
(5) whether it's through reading the newspapers, watching TV while reading online, it is unwise

12. Sentence 6: Hundreds and thousands of people, if not millions, may read your advertisement, while you are attending to your routine business.

Which correction should be made to sentence 6?

(1) delete the comma after <u>people</u>
(2) delete the comma after <u>advertisement</u>
(3) change <u>while</u> to <u>though</u>
(4) change <u>your</u> to <u>you're</u>
(5) no correction is necessary

13. Sentence 9: The way the farmer does it, planting his potatoes and corn, sowing his grain, and then going about something else.

Which correction should be made to sentence 9?

(1) add "This is the way" to the beginning of sentence 9.
(2) change potatoes to potatos
(3) delete the comma after The way the farmer does it
(4) delete the comma after grain
(5) delete then

14. Sentence 12: To make the most impact, it is important to advertise <u>regularly placing one ad in a Newspaper</u> is usually not effective.

Which of the following is the best way to write the underlined portion of sentence 12? If you think the original is the best way, choose option (1).

(1) regularly placing one ad in a Newspaper
(2) regularly; placing one ad in a Newspaper
(3) regularly placing one ad in a newspaper
(4) regularly; placing one ad in a newspaper
(5) regularly, placing one ad in a newspaper

15. Which revision would improve the flow of the passage?

(1) delete paragraph A
(2) move sentence 7 to the end of paragraph B
(3) move paragraph C to before paragraph B
(4) move paragraph D to before paragraph B
(5) delete paragraph C

Questions 16 through 23 refer to the following passage.

Dear Sir or Madam:

(A)

(1) I'm writing to express my interest in the Marketing Director position listed in the Times Journal. (2) I have always admired the work of Ogden & Pierce. (3) Including the award-winning soap bubble ad that played during last year's Super Bowl.

(B)

(4) I have over six years of experience as a marketing manager with Fieldings, Ltd., I helped to increase product recognition and loyalty. (5) During my time with the Company, I managed anywhere from four to six marketing and sales representatives. (6) Marketing Fieldings' services internationally have given me an overall knowledge of international business, directly applicable to your interest in increasing sales abroad.

(C)

(7) As Marketing Director at your organization, I would emphasize how each customer relationship is a critical component in a broader strategy of long-term growth, and steady gains in market share. (8) I would like to bring to you're company a blend of sales leadership, team management, and financial skill that combines efficiency with imagination to produce effective bottom-line results. (9) My team always met or exceeded sales forecasts.

(D)

(10) I would appreciate the opportunity to meet with you and discuss ways I could help your organization. (11) Their are several ways you may get in touch with me, including email and cell phone. (12) My contact information is available on the enclosed resume. (13) Thank you for your consideration.

Sincerely,

Kayla McHenry

16. Sentences 2 and 3: I have always admired the work of <u>Ogden & Pierce. Including</u> the award-winning soap bubble ad that played during last year's Super Bowl.

Which of the following is the best way to write the underlined portion of these sentences? If you think the original is the best way, choose option (1).

(1) Ogden & Pierce. Including
(2) Ogden & Pierce; including
(3) Ogden & Pierce. Including
(4) Ogden & Pierce including
(5) Ogden & Pierce, including

17. Sentence 4: I have over six years of experience as a marketing manager <u>with Fieldings, Ltd., I helped</u> to increase product recognition and loyalty.

Which of the following is the best way to write the underlined portion of Sentence 4? If you think the original is the best way, choose option (1).

(1) with Fieldings, Ltd., I helped
(2) with Fieldings, Ltd. I helped
(3) with Fieldings, Ltd. yet I helped
(4) with Fieldings, Ltd.; I helped
(5) with Fieldings, Ltd., helped

18. Sentence 5: During my time with the Company, I managed anywhere from four to six marketing and sales representatives.

Which correction should be made to sentence 5?

(1) change Company to company
(2) delete the comma after Company
(3) insert a comma after marketing
(4) change representatives to Representatives
(5) no correction is necessary

19. Sentence 6: Marketing Fieldings' services internationally have given me an overall knowledge of international business, directly applicable to your interest in increasing sales abroad.

Which correction should be made to sentence 6?

(1) change Fieldings' to fieldings'
(2) insert a comma after internationally
(3) change have to has
(4) delete the comma after business
(5) no correction is necessary

20. Sentence 7: As Marketing Director at your organization, I would emphasize how each customer relationship is a critical component in a broader strategy of long-term growth, and steady gains in market share.

Which correction should be made to sentence 7?

(1) change Marketing Director to marketing director
(2) delete the comma after organization
(3) delete the comma after growth
(4) change market share to Market Share
(5) no correction is necessary

21. Sentence 8: I would like to bring to you're company a blend of sales leadership, team management, and financial skill that combines efficiency with imagination to produce effective bottom-line results.

Which of the following is the best way to write the underlined portion of sentence 8? If you think that the original is the best way, choose option (1).

(1) to bring to you're company a blend of sales leadership, team management, and financial skill
(2) to bring to you're company a blend of sales leadership, team management and financial skill
(3) to bring to your company a blend of sales leadership, team management, and financial skill
(4) to bring to your company a blend of sales leadership team management and financial skill
(5) to bring to you're company a blend of sales leadership team management and financial skill

22. Which of the revisions below would most improve the flow of the cover letter?

(1) combine paragraphs C and D
(2) end paragraph B with a sentence beginning, "But I'm not going to go on and on about my experience…"
(3) end paragraph D with a sentence beginning, "I look forward to getting together for a chat…"
(4) move sentence 9 after sentence 5
(5) move sentence 5 after sentence 9

23. Sentence 11: <u>Their are several ways you may</u> get in touch with me, including email and cell phone.

Which of the following is the best way to write the underlined portion of Sentence 11? If you think the original is the best way, choose option (1).

(1) Their are several ways you may
(2) They're are several ways you may
(3) There are several ways one may
(4) Their are more than one way one may
(5) There are several ways you may

Questions 24 through 30 refer to the following passage.

(A)

(1) After a seven-year journey, the Cassini spacecraft approached the planet saturn in June 2004. (2) It's successful entry into orbit around the world represented the culmination of a vision that took more than 20 years to realize. (3) Launched amid controversy in October 1997, over one billion miles was covered by the spacecraft. (4) They're were great technological challenges, but the Cassini mission has been more successful than even its planners imagined.

(B)

(5) The Cassini mission resulted from the joint efforts of NASA (National Aeronautics and Space Administration), the European Space Agency, and the Italian Space Agency. (6) The Cassini spacecraft actually consisted of two parts; the first is the Cassini orbiter itself, designed to explore the moons, rings and atmosphere of Saturn. (7) The second is the Huygens probe.

(C)

(8) The Huygens probe was built to plunge into the atmosphere of Saturn's largest moon, Titan. (9) Fortunately, the launch of Cassini went off without a problem. (10) For seven years, the spacecraft traveled through the void of space. (11) Upon reaching Saturn, Cassini's instruments awoke from their long slumber. (12) Began transmitting data, including photographs of a giant hurricane system more than 500 miles across.

24. Sentence 1: After a seven-year journey, the Cassini spacecraft approached the planet saturn in June 2004.

Which correction should be made to sentence 1?

(1)   change <u>Cassini</u> to <u>cassini</u>
(2)   delete the comma after <u>journey</u>
(3)   change <u>planet saturn</u> to <u>Planet</u> <u>Saturn</u>
(4)   change <u>saturn</u> to <u>Saturn</u>
(5)   no correction is necessary

25. Sentence 2: <u>It's successful entry into orbit around the world</u> represented the culmination of a vision that took more than 20 years to realize.

Which of the following is the best way to write the underlined portion of Sentence 2? If you think the original is the best way, choose option (1).

(1)   It's successful entry into orbit around the world
(2)   It's successful entry into orbit around the World
(3)   It's successful entry into orbit around the world,
(4)   Its successful entry into orbit around the World
(5)   Its successful entry into orbit around the world

26. Sentence 3: Launched amid controversy in October 1997, <u>over one billion miles was covered by the spacecraft</u>.

Which of the following is the best way to write the underlined portion of Sentence 3? If you think the original is the best way, choose option (1).

(1) over one billion miles was covered by the spacecraft.
(2) over one billion miles was covered by the Spacecraft.
(3) the spacecraft traveled over one billion miles in its journey.
(4) it was the spacecraft that was traveling over one billion miles.
(5) the journey of the spacecraft was over one billion miles.

27. Sentence 4: They're were great technological challenges, but the Cassini mission has been more successful than even its planners imagined.

Which correction should be made to sentence 4?

(1) change <u>They're</u> to <u>There</u>
(2) change <u>They're</u> to <u>Their</u>
(3) change <u>They're were</u> to <u>They're was</u>
(4) change <u>They're were</u> to <u>There was</u>
(5) change <u>but</u> to <u>and</u>

28. Sentence 6: The Cassini spacecraft actually consisted of two parts; the first is the Cassini orbiter itself, designed to explore the moons, rings and atmosphere of Saturn.

Which correction should be made to sentence 6?

(1) delete the semicolon after <u>parts</u>
(2) replace the semicolon after <u>parts</u> with a comma
(3) change <u>Cassini</u> to <u>cassini</u>
(4) change <u>moons</u> to <u>Moons</u>
(5) insert a comma after <u>rings</u>

29. Which of the revisions below would most improve the flow of the passage?

(1) delete sentence 3
(2) delete paragraph C
(3) move sentence 8 to the end of paragraph B
(4) delete sentence 8
(5) move paragraph C before paragraph B

30. Sentences 11 and 12: Upon reaching Saturn, <u>Cassini's instruments awoke from their long slumber. Began transmitting data,</u> including photographs of a giant hurricane system more than 500 miles across.

Which of the following is the best way to write the underlined portion of these sentences? If you think the original is the best way, choose option (1).

(1) Cassini's instruments awoke from their long slumber. Began transmitting data
(2) Cassini's instruments awoke from their long slumber. And began transmitting data
(3) Cassini's instruments awoke from their long slumber, when they began transmitting data
(4) Cassini's instruments awoke from their long slumber, but they transmitting data
(5) Cassini's instruments awoke from their long slumber; began transmitting data

_____

_____

_____

_____

_____

_____

_____

_____

_____

_____

_____

_____

_____

_____

_____

_____

_____

Chapter 4
Writing
Drill Answers

ANSWERS AND EXPLANATIONS

1. **(4)** This is a subject/verb agreement problem. In the second clause, the subject is *they*. The problem is that it says: *they forms*. *Forms* is not in the correct form. You wouldn't say *they forms*; you'd use the plural form of the verb: *they form*. Answer choice (4) is the best answer.

2. **(1)** The subject/verb agreement is incorrect. The subject of this sentence is a single thing: *a boiling pot of gold*. Therefore, we need a plural verb, so we have to change *There are* to *There is*. Answer choice (1) is the best answer.

3. **(4)** This is a good example of a pronoun switch in mid-sentence. The sentence begins with the pronoun *you,* and then switches to *one* at the end. Since the sentence starts with *you*, and we cannot change that, we must change the *one* to *you* to be consistent. We do need the comma after *look*, because it is followed by *but* with an independent clause, so answer choice (4) is the best answer.

4. **(3)** This is a pronoun problem. The sentence is saying that a man's friends say that *the man* is looking for the pot of gold at the end of the rainbow. It is not the *friends* that are looking; it's the *man*. That said, the man's friends say that *he is looking*. There are distractors here with *there, they're,* and *their*, but none of these is correct anyway. The best answer is choice (3).

5. **(3)** We need the comma after *reflection* because there are two independent clauses in this sentence that must be separated by a comma with a connecting word. If we just changed the comma to a period, the second clause *while it is a refraction* wouldn't make sense by itself as sentence. The best connecting word is *but*, because the physicists believed one thing and found out that it was something else. The best answer is choice (3).

6. **(1)** Sentence 11, as it stands, is a fragment. There is no subject and really no verb. It's just part of a description that continues the idea from sentence 10. Answer choice (2) gives us a way to combine sentences 10 and 11 into one sentence, but look at how it would read if we did that by replacing the period with a comma: *Throughout the centuries people have explained the rainbow in various ways, as a miracle without physical explanation.*

   It doesn't make sense. We need more words no matter what we do. Answer choice (1) solves the problem, making sentence 11 read: *Some people accepted it as a miracle without physical explanation.*

7. **(3)** We want to move paragraph C before paragraph B because paragraph C introduces the idea of people trying to explain the rainbow with the topic sentence, *Throughout the centuries people have explained the rainbow in various ways*. This should go before paragraph B because the first sentence in paragraph B refers to *Others* explaining the rainbow. If there are *others*, someone else has to be mentioned first because *others* is a relative word. Paragraph C does the job of mentioning what some people think, and then paragraph B continues to talk about what *others* think. Answer choice (3) is the best answer.

8. **(4)** It is correct here to insert a comma after "depend" and "less" because the words "more or less" are extra information that could be taken out without making the sentence incomplete or incorrect. Take a look at the sentence without "more or less": *We all depend upon the public for our support.*

   See? No problem. So these words need to be set off by commas. Answer choice (4) is the best answer.

9. **(4)** We have two issues here. The first is *their goods*. This is the correct word to use here (as opposed to *there* or *they're*). It is the possessive form and that is what's needed here. Then we have the comma. Remember: When there are 3 or more items in a list, there is a comma after each item before the *and*. Answer choice (4) has *their* and the commas are correct, so it is the best answer.

10. **(2)** The correct form of your/you're is the possessive because it is *your customers*. Answer choice (2) is the best answer.

11. **(3)** There are two things going on here. First, we need the correct form of it's/its. Here we need the contraction of *it is*, so we need *it's*. Now it's between answers 1, 3, and 5. Answer 1 is wrong because when there are 3 or more items in a list, there is a comma after each item before the *or*. Only answer choice (3) has the comma correctly placed. Answer choice (5) throws *and* in, which changes the meaning and you want to avoid that.

12. **(5)** No correction is necessary. Yes, that happens! There is proper comma placement everywhere, with *if not millions* set off by commas because it's extra information and a comma before *while* because it joins two independent clauses.

13. **(1)** The second sentence, *The way the farmer does it*, is a fragment. It is all one long subject without any sign of a verb. All the "-ing" words are nouns. See how this is all one subject: *The way the farmer does it, planting his potatoes and corn, sowing his grain, and then going about something else is the best way to do it.*

See how it is all just one subject? So, to make it a sentence, you add the verb *is* with the rest of the phrase in answer choice (1).

14. **(4)** This is a run-on sentence and *Newspaper* is capitalized, which is incorrect. You would only capitalize *newspaper* if it were part of the name of a particular newspaper, such as "The New York Newspaper." Dumb name, but you get the point. So now we have to fix the run-on sentence with an un-capitalized *newspaper.* Answer choice (4) does the job nicely by separating the two independent clauses with a semicolon.

15. **(2)** Sentence 7 continues the same idea as those in paragraph B. Paragraph B talks all about placing ads, the great exposure you may get, and the fact that people may see your ads while you are doing other things. Sentence 7 adds that people may even see your ads while you sleep, so it makes sense to move Sentence 7 to paragraph B. Answer choice (2) is the best answer.

16. **(5)** Sentence 2 is only a fragment with no verb, so our choices are either to insert a verb or combine the sentences. Only answer choice (5) correctly combines the sentences with a comma and a connecting word, *including.*

17. **(4)** We have two independent clauses connected here with a comma only and no connecting word. We need either a comma with a connecting word, a semicolon, or we have to make two separate sentences. The only choice that does this correctly is (4).

18. **(1)** Remember: The word *company* is only capitalized when it is part of the name of an actual company. The word by itself is just a general term and should not be capitalized. Answer choice (1) is the best answer.

19. **(3)** The subject/verb agreement is incorrect. The subject is *marketing.* Remember, these -ing forms can often be nouns. Marketing is a singular noun (it's an activity), so it needs the singular form of the verb *has.* Answer choice (3) is the best answer.

20. **(3)** There is no need for a comma here. The word *and* is joining two things, so the comma should be deleted. You need a comma only if there are three or more items in a list.

21. **(3)** The word *your* is correct here because it is possessive: *your company*. Also, the three items in the list need to be separated with commas: *blend of sales leadership, team management, and financial skill*.

22. **(4)** Paragraph B is about how Kayla performed at Fieldings, what she did with her sales team, and her responsibilities. Sentence 9 is also about Kayla's accomplishments with her sales team, so it belongs in paragraph B, not C. C is all about what Kayla will do at Ogden & Pierce.

23. **(5)** The correct word here is *There*, as in *There are*. There is no reason to switch to *one* after Kayla used *you* in sentence 10, so answer choice (5) is the best answer.

24. **(4)** All planet names are capitalized, so *Saturn* must be capitalized. Answer choice (4) is the best answer.

25. **(5)** The correct word is *its* because it is possessive, as in *Its successful entry*. Also, *world* is not capitalized. Maybe you thought it is the name of our planet and should be capitalized, but it is not; Earth is the name of our planet.

26. **(3)** This is a modifier issue. The first part of the sentence, *Launched amid controversy in October 1997*, is describing something. It is describing the spacecraft, so *the spacecraft* must come right after the comma. Only answer choice (3) has *the spacecraft* right after the comma.

27. **(1)** The correct word is *There*, not *They're*. If it were *They're*, the sentence would read: *They are were great technological challenges,* which makes no sense. *Their* is the possessive form, so that is not correct either. It is incorrect to change it to *There was*, because the subject is *technological challenges*, which is a plural subject, and thus we need *were*.

28. **(5)** This is a list of three or more items, so we need a comma after each item before *and*. Answer choice (5) is the best answer.

29. **(3)** Moving sentence 8 to the end of paragraph B makes sense because sentence 7 in paragraph B introduces the Huygens probe. Sentence 8 further explains what the Huygens probe is, so it belongs after sentence 7.

30. **(3)** Combining these sentences using *when they* is the best choice. Answer choice (1) leaves sentence 12 a fragment. Answer choice (2) begins a sentence with *And*, which is not a good idea on the GED. There is no reason to insert *but*, as answer choice (4) suggests, because the sentence 12 does not introduce an opposite idea. Answer choice (5) leaves sentence 12 as a fragment.

Chapter 5
Reading
Comprehension

INTRODUCTION

For many test takers, the Language Arts, Reading test is the most enjoyable portion of the GED—that is, to the degree that anyone can "enjoy" any part of a lengthy standardized test, they enjoy this section. The fiction, poetry, and drama excerpts come from the work of many of our greatest writers, so they are written with flair and exquisite command of the English language, making these passages pleasurable to read. After all, these writers became famous for their ability to write well. Most people would prefer to read a compelling scene about, say, lovers caught in a web of international intrigue, rather than forge through a tedious scientific data table delineating the differences between igneous and sedimentary rock layers. Similarly, the nonfiction articles and business documents are usually realistic and engaging, and are easier to answer questions about than a treatise about the Taft-Hartley Labor Act.

That said, the Language Arts, Reading test does pose some unique challenges. The fiction, poetry, and drama selections were written principally for literary effect, rather than expressly for clarity. You may have trouble, especially at first, figuring out what the author of an excerpt is *trying to say*. But have no fear! This gets easier the more you read and the more you practice. Also, bear in mind that you won't be asked for any super-deep literary interpretations (like you were in high school English class). If you can figure out the overall idea of a passage, who the characters are and what happens to them, and what the author wants you to think about it all, then you're going to be fine. Plus, if you really don't get one particular part of a certain passage, hey, maybe there won't be a question about that exact part anyway!

Another hurdle you'll need to surmount is the vocabulary that the authors use. As you saw in the Introduction, cultivating your vocabulary is a huge step in GED preparation. So, you should have ready access to a good dictionary. That way you can look up words—like "surmount," in the first sentence of this paragraph—and immediately things start to make more sense. Of course you won't have access to a dictionary when you take the real GED, but that just means you need to make the most of it now.

Luckily, even without a dictionary, you can figure out a word's meaning from those that surround it. So, "surmount," hmm… Well, evidently it's what you do to "a hurdle," and a hurdle is a thing that you have to get over, or overcome, in order to move on. And you know we want you to do just that, so "surmount," as you may have figured out by now means "get over." Good job!

Keep it up, both the dictionary-investigation part and the context-clue part. Not only will this pay dividends on the GED, but it'll come in handy in your own life every day. You heard us: every day. The more words you know, the more words you have available to think with; the more, and better, words you have to think with, the better your thoughts; the better your thoughts, the smarter you are; the smarter you are, the smarter you get.

QUESTION TYPES

GED test writers ask four different types of questions about the passages: Comprehension questions, Analysis questions, Synthesis questions, and Application questions. Now, they don't label the questions as "Analysis" or "Synthesis," and you don't have to name the question type in order to get it right, but identifying which kind of question you're confronted with will help you figure out what you're being asked, and therefore what the right answer is. You certainly don't want to get the *right* answer to the *wrong* question, because that translates to the *wrong* answer. Recognizing the question types will also help you decide which questions to spend your time doing (the types of questions you're better at) and which to not worry much about (those types that you struggle with, or that take too long).

So, let's look at the kinds of questions you'll see on the GED, and how to answer each one.

Comprehension Questions

A comprehension question asks you to find something in the passage and then recognize that piece of information among the answer choices. The correct answer choice will be a rephrasing of what was in the passage, rather than a word-for-word copy, which would be a bit too easy. These questions are the most straightforward, and therefore the simplest to answer, on the Reading Test.

Synthesis Questions

A question of this type asks you to go one step further than a comprehension question does. Instead of finding a detail, you find clues that lead you to conclude what the answer must be. While a synthesis question's answer won't be there in black and white, it is still based on the facts as stated in the passage.

Application Questions

Application questions definitely demand deeper thought than previously described question types. First you must understand the information in the passage, and then apply that information to some other situation than the one depicted in the text. As in a synthesis question, you are looking for clues in the passage.

Analysis Questions

These questions ask you about the literary techniques the author has used to create an effect. Instead of asking *what* the author said, as a Comprehension or Synthesis question would, an Analysis question asks you *how* he said it, or *how* he achieved the effect that he wanted.

So, of the four types of questions you'll see on the Language Arts, Reading Test:

- Comprehension questions ask <u>what</u> the author says,
- Synthesis questions ask, given what the author says, <u>what must be</u> true,
- Application questions ask, given what the author says, <u>what would happen</u> under different circumstances,
- Analysis questions ask you <u>how</u> the author painted the picture in your mind.

No matter what the question type, you're always looking for <u>direct</u> and <u>specific</u> evidence from the passage to support your answer.

ANSWERING THE QUESTIONS

Let's focus on the process that's going to get us the correct answers to questions, no matter what type of passage we're being asked about. (We'll get to the specific types of passages soon.) Once you've given the passage a quick look, trying to identify the main idea and other key points, you're ready to tackle the questions.

Read the Question

First, *carefully read the question*. Does it ask about a particular part of the passage—for example, the second paragraph? If so, don't depend on your memory, which by this point in the test has been through a lot. Instead, *always go back to the passage and reread the part you're asked about*. However, it really helps to start reading a few lines up in the previous paragraph, and read all the way through to a few lines into the following paragraph. This method gives you the context for the second paragraph; it reminds you of what went on just before and what is going to happen next. After all, the second paragraph is just a portion of the bigger passage, so the more you can connect it to the larger action and the main idea, the better off you are. (And, not coincidentally, the greater your chances of getting the right answer.)

Answer the Question in Your Own Words

Second, once you've reread the portion of the passage and refreshed your memory of what's going on—and before you look at the answer choices—*answer the question in your own words*. Stick as close as possible to what the passage says and jot down your answer to the question right onto your scratch paper. This is a key step, because this is you saying: "I know what the answer is supposed to be and it's this!" When you perform this step, not only are you being more active in your problem-solving (which invariably leads to better results than being passive does), but you are also giving yourself a method for evaluating the answer choices the GED will offer you: The answer choice that you pick has got to match the answer that you found in the text itself.

This is similar to going into a restaurant and, when the waiter asks you what you want, you tell him "I want a cheeseburger with extra pickles and no tomatoes." This way, you have a much better chance of getting the delicious meal you desire than you would if you told the waiter, "Oh, just bring me any five things, and I'll try to like one of them." What are the chances that the second method will get you the food that you really want to eat? Not nearly as good as the first.

Use Process of Elimination

Once you've answered the question in your own words—and written down that answer on your scratch paper—now it's time to check out the answer choices. Use Process of Elimination: Does this answer choice match the answer that I found in the text? If it doesn't, get rid of it! ("This is not the cheeseburger that I ordered!") On your scratch paper, cross off the number of that bad answer. Go through each answer choice using the same POE strategy.

If you're down to one answer choice, fantastic! You've got a winner. If you get down to two answer choices that both seem to match what you've said is the right answer, then keep looking for what makes one of them <u>bad</u>. There must be something, some difference between the two. Don't start looking for what makes one answer *good*; keep trying to find the *badness* of the bad one. For one thing, badness is easier than goodness to actually pick out. For another thing, finding the badness is what has gotten you this far, so clearly that strategy is working: Stick with it.

If you're down to two possibilities and you really can't get any further, then take your best guess between them. Maybe you'll be right, and a good guess counts just as much as an answer that you knew all along.

So, let's review our strategy:

- Read the question.
- Go back to the passage, and read what you need.
- Answer the question in your own words, based on what the passage says.
- POE each answer choice against the answer you gave. Eliminate what doesn't match. Check *every* answer choice, and select the one that works best.

Sample Reading Test Questions

Let's look at a short fiction passage, and try out our overall strategy on the various question types. Some students might object that this process is time-consuming—and indeed it will be *at first*. However, keep two things in mind as you practice using this system.

First, although initially you'll spend a fair amount of time working through the steps, the more you practice the quicker you'll get.

Which brings us to the even more important consideration: *You can't get faster; you can only get better.* That is, if you just try to hurry (which is a natural impulse on a timed test), you'll end up missing questions that you otherwise would've gotten right. And that's exactly the tragic circumstance that we're trying to avoid!

On the other hand, as you focus on getting the question correct, and you practice and practice using the steps, you'll get faster without even realizing that you have! And you won't mess up on ones that are within your power to answer correctly. Remember: It's not how many questions you answer that gets you your score; it's how many you answer correctly.

Let's look at the passage and the questions.

HOW DOES THE DOG WISH ITS TAIL WOULD BEHAVE?

A DOG of a taciturn disposition said
to his Tail:

"Whenever I am angry, you rise
and bristle; when I am pleased, you wag;
(5) when I am alarmed, you tuck yourself in
out of danger. You are too mercurial—you
disclose all my emotions. My notion is that
tails are given to conceal thought. It is my
dearest ambition to be as impassive as the
(10) Sphinx.*"

"My friend, you must recognize
the laws and limitations of your being,"
replied the Tail, with flexions appropriate
to the sentiments uttered, "and try to be
(15) great some other way. The Sphinx has
one hundred and fifty qualifications for
impassiveness which you lack."

"What are they?" the Dog asked.

"One hundred and forty-nine tons of
(20) sand on her tail."

"And—?"

"A stone tail."

*The Sphinx, in Egypt, is an enormous statue of a creature that is part lion, part bird, and
part human.

— *The Tail of the Sphinx* by Ambrose Bierce

1. Why does the Dog wish his Tail would not
   wag?

   (1) He doesn't want his Tail to give
       away his thoughts.
   (2) The Sphinx is jealous of the Dog.
   (3) It hurts him when his Tail moves.
   (4) He envies the Sphinx because it is
       so much larger than the Dog.
   (5) The Sphinx despises the Dog
       because of its Tail.

This is a classic comprehension question. "You disclose all my emotions," the Dog tells the Tail. Let's match this answer—or, rather, get rid of what doesn't match this answer. (2) and (5) are no good, because the Sphinx, an enormous statue in Egypt, doesn't know anything or think anything about the Dog. (3) has no support in the passage—there's nothing in there about pain. And (4) starts out well—the Dog does wish he were more like the Sphinx—but not because of the Sphinx's size. Remember: The whole answer choice has to be right, not just part of it. So, (1) best answers the question according to what the passage tells us.

2. "Impassiveness" (line 17) could best be replaced with

(1) impressiveness
(2) stoicism
(3) wisdom
(4) passion
(5) slowness

Here is another comprehension question, this one perhaps slightly more challenging since it deals with vocabulary. Come up with your own answer: The Dog doesn't want his tail to give away his emotional state, so he says "It is my dearest ambition to be as *no-emotion-showing* as the Sphinx." Now eliminate what doesn't jive with "no-emotion-showing." (1) can go, because there's nothing about this advice that makes a big impact or elicits a ton of respect. (2), well, let's say you don't recognize that word—no big deal, leave it in for now, and see what happens. (3) doesn't work because the Dog isn't craving wisdom. (4) is the opposite of what we want, because *passion* is deeply felt emotion and we want no emotion. (5) can be eliminated because, even though the Sphinx is immobile and the Dog thinks his own Tail moves too much, it's more about showing emotion than it is about the speed of movement. So, even though (2) stoicism might be an unfamiliar word, you know it has to be right, since it's the only one left. And stoicism does indeed mean demonstrating no emotions.

3. The Tail's advice to the Dog could be best described as

(1) inefficient
(2) sarcastic
(3) emotional
(4) pragmatic
(5) unstated

This is a synthesis question, in that the answer is not directly stated in the passage; instead, you are asked to draw a conclusion about what has been said (a conclusion that's directly based on what is in the passage). So, what can we conclude about the Tail's advice? The Tail tells the Dog that he should recognize his own limitations, so we can say that this advice is practical—sensible and realistic, based on worldly (not theoretical) considerations. Let's get rid of what doesn't match. The Tail's statement isn't (1) *inefficient*, because it's not wasteful, nor is it at all (3) *emotional*, and it's definitely not (5) *unstated* (because, hey, it's right there on the page!). And, even though the conversation is humorous, we can't say that the Tail is being (2) *sarcastic*, because it doesn't mean the opposite of what it says. (4) is the correct answer here.

4. The Sphinx does not wag its tail because the Sphinx is

(1) lonely
(2) wise
(3) unable
(4) too old
(5) sad

Here's another synthesis question. The Dog envies the Sphinx because the Sphinx's tail doesn't betray its emotional state the way the Dog's does. The Tail informs the Dog that it's not that the Sphinx *doesn't* wag its tail, but rather that the Sphinx's tail is buried in sand and made of stone—so the Sphinx *can't* wag its tail. So, it's not about the Sphinx being (1) *lonely* or (5) *sad*. And while the Sphinx is (4) *old* and, according to myth, (2) *wise*, these are not the reasons for its immobility. Choice (3) accurately captures the Tail's sentiment.

5. If the Sphinx and its own Tail had a similar conversation in which the Sphinx wished that its Tail could move, the Tail would probably respond by

(1) saying that the Sphinx too should be conscious of its limitations
(2) turning into sand
(3) turning into stone
(4) wagging vigorously
(5) wishing that it were more like the Dog's Tail

Like any application question, this asks you to take what you know from the passage and apply it to a different situation. Given the passage, what do we know about Tails? That they can only do what they are able to do. The Dog's Tail is free to wag as it pleases, and so it does. The Sphinx's Tail is made of stone and buried under tons of sand, so it can't do anything—and that is what the Sphinx's Tail would surely tell the Sphinx. So, it wouldn't (2) *turn into sand,* nor would it (3) *turn into stone* (especially since it already *is* stone). It wouldn't (4) do any wagging, because it simply cannot. There's no reason to think that the Sphinx's Tail would (5) wish it were more like the Dog's, so eliminate that too. Thus, choice (1) is the best answer. It seems that Tails are content to be what they are, whereas their owners wish to be otherwise.

6. The Dog and his Tail speak to one another in English. This is an example of

    (1) simile
    (2) personification
    (3) metaphor
    (4) alliteration
    (5) digression

Answer: (2). This is an analysis question, which asks you about the technique a writer uses to achieve his goal. In this tale, a dog speaks to its tail, and the tail talks back. So, the writer has given human qualities to nonhuman things—therefore, he has used (2) *personification*. He has not compared one thing to another, which eliminates (1) and (3), both of which are techniques involving comparisons. He does not repeat the same sound in a sequence of words, so it's not (4) *alliteration*. The story doesn't wander off on a tangent, so there has been no (5) *digression*.

Note: Although in this particular exercise the questions went in comprehension—synthesis—application—analysis order, don't expect any such order on the GED (or, for that matter, on any subsequent drill). When you have a passage and questions about it, it's up to you to decide in what order you want to do those questions. Since, for most test takers, a comprehension question is easier than an application question, usually the best thing to do is check out **all** the questions about a given passage, then decide which order is going to work best for *you*. Find the question types **you** are best at (again, comprehension or synthesis questions are usually your best bet) and take the time answering those questions correctly. Then, deal with the harder questions once you know you've knocked out the easier ones—either doing your best to answer them if you have time, or guessing at those that you have the least chance at getting right anyway. The last thing you'd want to have happen is to run out of time on a section because you spent too long wrestling with a hard question when there were way easier questions that you didn't even get to.

TYPES OF PASSAGES

You will see four types of passages on the GED: Fiction passages, which are either complete short stories or, more likely, excerpts from longer works of fiction; Drama passages, which, like the fiction passages, are either complete works or sections of longer plays; Poetry, which tend to be complete poems (since, after all, most of them are rather short and therefore easily fit on a page or two) but might be excerpts from longer poetry (since some poets aren't as succinct as others); and Nonfiction, which could be business or government documents, performance or book reviews, magazine articles, and so on—pretty much any kind of, well, not fictional writing (hence the name). We're going to use essentially the same techniques to answer the questions to all of these forms of writing, but let's take a moment to think about the salient differences in the way each kind of passage works, and consider how to read each one.

Each passage is headed with a question in all capital letters. This question indicates a central point in the passage—as you read, try to answer this question. It helps a lot, especially in figuring out the main idea of the passage; however, this will NOT be one of the exact multiple-choice questions that will follow the passage.

FICTION

Here, a writer tells a made-up story using plot, characters, and descriptions. A well-written piece of fiction creates a real-seeming world in the mind of the reader.

When you read fiction on the GED, ask yourself the following Big Questions ("Big" because knowing these answers will help you out on whatever multiple-choice questions the GED will ask):

Who's telling the story?

Is the story told by one of the characters taking part in it—an "I"—or is it told by someone outside the action? When a story is told by an "I," we call this a "first-person narrator." Such "first-person narrators" are not always reliable—sometimes the character telling the story has a vested interest in it, and so will tell you, the reader, not the whole truth, but rather only what he wants you to know. A "third-person narrator," on the other hand, provides an unbiased, all-seeing, "God's-eye" view of the action.

What's happening?

The plot consists of what happens in the story: the physical actions, the dialog, even what goes on inside a character's head (choices, decisions, revelations). This action is the main idea of the fictional piece.

Who are the main characters?

In GED passages, there will be only two or three main characters. Who are they? How does the author describe them? What do they think of each other? What do the minor characters, the ones on the outskirts of the action, think about these main characters?

What's the mood?

Is it funny or sad? Is it about heavy stuff or is it more lighthearted? What feeling does it stir inside of you? Questions about mood are Analysis questions, because they deal with how the author created this feeling.

What is the setting?

Where a story takes place might be important or irrelevant. If it is important—and you'll know that it is if the author takes a lot of time describing the surroundings—what does the setting tell you about the action?

Take a look at this fiction passage. First, we'll work on answering the above Big Questions, to make sure we have a good grip on what's going on in this story. Then, we'll look at the specific multiple-choice test questions.

HOW DO WALLACE AND DE VILLE BATTLE EACH OTHER?

He was the Leopard Man, but
he did not look it. His business in life,
whereby he lived, was to appear in a
cage of performing leopards before vast
(5) audiences, and to thrill those audiences
by certain exhibitions of nerve for which
his employers rewarded him on a scale
commensurate with the thrills he produced.

As I say, he did not look it. He was
(10) narrow-hipped, narrow-shouldered, and
anaemic, while he seemed not so much
oppressed by gloom as by a sweet and
gentle sadness, the weight of which was
as sweetly and gently borne. For an hour
(15) I had been trying to get a story out of him,
but he appeared to lack imagination. To
him there was no romance in his gorgeous
career, no deeds of daring, no thrills—
nothing but a gray sameness and infinite
(20) boredom.

Lions? Oh, yes! he had fought with
them. It was nothing. All you had to do was
to stay sober. Anybody could whip a lion
to a standstill with an ordinary stick. He
(25) had fought one for half an hour once. Just
hit him on the nose every time he rushed,
and when he got artful and rushed with
his head down, why, the thing to do was
to stick out your leg. When he grabbed at
(30) the leg you drew it back and hit hint on the
nose again. That was all.

With the far-away look in his eyes
and his soft flow of words he showed
me his scars. There were many of them,
(35) and one recent one where a tigress had
reached for his shoulder and gone down to
the bone. I could see the neatly mended
rents in the coat he had on. His right arm,
from the elbow down, looked as though
(40) it had gone through a threshing machine,
what of the ravage wrought by claws and
fangs. But it was nothing, he said, only the
old wounds bothered him somewhat when
rainy weather came on.

(45)　　　Suddenly his face brightened with a recollection, for he was really as anxious to give me a story as I was to get it.

　　　"He was a little, thin, sawed-off, sword-swallowing and juggling Frenchman.
(50) De Ville, he called himself, and he had a nice wife. She did trapeze work and used to dive from under the roof into a net, turning over once on the way as nice as you please.

(55)　　　"De Ville had a quick temper, as quick as his hand, and his hand was as quick as the paw of a tiger. The word went around to watch out for De Ville, and no one dared be more than barely civil to his
(60) wife. And she was a sly bit of baggage, too, only all the performers were afraid of De Ville.

　　　"But there was one man, Wallace, who was afraid of nothing. He was the
(65) lion-tamer, and he had the trick of putting his head into the lion's mouth. He'd put it into the mouths of any of them, though he preferred Augustus, a big, good-natured beast who could always be depended upon.

(70)　　　"As I was saying, Wallace—'King' Wallace we called him—was afraid of nothing alive or dead. He was a king and no mistake.

　　　"Madame de Ville looked at King
(75) Wallace and King Wallace looked at her, while De Ville looked at them darkly. We warned Wallace, but it was no use. He laughed at us, as he laughed at De Ville.

　　　"But I saw a glitter in De Ville's eyes
(80) which I had seen often in the eyes of wild beasts, and I went out of my way to give Wallace a final warning. He laughed, but he did not look so much in Madame de Ville's direction after that.

(85)　　　"Several months passed by. Nothing had happened and I was beginning to think it all a scare over nothing. We were West by that time, showing in 'Frisco. It was during the afternoon performance, and the
(90) big tent was filled with women and children.

"Passing by one of the dressing tents I glanced in through a hole in the canvas: in front of me was King Wallace, in tights, waiting for his turn to go on with his
(95) cage of performing lions. I noticed De Ville staring at Wallace with undisguised hatred. Wallace and the rest were all too busy to notice this or what followed.

"But I saw it through the hole in the
(100) canvas. De Ville drew his handkerchief from his pocket, made as though to mop the sweat from his face with it (it was a hot day), and at the same time walked past Wallace's back. The look troubled me at
(105) the time, for not only did I see hatred in it, but I saw triumph as well.

"De Ville will bear watching," I said to myself, and I really breathed easier when I saw him go out the entrance to the
(110) circus grounds. A few minutes later I was in the big tent. King Wallace was doing his turn and holding the audience spellbound. He was in a particularly vicious mood, and he kept the lions stirred up till they were
(115) all snarling, that is, all of them except old Augustus, and he was just too fat and lazy and old to get stirred up over anything.

"Finally Wallace cracked the old lion's knees with his whip and got him
(120) into position. Old Augustus, blinking good-naturedly, opened his mouth and in popped Wallace's head. Then the jaws came together, *crunch*, just like that."

The Leopard Man smiled in a
(125) sweetly wistful fashion, and the far-away look came into his eyes.

"And that was the end of King Wallace," he went on in his sad, low voice. "After the excitement cooled down
(130) I watched my chance and bent over and smelled Wallace's head. Then I sneezed."

"It . . . it was . . .?" I queried with halting eagerness.

"Snuff—that De Ville dropped on
(135) his hair in the dressing tent. Old Augustus never meant to do it. He only sneezed."

Adapted from *Leopard man's story* by Jack London

Who's telling the story?

The story of King Wallace and De Ville the knife-thrower is told by the Leopard Man, who worked with both of them at the circus. The way the Leopard Man is described—as sweet and soft-spoken—indicates that he probably would give a trustworthy account of the action. After all, the writer says that the Leopard Man doesn't think his own life is exciting or interesting.

What's happening?

The Leopard man describes a love triangle that ends in a very atypical murder, in which De Ville gets the old lion to kill his rival (which is pretty darn impressive, when you think about it).

Who are the main characters?

Which characters are mentioned most often? Which characters make an impact on the action? Wallace and De Ville, as well as the Leopard Man himself. De Ville's wife is, in a sense, important (since the men's conflict is over her), but she never actually appears in the narrative.

What's the mood?

Well, knife-throwing, wild animals, romance, jealousy, not to mention heads getting chomped off…shall we say the mood is one of adventure? Of action and daring?

What is the setting?

The setting is, of course, the big top of a travelling circus, and clearly this setting is quite important to the story. Not too many people get their heads bitten off in the public library or at the bus stop.

Now that we've covered our Big Questions, let's check out some test questions.

1. Old Augustus kills Wallace because

    (1)   the lion is angry about the lion tamer's brutality
    (2)   Augustus hates De Ville's wife and wants her to be unhappy
    (3)   De Ville causes an involuntary response in the lion
    (4)   The Leopard Man is unable to stop him in time
    (5)   De Ville has trained him to do so

Answer: (3). This question tests your understanding of the main plot idea of the story. De Ville, who can't beat the bigger, tougher Wallace in a flat-out fight, figures out a way to get a lion to do his dirty work for him. So, let's use POE. (1) and (2) can go, since the old lion has nothing against Wallace—in fact, we're told that Augustus is the most dependable of all the big cats. (4) is no good, since the Leopard Man didn't know what De Ville's trap was until he investigated later. And (5) might look good for a moment, until we remember that De Ville didn't *train* the lion (as Wallace or the Leopard Man might), but rather just got the animal to sneeze at the worst (or best, depending who you're rooting for) possible time. So, we're left with (3).

2. The description of the Leopard Man depicts him as

    (1)   surprisingly good-natured and soft-spoken
    (2)   deeply jealous and hot tempered
    (3)   exceptionally bold and violent
    (4)   unusually treacherous and conniving
    (5)   inherently fearful and suspicious

Answer: (1). This comprehension question can be answered by looking at the author's early description of the Leopard Man, who "did not look" like a wild animal tamer. He is described as "sweetly and gently" bearing the weight of sadness—the very opposite of what one expects of a man who risks so much doing his job. The other answer choices describe other characters in his story, but not the Leopard Man himself. Don't be fooled by such answer choices: Read the question carefully, and make sure you know who you're being asked about.

3. The Leopard Man says Wallace was "a king and no mistake" (lines 72–73) in order to demonstrate Wallace's

   (1) superior wealth
   (2) fearlessness
   (3) claim to a throne
   (4) power over other circus performers
   (5) skill at playing games

Answer: (2). Just before this line, the Leopard Man says that Wallace "was afraid of nothing alive or dead," and that that's why he was called "King." So, eliminate (1), (3), and (5), which are not supported by the text. As for (4), well, the other performers definitely respect Wallace, but we can't really say that he exerts any "power over" them. So, (2) is the best answer.

4. When he says "De Ville will bear watching," (line 107) the Leopard Man means De Ville

   (1) is going to look at the bear cages
   (2) can't take care of himself
   (3) doesn't realize how late in the day it is
   (4) will not allow himself to be seen
   (5) should be observed carefully

Answer: (5). The Leopard Man sees De Ville acting suspiciously, and thinks that he's about to do something evil to Wallace. The Leopard Man thinks he had better watch De Ville closely, in case he does try something; when the knife-thrower does go off towards town, the Leopard Man is relieved. So, "bear watching" means "I'd better keep my eye on that guy." Let's eliminate what doesn't match. Even though the word "bear" is used, it's not the same kind of bear as the animal, so (1) can be eliminated. He doesn't mean that De Ville needs to be watched for *his own good,* so it's not (2). It's not (3) either, since this isn't the time-keeping kind of "watch." Nor is (4) any good, since De Ville does go about openly, and is in full view of the public as he leaves what will soon be the scene of the crime. So, (5) best translates the line we're being asked about.

5. The author puts the word "crunch" in italics in order to

    (1) emphasize the drama of the moment
    (2) show the humor of the incident
    (3) make the noise seem louder than it actually was
    (4) draw the reader's attention to a foreign word within the English text
    (5) indicate that this word is not meant literally

Answer: (1). This is an analysis question, which asks why the writer does what he does—how he creates the effect he desires. Here, in the climactic moment of the story, the old lion bites down on Wallace's head. The writer italicizes the "crunch" to make the reader hear—or even feel (kind of)—this, which the whole story has lead up to. So, it's there—and in italics—to increase the impact (no pun intended) of the story's climax. Let's see what we can eliminate. (2) is no good, because this is definitely not funny (although De Ville was probably laughing). As for (3), our answer has to do with emphasizing the sound, but the writer is not trying to *make it louder,* just to make us really notice it. And, while foreign words are often italicized, "crunch" is not such a word, so we can lose (4). (5) doesn't work either, since the writer does literally mean that Augustus's jaws went *crunch* onto King Wallace's head.

DRAMA

Drama is a similar form to fiction in that each tells an imaginary story using dialog and action. What makes reading a play different from reading a work of fiction is that, while fiction is written to be read, drama is intended to be performed on stage; so, in fiction, the words on the page are meant to be just that, words on a page—whereas the words on the page of a play are meant to be coming out of people's mouths. Therefore, as you read a drama passage, the best thing to do is imagine the play being performed in front of you. Give different voices to the various characters: You might even picture famous actors playing the roles. This way, you're "seeing" it the way the writer wants you to—meaning you're more likely to "get it."

Since a play is meant to be performed, it has much more dialog than description. The dialog *reveals* the plot and characterization. As you read the dialog, imagine the actors' actions that would accompany what they're saying.

Keep these Big Questions in mind, many of which are largely the same as those you asked yourself about the fiction passages:

What's happening?

As in fiction, there will be some plot—some action, some conflict—but keep in mind, the "action" is likely to be portrayed via the dialog, rather than through description.

Who are the main characters?

Drama passages will only have two or three main characters, though you may also see several minor characters, who are there to move the action along or perform some background function. Concentrate on the main characters, though: What are they doing? What are they feeling? What is their relationship to one another? How do the minor characters behave toward the main characters?

Here's a useful tool to figure out what characters think of each other: Are they really listening to each other? If they're actually *speaking* to each other, then they have a more respectful relationship; if they're just yammering on—speaking more to the audience, or just to hear their own selves talk—rather than actually interacting, then that tells you that they might not care much for each other. If one character is responding to another, but not vice versa, then you can deduce that their relationship is more one-sided.

What's the mood?

In drama, this translates to: What are the emotional states of the main characters? Is the dialog frantic, with characters interrupting one another and trying to talk over each other? Is it funny, with characters trading jokes and making fun of each other? Is it sad or mournful, with pauses, and more emotionally loaded words being exchanged? All of these help you define the mood of the play.

What is the setting?

Usually a brief description of the setting is given at the beginning of the passage, which gives you a great place to start answering this question. But don't stop there—see if the characters actually interact with the setting. The more they do so, the more integral that setting probably is to the drama's main idea. If, on the other hand, the setting is "a room," and the action of the text plays out with no other specific reference to the set itself, then it's likely less important to "getting the point."

Let's look at an example of the kind of Drama passage you'll see on the GED. Read through this excerpt from a play, and then answer the Big Questions. Once we do that, we'll be ready for the specific multiple-choice test questions.

WHAT IS ERNEST TRYING TO HIDE FROM ALGERNON?

Ernest has come to visit Algernon. The two plan to have tea with Algernon's Aunt Augusta and cousin Gwendolen. Ernest tells Algernon that he plans to propose to
(5) Gwendolen.

Algernon. You behave as if you were married to her already. You are not married to her already, and I don't think you ever will be.

(10) **Ernest.** Why on earth do you say that?

Algernon. Well, in the first place girls never marry the men they flirt with. Girls don't think it right.

Ernest. Oh, that is nonsense!

(15) **Algernon.** It isn't. It is a great truth. It accounts for the extraordinary number of bachelors that one sees all over the place. In the second place, I don't give my consent.

(20) **Ernest.** Your consent!

Algernon. My dear fellow, Gwendolen is my first cousin. And before I allow you to marry her, you will have to clear up the whole question of Cecily.

(25) [Rings bell.]

Ernest. Cecily! What on earth do you mean? What do you mean, Algy, by Cecily! I don't know any one of the name of Cecily.

(30) [Enter Servant.]

Algernon. Bring me that cigarette case Mr. Worthing left in the smoking-room the last time he dined here.

Servant. Yes, sir. [Servant goes out.]

(35) **Ernest.** Do you mean to say you have had my cigarette case all this time? I wish to goodness you had let me know. I have been writing frantic letters to Scotland Yard about it. I was very
(40) nearly offering a large reward.

Algernon. Well, I wish you would offer one. I happen to be more than usually hard up.

Ernest. There is no good offering a large
(45) reward now that the thing is found.

[Enter Servant with the cigarette case on a tray. Algernon takes it at once. Servant goes out.]

Algernon. I think that is rather mean of
(50) you, Ernest, I must say. [Opens case and examines it.] However, it makes no matter, for, now that I look at the inscription inside, I find that the thing isn't yours after all.

(55) **Ernest.** Of course its mine. [Moving to him.] You have seen me with it a hundred times, and you have no right whatsoever to read what is written inside. It is a very ungentlemanly thing
(60) to read a private cigarette case.

Algernon. Oh! it is absurd to have a hard and fast rule about what one should read and what one shouldn't. More than half of modern culture depends
(65) on what one shouldn't read.

Ernest. I am quite aware of the fact, and I don't propose to discuss modern culture. It isn't the sort of thing one should talk of in private. I simply want
(70) my cigarette case back.

Algernon. Yes; but this isn't your cigarette case. This cigarette case is a present from some one of the name of Cecily, and you said you didn't know
(75) any one of that name.

Ernest. Well, if you want to know, Cecily happens to be my aunt.

Algernon. Your aunt!

Ernest. Yes. Charming old lady she is,
(80) too. Just give it back to me, Algy.

Algernon. [Retreating to back of sofa.] But why does she call herself little Cecily if she is your aunt? [Reading.] From little Cecily with her fondest love.

(85) **Ernest.** [Moving to sofa and kneeling upon it.] My dear fellow, what on earth is there in that? Some aunts are tall, some aunts are not tall. That is a matter that surely an aunt may (90) be allowed to decide for herself. You seem to think that every aunt should be exactly like your aunt! That is absurd! For Heavens sake give me back my cigarette case. [Follows (95) Algernon round the room.]

Algernon. Yes. But why does your aunt call you her uncle? From little Cecily, with her fondest love to her dear Uncle Jack. There is no objection, I admit, to (100) an aunt being a small aunt, but why an aunt, no matter what her size may be, should call her own nephew her uncle, I can't quite make out. Besides, your name isn't Jack at all; it is Ernest.

(105) **Ernest.** It isn't Ernest; it's Jack.

Algernon. You have always told me it was Ernest. I have introduced you to every one as Ernest. You answer to the name of Ernest. You look as if (110) your name was Ernest. You are the most earnest-looking person I ever saw in my life. It is perfectly absurd your saying that your name isn't Ernest. It's on your cards. Here is (115) one of them. [Taking it from case.] Mr. Ernest Worthing, B. 4, The Albany. I'll keep this as a proof that your name is Ernest if ever you attempt to deny it to me, or to Gwendolen, or to any one (120) else. [Puts the card in his pocket.]

Ernest. Well, my name is Ernest in town and Jack in the country, and the cigarette case was given to me in the country.

(125) **Algernon.** Come, old boy, you had much better have the thing out at once.

Ernest. Well, produce my cigarette case first.

(130) **Algernon.** Here it is. [Hands cigarette case.] Now produce your explanation, and pray make it improbable. [Sits on sofa.]

Ernest. My dear fellow, there is nothing improbable about my explanation at (135) all. In fact it's perfectly ordinary. Old Mr. Thomas Cardew, who adopted me when I was a little boy, made me in his will guardian to his grand-daughter, Miss Cecily Cardew. Cecily, (140) who addresses me as her uncle from motives of respect that you could not possibly appreciate, lives at my place in the country under the charge of her admirable governess, Miss Prism.

(145) **Algernon.** Now, go on. Why are you Ernest in town and Jack in the country?

Ernest. My dear Algy, I don't know whether you will be able to understand (150) my real motives. You are hardly serious enough. When one is placed in the position of guardian, one has to adopt a very high moral tone on all subjects. It's one's duty to do so. And (155) as a high moral tone can hardly be said to conduce very much to either one's health or one's happiness, in order to get up to town I have always pretended to have a younger brother (160) of the name of Ernest, who lives in a hotel here in the city, and gets into the most dreadful scrapes. That, my dear Algy, is the whole truth pure and simple.

(165) **Algernon.** The truth is rarely pure and never simple. Modern life would be very tedious if it were either, and modern literature a complete impossibility!

—Adapted from Wilde's "Importance of Being Earnest"

What's happening?

Ernest goes to visit his friend Algernon, who says he's found Ernest's cigarette case—but it's inscribed not to Ernest, but to a mysterious "Jack." Algernon demands an explanation, and Ernest tries to avoid giving him one (as they chase each other, both physically and verbally, around the room). Finally, Ernest spills the beans: He has, essentially, been living a double life, having one identity when in the country ("Jack") and another when in town ("Ernest").

Who are the main characters?

As we've said, it's really only Algernon—the witty one whose house the scene is in—and Ernest (a.k.a. Jack), his friend. Other characters are mentioned (specifically Gwendolen and Cecily), and a servant appears briefly, but Algy and Ernest are the main players here.

What's the mood?

What can we say about the mood? The two men are chasing each other around, almost "Tom and Jerry"-style. So, it's certainly funny, even a bit silly—this tone really comes across when you picture two famous comic actors doing the scene, talking very quickly as they run around the sofa and chairs.

Remember: Picturing actual actors playing the roles helps out massively when it comes to drama passages. Doing this makes you "see" the action, rather than just reading it—and plays are meant to be seen.

What is the setting?

As we're told at the beginning, this scene takes place in Algernon's house. The characters do interact with the setting, as they chase each other around the room. Another clue: they talk about "town" (where this scene takes place) versus "country" (where Ernest uses his alternate identity, "Jack")—so the setting is likely an important element.

Now let's check out the test questions.

1. Which of the following best describes Ernest and Algernon's relationship?

   The two men are

   (1) rivals for Gwendolen's affection
   (2) cousins who live in the country
   (3) strangers who just met
   (4) friends who are sometimes in conflict
   (5) enemies, though each envies the other

Answer: (4). Even though this excerpt is comprised of a lengthy and comical argument between the two characters, the evidence shows that they are friends who have known one another for some time. [For instance, Algernon says "You have always told me it was Ernest. I have introduced you to every one as Ernest." Ernest calls Algernon by an affectionate nickname—Algy, and says that Algernon has seen him with the cigarette case "a hundred times." All of this demonstrates their longstanding friendship.] So, eliminate (2), since the men are not related, (3) for obvious reasons, and (5) since they are not enemies. Get rid of (1), since Ernest is interested in Gwendolen while Algernon is simply her cousin.

2. Ernest repeatedly demands his cigarette case back from Algernon. This repetition demonstrates that Ernest

   (1) needs to escape before Gwendolen arrives
   (2) desires to end the conversation without explaining himself fully
   (3) is unable to go without smoking cigarettes
   (4) lacks imagination in his conversation
   (5) has forgotten why he came to see Algernon

Answer: (2). Much of this scene is devoted to Algernon playing "keep away" with Ernest's cigarette case. Ernest clearly doesn't want to reveal the reason that the case is inscribed to "Jack" rather than "Ernest." His continued requests for the case show how much he wants the entire matter to just go away. So, we can say that (1) is wrong, since Ernest is not trying to escape from Gwendolen, but rather to avoid having the cigarette case controversy brought up in her presence. (3) is no good, since it's about the case, and its inscription, rather than cigarettes themselves. Nor does (4) work, since nothing indicates that Ernest couldn't carry on a more varied conversation under different circumstances. And (5) is no good either, because Ernest hasn't forgotten why he came—his attempts to get the case back are directly related to why he came.

3. Ernest's attempts to explain the inscription are unconvincing to Algernon because

    (1) Ernest doesn't know the truth about the inscription

    (2) Ernest has not told the police that the case is missing

    (3) Ernest's stories don't completely make sense

    (4) Algernon has known for years that Ernest is a liar

    (5) Algernon knows the real truth already

Answer: (3). Algernon refuses to let go of the cigarette case (both literally and figuratively) until Ernest tells him the truth about it. After pretending he doesn't know about the inscription, Ernest tries a series of false or incomplete explanations, but Algernon won't let him get away with them. Every time he tries one, Algernon cross-examines him. (For example: "But why does your aunt call you her uncle?" and "Why are you Ernest in town and Jack in the country?") So, we can say that whenever Ernest's explanations don't totally add up, Algernon pounces on them. So, eliminate (1), because Algernon knows that Ernest does know, and is purposely hiding the truth. (2) can be cut, since Ernest does say he has notified Scotland Yard (who are the police). And (4) is not supported by the text: Algernon is genuinely surprised that his friend has such a secret. Algernon, however, definitely does not know the real truth already—in fact he very much wants to find it out; therefore we can eliminate (5). (3) is the answer best supported by the text.

4. When he does finally explain the fact that the inscription on his cigarette case refers to him as "Jack," Ernest says that

    (1) he created an imaginary person, in order to escape from some of his responsibilities

    (2) he plans to return the cigarette case, now that he knows it isn't really his

    (3) he stole it from someone named Jack

    (4) the engraver made a mistake, and inscribed the wrong name on it

    (5) he inherited it from his uncle Jack

Answer: (1). This comprehension question can be answered in a straightforward manner—the trick is figuring out where to find the information. Use the clue in the question—the word "finally"—and go to the end of the passage, where we find Ernest's eventual explanation for the inscription on the case. He says he invented "Ernest," to give him an excuse to come to town, instead of being stuck out in the country. Let's use POE. Get rid of (2) and (3), since the cigarette case is in fact his. (4) can go, since "Jack" and "Ernest" are in fact the same person. (1) best answers the question.

5. Algernon's words in lines 106-114 ("You have ... cards) primarily serve to

(1) show that Ernest's name is really Jack
(2) prove that nothing Ernest has told him is true
(3) convince Ernest to marry Cecily instead of Gwendolen
(4) offer evidence to rebut Ernest's previous claim
(5) demonstrate the necessity of proper identification

Answer: (4). Ernest tells Algernon that his name is really Jack. Ernest doesn't believe it, and, in these lines, gives a bunch of reasons why Ernest's name must be Ernest. So, get rid of (1), since that's the opposite of Algernon's intention. (2) is too strong: "nothing is true"? This is just one instance, not a denial of everything the man has ever said. (3) is not what Algernon is trying to do at all, as he has never met Cecily. (5) doesn't answer the question, because we're only talking about one man and his identity, not everyone everywhere. (4) appropriately sums up the lines. As a side note, the word *rebut* means argue against or disprove.

6. The title of this play is "The Importance of Being Earnest," and the word earnest means "straightforward and truthful." Why does the playwright have a dishonest character named "Ernest?"

The playwright most likely does this because he

(1) accidentally chose a word and a name that sound the same
(2) wishes to draw an ironic contrast between a character and his name
(3) wants to show that our understanding of the word is incorrect
(4) does not understand the word's definition
(5) wants to show how words' definitions change over time

Answer: (2). Analysis questions—those about why an author does what he does—can be tougher to answer in your own words. But, we can get rid of answers that don't work, and then see what we've got left. So: (1) and (4) are no good, because authors (good ones, like those whom the GED excerpts) definitely know what they're doing; (3) doesn't work either, because we do know what "earnest" means; and (5) gets the axe as well, because the word's definition has not changed (and there's nothing in the passage to suggest that it has). So, we're left with (2), that the author is being deliberately ironic—using a word to mean its opposite, for literary effect.

NON-FICTION

Non-fiction passages on the GED come in a few varieties. One of them will definitely be a business or government document, while others could be magazine articles and performance reviews. All in all, these are not much different from the kind of reading you're doing in the Social Studies and Science sections, so your approach to the Reading Test non-fiction will be pretty similar to that which you used on the Social Studies and Science sections. On the other hand, the Language Arts, Reading non-fiction passages are likely a lot more interesting than those were. (Well, maybe not the government documents—those aren't exactly a thrill a minute. But let's just say they'll be no worse than the ones about seed germination in the Science section.)

Here's what you should be thinking about as you read these passages:

What is the main idea?

Every non-fiction passage has a main idea. Whether it's stated outright or in a more subtle fashion, it's definitely there. Find that main idea: It'll help you answer most or even all of the questions (even if none of the questions is "What is the main idea?).

Note that the main idea is not just the topic of the passage, but also what the writer says (in an overall way) about the topic. So, if a passage is about kickboxing, the main idea isn't "kickboxing," or "kickboxing is an activity," but something more like "kickboxing is the sport of the future," or "kickboxing is a superior workout." (Or, maybe more likely, "kickboxing is extremely dangerous if done without proper instruction and equipment.")

How is the main idea supported?

Does the author use specific examples to back up her position? Does she cite statistics? Does she use anecdotes (that is, brief stories) to support her point? Or does she offer moral or ethical arguments.

In the government documents, what specifics are given? Are there steps to follow, or a list of "do's and don'ts"?

What does the author think about the topic?

Does the author agree or disagree with the main idea, or is she undecided? What is the tone of the piece: Positive? Neutral? Negative? Ironic? (Irony—that is, sarcasm—is popular in non-fiction passages. As in real-life conversation, irony in these passages occurs when the speaker really means the opposite of the words she's using.)

Read through the following non-fiction passage, asking yourself those Big Questions, and then we'll take a look at the multiple-choice questions.

WHY IS IT DIFFICULT TO COMPILE THIS CD?

The following CD review appeared in the pages of Soul Blues Magazine

Even by genre standards, Texas bluesman Sam "Lightnin" Hopkins released a stupefying amount of material during his lengthy career. As a guitar player, he was
(5)   never what one would call a perfectionist; few of his recordings are free of off-notes or mis-fretted chords, and he had no compunction about putting out version after version of the same song, either under the
(10)   same or different titles.

For such reasons, many fans feel that Hopkins is better served by "Best of" compilations than by individual albums. But how is one to choose which tracks to
(15)   include on a compilation CD, when there is such a surfeit of material? How can one select the best, say, "Mojo Hand," when there are 30-odd recordings of it floating around? Seemingly every time he sat down
(20)   to record, he'd do another run through "Mojo Hand." Every time he recorded the song he played it a little differently: each has its recommendations, each its shortcomings. And every one of those
(25)   takes has been released at some point over the years.

Since so many versions of the song were released, none sold appreciably better than the others—making "popular acclaim"
(30)   a moot point. No particular recording can be called a "Greatest Hit," even though the song itself is probably his best known composition.

So, when it's time to put out another
(35)   "Lightnin" Hopkins compilation CD, that means it's time to decide upon a "Mojo Hand" to include on it.

It would seem that all the intrepid compiler can do is choose one version
(40)   of "Mojo Hand" that is just as good as

(although admittedly no better than)
many others … and then do the same
for "Katie Mae," and again for "Lightnin's
Boogie," and on and on … thus rendering
(45) any purported "Best of" album less
representative of Sam "Lightnin" Hopkins
than of the person putting it together.

So it is with this most recent album:
the song titles are there, and a fan finds
(50) few surprises among them. But do you
need *this* album? Do you need these
particular versions, culled from various
sessions spanning five decades? Do you
need yet another "Lightnin" Hopkins CD
(55) titled—you guessed it—MOJO HAND?

Once again, let's think about those Big Questions before we get to the specific ones.

What is the main idea?

The question at the top of the page definitely gives us a big hint about the main idea here. The writer is reviewing a "Best of Lightnin' Hopkins" CD, and says that it's hard to put together a quality CD of the "Best of" Lightnin' Hopkins: Since the musician did so many versions of his various songs, it's really hard to choose the "best" one, and a lot of people will disagree with whichever version of a song a CD does include.

How is the main idea supported?

The writer gives us some titles of songs that Hopkins recorded many different times. So, specific examples are given to back up the main point.

What does the author think about the topic?

Look at the last couple of paragraphs to answer this question. The writer says that whichever version of a song *is* chosen is probably no better than those *not* chosen. He then asks whether the reader needs "this album." What's he implying? That the reader probably doesn't need this album.

Now that we know the overall stuff, we can tackle the multiple-choice questions.

1. The writer indicates that deciding on a good version of "Mojo Hand" is

    (1) impossible
    (2) subjective
    (3) unpopular
    (4) confusing
    (5) uncommon

Answer: (2). The writer says more than 30 recordings of the song exist, and that each could be considered for a "Best of" compilation. So, while it might be impossible to say which is the greatest version, it is very possible to find a good one—eliminate (1), (4), and (5). There's no reason to think that a good version would be unpopular, so get rid of (3). Since a listener might prefer any number of the existing versions, (2) is the best answer.

2. The main idea of this passage is that Lightnin' Hopkins

    (1) recorded more songs than any other blues musician
    (2) made too many mistakes for his records to be considered good
    (3) presents several problems for blues fans
    (4) resists easy song selection processes
    (5) cannot be accurately represented on CD

Answer: (4). The passage is concerned with the difficulty of deciding upon the best version of any given Lightnin' Hopkins song. It never says that he recorded more than any other musician, so get rid of (1). While it says that Hopkins's songs often contained mistakes, it doesn't say there were too many mistakes, so eliminate (2). While Hopkins's work is problematic, it's problematic for people who want to put together "Best of" CDs, not for people who want to listen to them, so (3) is not correct. Remember: Every word of an answer choice has to be right. (5) is too extreme; just because multiple versions of songs exist doesn't make it impossible to represent the artist's work. Choice (4) best captures the main idea.

3. "Intrepid" (line 38) can best be replaced with

   (1) foolish
   (2) misguided
   (3) intelligent
   (4) adventurous
   (5) artistic

Answer: (4). "Intrepid" is an adjective usually applied to daring explorers who blaze new trails through the wilderness. If you know that, then this question is quite easy. If, however, you don't know the vocab, then use the context to give yourself a fighting chance. What do we know? Well, the compiler has to search through a ton of versions of a song to find what to her is the best one. So, neither (1) nor (2) is a good fit. Intellectual ability isn't really what this is about either—it's a matter of taste more than book-learning, so eliminate (3). And the compiler is principally involved in a search, not in making her own artistic statement, so (5) is not as good an answer as choice (4).

4. The writer implies that "Katie Mae"

   (1) was recorded after "Mojo Hand"
   (2) is better than "Lightnin's Boogie"
   (3) exists in multiple versions
   (4) was recorded by other singers as well
   (5) has been overshadowed by Hopkins's other songs

Answer: (3). When you're asked about what an author implies, look for what *must be* true, not what *could be*. What do we know about the song "Katie Mae"? The writer described a process of sifting through many competing versions of "Mojo Hand," and then says one would have to do the same for "Katie Mae." Therefore there must be a whole bunch of different recordings of "Katie Mae" as well. Get rid of (1), since we don't know about which song came first; get rid of (2) and (5), since we're not comparing one song to another, just different versions of the same song; (4) is no good, as only Lightnin' Hopkins is referred to, not any other singers. (3) is the only one that is supported by the passage.

5. The series of questions in the final paragraph serves which of the following functions?

    The questions are intended to make the reader

    (1) wonder if compilation CDs serve any purpose
    (2) realize that Hopkins was less talented than many listeners believe
    (3) see that this compilation CD may not be a necessary addition to Hopkins's discography
    (4) recognize the lack of imagination of the people who compiled this CD
    (5) understand that nobody can predict which version of a song will sell the most copies

Answer: (3). With these questions, the writer reinforces the point that, since Lightnin' Hopkins recorded a bunch of versions of the same songs, the versions included on this CD are not necessarily as good as others that are available—hence the "Do you need *this* album?" So, get rid of what doesn't match. (1) can be eliminated, because this article is only about Lightnin' Hopkins compilation CDs, not compilation CDs in general. (2) is no good, since it's not Hopkins's talent that's at issue, just the selections made by his compilers. (4) is needlessly harsh on those compilers—it's not that they lack imagination, just that their selections may be questionable. And (5) can go, since we're not talking about what *sells*, but rather what *has artistic merit*.

POETRY

First, read the poem. Then, read it again. Reading a poem twice makes a *huge* difference in how well you understand it. The first time you read it, you're looking for what happened—because even in poetry, something happens. The second time you read it, since now you know what happened, you're finding out how it happened. How does the poet use language to make her point?

A poem is a bit like a mystery: The first time you read it, you see wild and seemingly inexplicable events occurring. The poem may contain weird sentence structure or odd syntax—it's a poem, so it's allowed to play by somewhat looser rules than prose does. (This looseness is what's meant by the phrase "poetic license.") But don't get tangled up in any linguistic weirdness on your first reading of the poem. Instead, concentrate on figuring out *what happened*. Then, immediately reread the poem: The second time you read the poem, figure out *how it happened*. Now you're Sherlock Holmes, putting together the clues, seeing the way the puzzle pieces fit together.

Putting it a slightly different way: First, read the poem for its literal (surface level) meaning. If it's about a river, just consider it as a piece of writing about a river. On the second reading, think about the figurative (deeper, symbolic) meaning. Does the river represent the flow of life, maybe?

Also, realize that even though some poems are harder to read than, say, a fiction passage, many times the questions about a poem are in fact easier than those about the other passages. (Again, the GED is *not necessarily* like high school English class.) So, if you "get" the literal meaning of a poem (the river as a river), but aren't too sure about the figurative meaning (what does the river symbolize?), you'll probably still be in good shape to answer a lot of the questions.

One question you definitely need is: *Who is speaking?* Many poems are told from a certain perspective—much as a piece of fiction often has a "narrator," a poem often has a "speaker." (Those two are the same thing: In a poem, the narrator is called the speaker. In both cases, it's the "I" of the passage.) Who is this speaker? A lot of times the "I" of a poem is the poet himself—a lot of times, but not always. Look for clues in the poem that tell you about the speaker.

Worst case scenario, you get a poem that you really have a hard time understanding on almost any level. Even then, there's something you can do. Think about the mood: Is it sad, joyous, nostalgic, or silly? Just knowing what the overall tone of the poem is can be enough to eliminate a bunch of answer choices, thereby allowing you to make strong guesses on many questions.

Let's check out an example. Read this poem once, and then read it again, and let's see what we can figure out.

> Little Fly,
> Thy summer's play
> My thoughtless hand
> Has brushed away.
>
> (5)   Am not I
> A fly like thee?
> Or art not thou
> A man like me?
>
> For I dance
> (10) And drink and sing,
> Till some blind hand
> Shall brush my wing.
>
> If thought is life
> And strength and breath,
> (15) And the want
> Of thought is death,
>
> Then am I
> A happy fly,
> If I live
> (20) Or if I die.
>
>   —Blake: *The Fly*

Okay, let's see what we've got. You *did* read it twice, right? Great.

This is an old poem, and it uses some antiquated language (like *thy* instead of *your*, and *thee* and *thou* in place of *you*), but don't let that stop you.

What's happening on the surface-level of the poem?

The speaker of the poem—who does seem to be the poet himself—thoughtlessly smashes a fly. Then he thinks that he could be swatted by something that's as much bigger than he is as he is bigger than the fly.

What is the mood?

The poet considers life and how fleeting it is, that his own is no more assured than a fly's. So, we can say that the tone is contemplative (that is, deep-thinking) and serious, maybe even a little sad.

Now let's use what we've found on some test questions.

1. The poet compares himself to the fly because

   (1) he has trouble concentrating
   (2) he feels insignificant
   (3) he desires flight
   (4) he can't stay still
   (5) he sees his own life as tenuous

Answer: (5). In the poem, the speaker absent-mindedly swats a fly. He then thinks that he himself is like the fly, pursuing his own activities until someone—or something—bigger than he will swat him. So, his existence is fragile, when compared to the greater powers in life; just as the fly's existence is so fragile that the poet affects it without even realizing he has. Look for an answer that matches this idea: Neither (1) nor (3) work at all. While he says he'll "dance and drink and sing," it's not movement that the writer is mainly concerned with; it's life itself. Eliminate (4). (Also, just because he doesn't stay still *doesn't* mean he *can't*.) So, we're down to (2) and (5): What's the difference between them: (2) uses the word "insignificant," or meaningless. Is this what the poet is referring to? No, it's not the (un)importance of his life—or the fly's—that worries him. It's how easily such a life can be ended. Choice (5), therefore, works best.

2. What does "The want of thought" (lines 15-16) mean?

   (1) the desire for learning
   (2) the need for education
   (3) the lack of mental activity
   (4) the wish for someone to care
   (5) the urge for adventure

Answer: (3). Using *want* to signify *lack*, or *insufficient amount*, is an archaic usage unfamiliar to many modern readers. Nevertheless, we can use context to help us answer the question. The poet says that *Thought is life and strength and breath*—so, when you are thinking then you are living—and then says that something else is *Death*: So, that something else must be the opposite of thinking, since death is the opposite of life. We need the opposite of thinking, so eliminate (4) and (5). Look again at (1), (2), and (3). The desire and the need for learning/education aren't the opposite of thinking. Get rid of those two, and you're left with (3).

3.   What is "some blind hand" (line 11)?

     (1)   a power greater than the author
     (2)   a disabled person
     (3)   an unfortunate game of cards
     (4)   an enemy of the author
     (5)   the author's father

Answer: (1). This question involves the main idea of the poem—that the writer, having swatted a fly without even realizing that he had, now worries that something will thoughtlessly swat *him*, something as much bigger and more powerful than he as he is than the fly. Which answer choices don't match this? (2) and (3) have no relevance, so get rid of those. (5) doesn't work either, since the author, as an adult, couldn't be swatted by his own father. What about (4)? His enemies would have reasons to do harm to the poet—therefore, if one did "raise his hand" against the writer, it wouldn't be done *blindly* (that is, thoughtlessly), but rather *on purpose*. So, (4) doesn't work. Choice (1) is the best answer.

Now that we've seen examples of all four types of passages and learned how to work through them, you have a decent idea about which types of passages work best for you. Naturally, as you keep practicing you'll be getting better at both the kinds of passages that you're good at, and the kinds that you're not as good at.

As you go through the practice drills that follow, keep using the techniques we've been working on. It's not just practice that makes perfect, it's the *right kind* of practice.

Always stick to the techniques: They are the processes that get you the right answers.

FICTION DRILL

WHAT DOES THE AUTHOR THINK ABOUT HIS CHARACTER'S PHILOSOPHY?

Memnon one day took it into his head to become a great philosopher. "To be perfectly happy," said he to himself, "I have nothing to do but to divest myself
(5) entirely of passions; and nothing is more easy, as everybody knows. In the first place, I will never be in love; for, when I see a beautiful woman, I will say to myself, these cheeks will one day grow sallow
(10) and wrinkled, these eyes be encircled with vermilion, that bosom become lean and emaciated, that head bald and palsied. Now I have only to consider her at present in imagination as she will afterwards appear
(15) in reality, and certainly a fair face will never turn my head.

"In the second place, I shall always be temperate. It will be in vain to tempt me with good cheer, with delicious wines, or
(20) the charms of society, I will have only to figure to myself the consequences of excess — an aching head, a loathing stomach, the loss of reason, of health, and of time: I will then only eat to supply the
(25) waste of nature; my health will be always equal, my ideas pure and luminous. All this is so easy that there is no merit in accomplishing it."

"But," says Memnon, "I must think
(30) a little of how I am to regulate my fortune: why, my desires are moderate, my wealth is securely placed with the Receiver General of the finances of Nineveh. I have wherewithal to live independent; and that
(35) is the greatest of blessings. I shall never be under the cruel necessity of dancing

attendance at court. I will never envy any one, and nobody will envy me. Still all this is easy. I have friends, and I will
(40) preserve them, for we shall never have any difference. I will never take amiss anything they may say or do; and they will behave in the same way to me. There is no difficulty in all this."

(45) Having thus laid this little plan of philosophy in his closet, Memnon put his head out of the window.

Adapted from *Memnon*, the Philosopher by Voltaire

1. Memnon plans to resist overeating by

   (1) staying away from all food
   (2) reminding himself of what it will lead to
   (3) eating only food that he dislikes
   (4) giving his food away to the poor
   (5) not having enough money to dine well

2. The word "fair" (line 15) could best be replaced by

   (1) legal
   (2) even
   (3) ethical
   (4) pretty
   (5) celebratory

3. Memnon would define his philosophy principle as

   (1) unrealistic
   (2) problematic
   (3) moderate
   (4) impractical
   (5) friendly

4. The author views Memnon's attempt at philosophy as

   (1) naive and unrealistic
   (2) praiseworthy and noble
   (3) wise and thoughtful
   (4) evil and malicious
   (5) uncommon and incomprehensible

ANSWERS AND EXPLANATIONS TO FICTION DRILL

1. **(2)** When confronted with good food and drink, Memnon says he'll "figure the consequences" of overindulgence, consequences like an upset stomach and ill health. POE bad answers: it's not (1), because he's not going to starve himself. (3) won't work either, since he doesn't mention any such course of action, nor does he plan to (4) give his food away. While he does mention living without much money, that's not how he says he'll regulate his diet, so get rid of (5). (2) is the answer that best comports to the information in the passage.

2. **(4)** Memnon says "When I see a beautiful woman, I will say to myself, these cheeks will one day grow sallow and wrinkled," and so he will not be swayed by attractive women. So when he says "a fair face," we know he's talking about physical beauty. Let's get rid of what doesn't work. Goodbye to (1), (2), (3), and (5), none of which have to do with sex appeal. [Though all of these could be synonyms for "fair" under different circumstances—which shows why you always must go back to the passage, instead of just looking at the question and then searching the answer choices for a match.]

3. **(3)** Memnon wants to get rid of passions and desires in order to be happy. He doesn't want to fall head-over-heels in love, he doesn't want to drink or eat too much, or to crave money (or suffer from having too little), or to envy or be envied. So Memnon himself would say that he's after a kind of "medium-ness" in life. So, let's POE. (1), (2) and (4) can all go, because those are the opposite of how Memnon views his philosophy. And while Memnon does seem to be (5) friendly, that trait has nothing really to do with his philosophy. So, (3) is the best answer.

It's very important to realize that the question asks what Memnon thinks of his philosophy, not what the author thinks of Memnon's philosophy, which would lead to a very different answer.

4. **(1)** Now we're asked what the author thinks about Memnon's philosophy. So what evidence to we see? The first line says that the character "took it into his head to become a great philosopher"—which is a pretty disparaging (that is, belittling or insulting) way to speak of someone's ideas. Essentially, the writer is saying "Hey, this guy had the passing notion that he wanted to be a genius. Ha ha, what a knucklehead." We can be pretty sure that the author thinks much less of Memnon's supposed "philosophy" than Memnon himself does. More evidence comes when we check out the words the author puts in his character's mouth: Memnon considers deep, important questions and answers them with "Well, I'll just do this, and it'll be easy as pie." (Okay, we're paraphrasing here, but this is certainly the author's tone.) So, let's find an answer choice that says "Memnon is not nearly so bright as he thinks he is." Not (2) or (3), both of which are quite positive. Nor is it (4), because the author thinks Memnon is foolish, not an arch-criminal. And (5) doesn't work well, because his philosophy isn't incomprehensible (that is, impossible to understand)—if anything, it's way too simple to take seriously. So, (1) is the best fit.

DRAMA DRILL

WHY DOESN'T THE KING TRUST THE PROPHET?

The city of Thebes has been cursed with a plague ever since the murder of its previous king, Laius. Oedipus, the new king of Thebes, is trying to find out the identity

(5) of his predecessor's murderer. Attempting to get to the bottom of the mystery, he calls for Teiresias, the blind prophet.

[Enter TEIRESIAS led by a small BOY]

OEDIPUS: Teiresias, you who understand
(10) all things—what can be taught and what cannot be spoken of, what goes on in heaven and here on the earth— you know, although you cannot see, how sick our state is. The only cure for
(15) this infecting pestilence is to find the men who murdered Laius and kill them or else expel them from this land as exiles.

So do not withhold from us
(20) your prophecies. Save this city and yourself. Rescue me. Deliver us from this pollution by the dead. We are in your hands.

TEIRESIAS: Alas, alas! How dreadful it
(25) can be to have wisdom when it brings no benefit to the man possessing it. This I knew, but it had slipped my mind.

OEDIPUS: What's wrong? You seem so
(30) sad.

TEIRESIAS: Let me go home. You must bear your burden to the very end, and I will carry mine.

OEDIPUS: If you know something, then,
(35) by heaven, do not turn away. We are your suppliants—all of us—we bend our knees to you.

TEIRESIAS: You are all ignorant. I will not reveal the troubling things inside
(40) me.

OEDIPUS: What are you saying? Do you know and will not say? Do you intend to betray me and destroy the city?

TEIRESIAS: I will cause neither me
(45) nor you distress. Why do you vainly question me like this? You will not learn a thing from me.

OEDIPUS: You most disgraceful of disgraceful men! Will you not speak
(50) out? Will your stubbornness never have an end? What man who listened to these words of yours would not be enraged—you insult the city!

TEIRESIAS: Yet events will still unfold, for
(55) all my silence.

OEDIPUS: Since they will come, you must inform me.

TEIRESIAS: I will say nothing more. Fume on about it, if you wish, as
(60) fiercely as you can.

OEDIPUS: I will! In my anger I will not conceal just what I make of this. You should know I get the feeling you conspired in the act, and played your
(65) part, as much as you could do, short of killing him with your own hands. If you could use your eyes, I would have said that you had done this work all by yourself.

(70) **TEIRESIAS:** Is that so? Then I would ask you to stand by the very words which you yourself proclaimed and from now on not speak to me or these men. For the accursed polluter of this land is
(75) you.

OEDIPUS: You dare to utter shameful words like this? Do you think you can get away with it?

TEIRESIAS: I am getting away with it.
(80)   The truth within me makes me strong. I
         did not want to speak, but you incited
         me.

OEDIPUS: What do you mean? Speak it
         again, so I can understand you more
(85)   precisely.

TEIRESIAS: Did you not grasp my words
         before, or are you trying to test me
         with your question?

OEDIPUS: I did not fully understand your
(90)   words. Tell me again.

TEIRESIAS: I say that you yourself are
         the very man you're looking for.

Adapted from *Oedipus Rex,* by Sophocles,

translated by Ian Johnson

1. What does King Oedipus plan to do with
    the Laius's murderers once he discovers
    their identities?

    He says he will

    (1)   expose them to the plague that
          infects the city
    (2)   forgive them if the curse is lifted
    (3)   either kill them or banish them from
          the land
    (4)   keep silent, for the good of the
          community
    (5)   force them to admit their guilt

2. Which of the following best describes the
    Oedipus's conversation with Teiresias in
    this passage?

    (1)   In the beginning Oedipus offers to
          help Teiresias, until he realizes that
          the man is a fraud
    (2)   First Oedipus compliments the
          prophet, then Oedipus gets angry
          and insults and harasses him.
    (3)   Initially Oedipus cannot understand
          the blind man, but later he sees that
          the man is not who he claims to be
    (4)   First Oedipus questions Teiresias's
          powers, then he comes to believe in
          them
    (5)   In the beginning Oedipus does not
          know who Teiresias is, but he figures
          out the man's identity over time

3. Teiresias repeatedly refuses to reveal what
    he knows about Laius's murder. What
    finally convinces him to talk?

    Teiresias only tells Oedipus about Laius's
    murder once

    (1)   Oedipus threatens to imprison
          Teiresias
    (2)   Oedipus says he will kill Teiresias's
          boy if the prophet doesn't speak up
    (3)   Oedipus begs Teiresias on behalf of
          the entire city
    (4)   Teiresias remembers who the real
          culprit is
    (5)   Oedipus accuses Teiresias of being
          involved in the crime

4. According to Teiresias, who is responsible for Laius's death?

   (1) Oedipus's wife
   (2) Laius himself
   (3) Teiresias
   (4) Oedipus himself
   (5) Laius's bodyguards

5. The word "grasp," in line 86, could best be replaced by which of the following?

   (1) Hug tightly
   (2) Fully comprehend
   (3) Make stronger
   (4) Hold onto
   (5) Repeat precisely

ANSWERS AND EXPLANATIONS TO DRAMA DRILL

1. **(3)** "The only cure," says the king, "is to find the men who murdered Laius and kill them or else expel them from this land as exiles." So, let's match that. It's not (1), since everyone is already exposed to the plague. Get rid of (2) and (4) too, considering that Oedipus demonstrates an utter lack of forgiveness and discretion. He doesn't even say anything about needing a confession from the perpetrators, so (5) has no support in the text. (3) best reflects what the passage says.

2. **(2)** In the opening lines Oedipus praises the blind man, but he soon gets annoyed with the man's unwillingness to give any information. What answer choices does this eliminate? (1) can go, since Teiresias never required any help from Oedipus—really, it's more the other way around. (3) doesn't work, because Oedipus doesn't understand Teiresias's words at the end, not the beginning. (4) pretty much reverses the flow, since the passage shows that Oedipus was more accepting of the prophet at *first*, and *later* came to doubt them. And (5) definitely doesn't work: The king never wonders about Teiresias's identity, but rather that of the murderers.

3. **(5)** Oedipus doesn't get anything out of Teiresias until he says (line 62) "I get the feeling you conspired in the act, and played your part, as much as you could do, short of killing him with your own hands." So, Oedipus says he thinks the blind prophet was in on the murder. This accusation gets a response a response from Teiresias.

4. **(4)** This is clearly stated at the end of the passage. Teiresias says "you yourself are the very man you're looking for." So, Oedipus is the one to blame. Not (1), (2), (3), or (5).

5. **(2)** Teiresias utters the surprising statement that Oedipus himself is the culprit. Oedipus, in disbelief, asks him to repeat himself. "Did you not grasp my words?" Teiresias asks. No, says Oedipus, "I did not fully understand them." So, "grasp," in this case, means "fully understand." Eliminate (1) and (4), which are different uses of "grasp." (3) doesn't work at all, and (5), even though the king is asking the prophet to repeat the words, doesn't relate to "grasp." (2) is the best answer.

WHY ARE THESE ITEMS RESTRICTED?
Bringing Food into the U.S.

We regret that it is necessary to take agricultural items from your baggage. They cannot be brought into the United States because they may carry animal and
(5) plant pests and diseases. Restricted items include meats, fruits, vegetables, plants, soil, and products made from animal or plant materials.

Agricultural pests and diseases are
(10) a threat to U.S. food crops and livestock. Some of these organisms are highly contagious animal diseases that could cause severe economic damage to the livestock industry and losses in production,
(15) which would mean increased costs for meat and dairy products. Other pests can affect property values by damaging lawns, ornamental plants, trees, and even homes.

The U.S. Department of Agriculture
(20) (USDA) and the Department of Homeland Security (DHS) are partners in this effort to protect American agriculture against the introduction of foreign plant and animal pests and diseases at our nation's ports
(25) of entry. USDA's Animal and Plant Health Inspection Service (APHIS) develops the policies that determine what agricultural products can come into the country and what products pose a risk and should
(30) be kept out. U.S. Customs and Border Protection (CBP) at ports of entry enforce these agricultural policies. Confiscated items are carefully destroyed in special CBP facilities. For additional information, please
(35) visit the CBP Web site. (www.cbp.gov)

Or write to:

U.S. Customs and Border Protection
Office of Field Operations
Agriculture Programs and Liaison
(40) 1300 Pennsylvania Ave, NW
Washington, DC 20229

For more information on agricultural policy, please visit APHIS' Plant Protection and Quarantine (PPQ) Web site. (APHIS'
(45) Plant Protection and Quarantine) Or call 1-866-SAFGUARD. If you have any questions please write to:

APHIS-PPQ
Quarantine Policy Analysis
and Support Staff
4700 River Road
Unit 60
Riverdale, MD 20737

1. Which of the following best describes the structure of this document?

(1) A source is cited, and the origin of that source is described
(2) A major point is given in the first two sentences, and contrasting views of that point are debated.
(3) A problem is cited, and reasons are given that the problem cannot be solved.
(4) A course of action is stated, and reasons for that action are given.
(5) A historical background is given to support an opinion

2. If a plant is removed from someone's luggage, that person can expect

    (1)   to have a new policy developed
    (2)   never to have that plant returned
    (3)   to be questioned about its origin
    (4)   the plant to be returned after inspection
    (5)   to be arrested

3. Which of the following is NOT a reason cited for restricting the introduction of foreign agricultural items?

    (1)   Raising prices
    (2)   Damaging insects
    (3)   Differing policies on livestock
    (4)   Decreasing land values
    (5)   Health concerns

4. From this document, it can be inferred that

    (1)   those responsible for implementing this policy are located in Washington, DC
    (2)   several agencies are involved in agricultural policy and enforcement
    (3)   the ports of entry to the US are regulated by private companies
    (4)   all imported agricultural products contain contagious or damaging pests and diseases
    (5)   enforcement of this policy is handled by the Animal and Plant Health Inspection Service

ANSWERS AND EXPLANATIONS TO NON-FICTION DRILL

1. **(4)** The first sentence says what's going to happen—that agricultural items will be removed from travelers' baggage—and the rest of the document describes why such plants are dangerous and how they'll be dealt with. So, look for an answer choice that matches—being careful that the *entire answer choice* is right. (1) is no good, since the origin of the source is not explored. (2) looks good at first, until we see that no *contrasting views* are offered. (3), similarly, starts out okay, but the "problem cannot be solved" part is the opposite of what is stated in the text. (5) doesn't work, since the passage is concerned with the present, not past history. (4) best describes the passage structurally.

2. **(2)** For the answer to this Comprehension question, look at the last couple of lines in the text, which says "confiscated items are carefully destroyed." So, (1) is not mentioned, and (4) is definitely not going to happen. The passage doesn't say anything about questioning, much less arresting, the importer of the foreign plant, so there goes (3) and (5). (2) is what the passage specifies.

   Note that (2) says "never," which is such a strong word that it is usually not part of correct answer choices. However, this document does definitely say that "confiscated items are carefully destroyed," so we know that such an item is never to be returned.

3. **(3)** When dealing with a "NOT" question, go through and eliminate all the things that *are* in the passage, and what you have left is what is *NOT* there. [These aren't difficult questions, except that you're doing the opposite of what you normally do.] So, what are the reasons cited? (1) is in line 15, (2) and (4) are in lines 16–18, and (5) is in line 11. (3) is the only one not mentioned.

4. **(2)**   Remember, on a test like the GED, when you're asked to "infer," look for what must be true considering what the passage says. All we can do here is go through the answer choices, and see which one *has to be* true, rather than just *could be* true. So, let's have at it. (1) certainly looks right—until we notice that the APHIS-PPQ mailing address listed is in fact in Maryland. (3) is definitely no good, since only government stuff is listed here. (4) is not backed up by the document, which says "some of these organisms…," not "all of these organisms." And we can eliminate (5), since it specifically says that the CBP enforces the policy, not the APHIS. What the document does say is that an alphabet-soup of various offices and agencies are involved in agriculture-importing policy and enforcement, so (2) is correct.

POETRY DRILL

WHAT IS THE POET'S ADVICE?

If you can keep your head when all about you
Are losing theirs and blaming it on you;
If you can trust yourself when all men doubt you,
But make allowance for their doubting too;
(5) If you can wait and not be tired by waiting,
Or, being lied about, don't deal in lies,
Or, being hated, don't give way to hating,
And yet don't look too good, nor talk too wise;

If you can dream—and not make dreams your master;
(10) If you can think—and not make thoughts your aim;
If you can meet with triumph and disaster
And treat those two imposters just the same;
If you can bear to hear the truth you've spoken
Twisted by knaves to make a trap for fools,
(15) Or watch the things you gave your life to broken,
And stoop and build 'em up with wornout tools;

If you can make one heap of all your winnings
And risk it on one turn of pitch-and-toss,
And lose, and start again at your beginnings
(20) And never breathe a word about your loss;
If you can force your heart and nerve and sinew
To serve your turn long after they are gone,
And so hold on when there is nothing in you
Except the Will which says to them: "Hold on";

(25) If you can talk with crowds and keep your virtue,
Or walk with kings—nor lose the common touch;
If neither foes nor loving friends can hurt you;
If all men count with you, but none too much;
If you can fill the unforgiving minute
(30) With sixty seconds' worth of distance run—
Yours is the Earth and everything that's in it,
And—which is more—you'll be a Man my son!

If, by Rudyard Kipling

1. The speaker in this poem is most likely

   (1) a general advising his troops
   (2) an older man speaking to a younger one
   (3) a liar trying to fool his audience
   (4) a king talking to a servant
   (5) an athlete conferring with his coach

2. What is "pitch-and-toss" (line 18)?

   (1) a gambling game
   (2) a sport similar to baseball
   (3) a singing exercise
   (4) tools for digging
   (5) a pile of money

3. Why does the writer call triumph and disaster "two imposters"?

   (1) neither is as extreme as it seems
   (2) each is disguised as the other
   (3) the writer believes he has been lied to
   (4) no one can tell the two apart
   (5) neither one is worth anything

4. The word "knaves" (line 14) most nearly means

   (1) cutting implements
   (2) unethical people
   (3) unintelligent people
   (4) parts of a church
   (5) moral teachers

5. In line 20, "breathe" could be best replaced with

   (1) inhale
   (2) blow
   (3) speak
   (4) weep
   (5) suffer

6. If he met a singer who bragged about receiving an award, the author of this poem would most likely

   (1) congratulate her on her performance
   (2) criticize her songwriting
   (3) contend that awards are of limited value
   (4) offer no opinion
   (5) believe that she should give the award back

ANSWERS AND EXPLANATIONS TO POETRY DRILL

1. **(2)** This poem offers advice on how to be a man, which is made especially clear in the final lines. Who gives such advice, and when? Neither a general nor a king would concern himself with the character of an inferior, so eliminate (1) and (4). The speaker isn't trying to deceive us, so eliminate (3), and an athlete wouldn't be giving advice to his coach (rather, it would be the other way around), so that eliminates (5). An older person often wishes to impart such wisdom to younger generations, so (2) is the best answer (although we don't know if this poem is addressed to the speaker's biological son or not, we know anybody called "my son" is almost certainly younger).

2. **(1)** This one is all about context. What does the poem tell us about "pitch-and-toss"? That it is something you risk your life's winnings on, and that you may lose at. In essence, we're talking about gambling. Get rid of (3) and (4). (5) is the stuff you might lose, not the activity itself, so that can be eliminated. And while one could gamble on baseball or similar sports, the poet indicates that "pitch-and-toss" is something you win or lose at in one turn, which doesn't match a prolonged game like baseball. (1) has the most support.

3. **(1)** One of the overall points that the poet makes is that what the outside world thinks of you is not very important. An imposter is someone or something wearing a disguise, trying to fool the world. So, when the writer says that these two polar opposite situations—winning and losing, essentially—are both imposters, he means that they're each faking their identities somehow—that you should not believe what's on their surface. He does not say that they resemble each other, so eliminate (2) and (4). Get rid of (3), since the writer is imparting the truth that he has learned. (5), while somewhat supported by the poem, goes much further than the text itself. (1) is the best answer.

4. **(2)** "Knaves" is an archaic (that is, old-fashioned) word, and therefore unfamiliar to many readers. But what do we know, given the word's context? They twist the truth to trap fools, so "knaves" must be people: therefore you can eliminate (1) and (4)—which are there because "knives" and "naves" superficially resemble the word in question. Now, what kind of people twist the truth? Not unintelligent ones; they who are the ones who get fooled, not the one doing the fooling—so eliminate (3). Similarly, teachers of morality would never manipulate the truth, so it can't be (5). Unethical people, however do exactly that.

5. **(3)** Don't just scan the answer choices for synonyms; instead, look at the context. Someone who has lost something important is advised not to let on how bad he feels about it—to keep his mouth shut. (1) and (2) can be eliminated, because neither involves keeping quiet. The poet doesn't want the listener to let on how he feels, so (4) can go. And while the loser may suffer, he doesn't do so because of "words about [his] loss," so eliminate (5). (3) is the best answer.

6. **(3)** This application question asks you to take what you know about this situation and apply it to a hypothetical one. So, what is the overall advice given by the poet? A big part of it is not putting too much stock in what other people believe about you (such as in lines 3, 6-7, 25-28, etc). So, if he met a singer who had received an award, he would almost certainly tell her that what other people think about her talent doesn't ultimately mean much. This eliminates (1) and (2), both of which emphasize the importance of the award, which this poet does not believe in. Get rid of (4), because he certainly would have an opinion (after all, he seems to have an opinion on everything else). And, while the writer says that it's what you yourself think that truly matters, there's no reason to think that he would want the singer to reject an award, so you can reject (5). (3) is the choice that best reflects the author's attitude.

READING COMPREHENSION DRILL

WHAT ITEMS OF CLOTHING ARE ALLOWED ON WHICH DAYS?

This memo was sent to all employees of Dubrawsky & Weybright, Inc.

Philosophy and Purpose:

It is management's intent that work attire should complement an environment that reflects an efficient, orderly, and professionally operated organization. This policy is intended to define appropriate "business attire" during normal business operations and "casual business attire" on Fridays.

According to many sources, the increasing popularity of casual business dress has a variety of positive effects, including: boosting employee morale, improving quality, encouraging more open communication, and increasing productivity—thereby creating a more comfortable work environment. Dubrawsky & Weybright, Inc. recognizes this; therefore, casual business attire will be permitted on Fridays. Dubrawsky & Weybright, Inc. reserves the right to continue, extend, revise or revoke this policy at its discretion.

Enforcement of this guideline is the responsibility of Company management and supervisory personnel.

The key point to sustaining an appropriate causal business attire program is the use of common sense and good judgment, and applying a dress practice that Dubrawsky & Weybright, Inc. deems conducive to our business environment. If you question the appropriateness of the attire, it probably isn't appropriate.

Requests for advice and assistance in administrating or interpreting this guideline should be directed to Megan Sheffer in Human Resources.

Appropriate Business Attire

Business attire is to be worn Monday through Friday. Appropriate business attire for employee includes the following:

Men

- Blazers, suits, or sport coats
- Dress slacks
- Ties
- Dress shirts with buttons and collars
- Dress shoes

Women:

- Dresses
- Skirts or skorts*
- Dress slacks
- Blouses
- Dress shoes
- Sweaters
- Nylons or stockings

* Skorts are defined as non-tailored split skirts. They do not include walking shorts or Bermuda shorts.

Appropriate Casual Business Attire

Casual business attire may be worn on Friday of each week. Appropriate casual business attire for employees includes the following:

Men:

- Sport coats or blazers
- Slacks, Chinos or Dockers
- Polo shirts with collars
- Oxford button-down shirts
- Sweaters and cardigans
- Loafers and huaraches
- Sweaters

Women

- Slacks
- Stirrup pants
- Walking shorts
- Polo shirts
- Culottes, skorts, or splint skirts
- Loafers and huaraches
- Sweaters

Unacceptable Attire

- Plain or pocket T-shirts
- Cutoffs
- T-shirts with logos
- Athletic wear
- Thongs of any kind
- Blue denim jeans
- Spandex or Lycra such as biker shorts
- Tennis shoes
- Tank tops, tube tops, halter tops with spaghetti straps
- Deck shoes
- Underwear as outerwear
- Beach wear
- Midriff length tops
- Provocative attire
- Off-the-shoulder tops
- Workout clothes or shoes
- Evening wear

Enforcement

Department managers and supervisors are responsible for monitoring and enforcing this policy. The policy will be administered according to the following action steps:

1. If questionable attire is worn in the office, the respective department supervisor/manager will hold a personal, private discussion with the employee to advise and counsel the employee regarding the inappropriateness of the attire.

2. If an obvious policy violation occurs, the department supervisor/manager will hold a private discussion with the employee and ask the employee to go home and change his/her attire immediately.

3. Repeated policy violations will result in disciplinary action, up to and including termination.

Distribution

All employees will be provided with a copy of this policy.

Review and Revision

Dubrawsky & Weybright, Inc. reserves the right to rescind and/or amend this, and all Dubrawsky & Weybright, Inc. policies, at any time.

1. According to the dress code, which of the following women's items would be appropriate on Friday, but not on other workdays?

    (1) Tennis shoes
    (2) Culottes
    (3) Skorts
    (4) Halter tops
    (5) Sweaters

2. Dubrawsky & Weybright, Inc. allows casual business attire on Fridays. Which of the following is NOT one of the reasons given for allowing such attire?

(1) Fostering better communication
(2) Improving morale
(3) Administering an inviolable policy
(4) Cultivating a more comfortable work environment
(5) Raising productivity

3. If a male employee wore a T-shirt to work on a Friday, what would most likely happen to that employee?

The department supervisor/manager would have a private discussion with the employee, and then the employee

(1) would resume working.
(2) would be sent home without pay.
(3) would be provided with a copy of the dress code policy and required to sign it.
(4) would be sent home to change his clothes.
(5) would be immediately fired.

4. Which of the following items of clothing is given a specific definition in the policy?

   (1) Blazers
   (2) Skorts
   (3) Cardigans
   (4) Slacks
   (5) Huaraches

5. According to the memo, for how long will this dress code be in effect?

   (1) For one year
   (2) For as long as the company exists
   (3) Until there are no violations
   (4) Until it is changed, which could happen at any time
   (5) Until there are too many violations

WHAT DOES THIS BOY DO TO TAKE CARE OF HIS FAMILY?

One day as George Pillgarlic was going to his tasks, and while passing through the wood, he spied a tall man approaching in an opposite direction along (5) the highway.

"Ah!" thought George, in a low, mellow tone of voice, "whom have we here?"

"Good morning, my fine fellow," (10) exclaimed the stranger, pleasantly. "Do you reside in this locality?"

"Indeed I do," retorted George, cheerily, doffing his cap. "In yonder cottage, near the glen, my widowed mother and her (15) thirteen children dwell with me."

"And is your father dead?" exclaimed the man, with a rising inflection.

"Extremely so," murmured the lad, "and, oh, sir, that is why my poor mother is (20) a widow."

"And how did your papa die?" asked the man, as he thoughtfully stood on the other foot a while.

"Alas! sir," said George, as a large (25) hot tear stole down his pale cheek and fell with a loud report on the warty surface of his bare foot, "he was lost at sea in a bitter gale. The good ship foundered two years ago last Christmastide, and father was (30) foundered at the same time. No one knew of the loss of the ship and that the crew was drowned until the next spring, and it was then too late."

"And what is your age, my fine (35) fellow?" quoth the stranger.

"If I live till next October," said the boy, in a declamatory tone of voice suitable for a Second Grader, "I will be seven years of age."

(40) "And who provides for your mother and her large family of children?" queried the man.

"Indeed, I do, sir," replied George, in a shrill tone. "I toil, oh, so hard, sir, for (45) we are very, very poor, and since my elder sister, Ann, was married and brought her husband home to live with us, I have to toil more assiduously than heretofore."

"And by what means do you obtain (50) a livelihood?" exclaimed the man, in slowly measured and grammatical words.

"By digging wells, kind sir," replied George, picking up a tired ant as he spoke and stroking it on the back. "I have a good (55) education, and so I am able to dig wells as well as a man. I do this day-times and take in washing at night. In this way I am enabled barely to maintain our family in a precarious manner; but, oh, sir, should my (60) other sisters marry, I fear that some of my brothers-in-law would have to suffer."

"And do you not fear the deadly fire-damp*?" asked the stranger in an earnest tone.

(65) "Not by a damp sight," answered George, with a low gurgling laugh, for he was a great wag.

"You are indeed a brave lad," exclaimed the stranger, as he repressed (70) a smile. "And do you not at times become very weary and wish for other ways of passing your time?"

"Indeed, I do, sir," said the lad. "I wish I could run and romp and be like other (75) boys, but I must engage in constant manual exercise, or we will have no bread to eat, and I have not seen a pie since papa perished in the moist and moaning sea."

"And what if I were to tell you that
(80) your papa did not perish at sea, but was
saved from a humid grave?" asked the
stranger in pleasing tones.

"Ah, sir," exclaimed George, in a
genteel manner, again doffing his cap, "I
(85) am too polite to tell you what I would say,
and besides, sir, you are much larger than
I am."

"But, my brave lad," said the man in
low musical tones, "do you not know me,
(90) Georgie? Oh, George!"

"I must say," replied George, "that
you have the advantage of me. Whilst I
may have met you before, I can not at this
moment place you, sir."

(95) "My son! oh, my son!" murmured
the man, at the same time taking a large
strawberry mark out of his valise and
showing it to the lad. "Do you not recognize
your parent on your father's side? When our
(100) good ship went to the bottom, all perished
save me. I swam several miles through the
billows, and at last, utterly exhausted, gave
up all hope of life. Suddenly I stepped on
something hard. It was the United States.

(105) "And now, my brave boy," exclaimed
the man with great glee, "see what I have
brought for you." It was but the work of
a moment to unclasp from a shawl-strap
which he held in his hand and present to
(110) George's astonished gaze a large forty-
cent watermelon, which until now had been
concealed by the shawl-strap.

*fire-damp is a poisonous gas found in mines

Adapted from *The Grammatical Boy,* by William Nye

6. How does George think that his father
died?

George believes that his father died

(1) in a mining accident
(2) in a shipwreck
(3) from starvation
(4) in a crash on a highway
(5) trying to find his daughter Ann

7. The author's tone in this story could best be
described as

(1) jubilant
(2) funereal
(3) apathetic
(4) satirical
(5) melancholy

8. George says that, although he would like
to run and play like other boys his age,
instead he engages in "constant manual
exercise." By "constant manual exercise,"
George means that he

(1) must always work long hours to
support his family
(2) needs to keep up with his schoolwork
(3) tries to stay physically fit
(4) is saving money to try to find his
father
(5) must wait for his mother to return
before answering

9. George indicates that his brother-in-law

    (1)   has moved away to a different town
    (2)   was lost at sea and is presumed dead
    (3)   has never held a job
    (4)   is not contributing financially to the family
    (5)   will soon become a miner

10. George describes his family as

    (1)   small but happy
    (2)   lost at sea
    (3)   large and poverty-stricken
    (4)   modest and hard-working
    (5)   scattered around the country

WHO IS THE MAN TAKING NOTES?

[London at night. A torrential rain falls, and a group of pedestrians has taken refuge under an outdoor roof. The group includes an older man dressed (5) in military attire, a man preoccupied with scribbling notes in a notebook, and several others. A girl is selling flowers]

LIZA, THE FLOWER GIRL: [taking advantage of the military gentleman's (10) proximity to establish friendly relations with him]. If it's worse it's a sign it's nearly over. So cheer up, Captain; and buy a flower off a poor girl.

THE GENTLEMAN: I'm sorry, I haven't (15) any change.

LIZA: I can give you change, Captain,

THE GENTLEMAN: For a sovereign*? I've nothing less.

LIZA: Garn! Oh do buy a flower off me, (20) Captain. I can change half-a-crown*. Take this for tuppence*.

THE GENTLEMAN: Now don't be troublesome: there's a good girl. [Trying his pockets] I really haven't any (25) change—Stop: here's three ha'pence*, if that's any use to you [he retreats to the other pillar].

LIZA: [disappointed, but thinking three halfpence better than nothing] Thank (30) you, sir.

THE BYSTANDER: [to the girl] You be careful: give him a flower for it. There's a bloke here behind taking down every blessed word you're (35) saying. [All turn to Professor Higgins, the man who is taking notes].

LIZA: (springing up terrified) I ain't done nothing wrong by speaking to the gentleman. I've a right to sell flowers (40) if I keep off the curb. (Hysterically) I'm a respectable girl: so help me, I never spoke to him except to ask him to buy a flower off me. Oh, sir, don't

(45) let him charge me. You dunno what it means to me. They'll take away my character and drive me on the streets for speaking to gentlemen! They—

PROFESSOR HIGGINS: (coming forward on her right, the rest crowding after (50) him) There, there, there, there! Who's hurting you, you silly girl? What do you take me for?

THE BYSTANDER: It's all right: he's a gentleman: look at his boots. (55) (Explaining to Prof. Higgins) She thought you was a copper's nark, sir.

HIGGINS: (with quick interest) What's a copper's nark?

THE BYSTANDER: (inept at definition) It's (60) a-- well, it's a copper's nark, as you might say. What else would you call it? A sort of informer.

LIZA: (still hysterical) I take my Bible oath I never said a word—

(65) **HIGGINS:** (overbearing but good-humored) Oh, shut up, shut up. Do I look like a policeman?

LIZA: (far from reassured) Then what did you take down my words for? How do I (70) know whether you took me down right? You just show me what you've wrote about me. (The Professor opens his book and holds it steadily under her nose). What's that? That ain't proper (75) writing. I can't read that.

HIGGINS: I can. (Reads, reproducing her pronunciation exactly) "Cheer ap, Keptin; n' haw ya flahr orf a pore gel."

LIZA: (much distressed) It's because I (80) called him Captain. I meant no harm. (To the gentleman) Oh, sir, don't let him lay a charge against me for a word like that. You--

THE GENTLEMAN: Charge! I make (85) no charge. (To Professor Higgins)

Really, sir, if you are a detective, you need not begin protecting me against molestation by young women until I ask you. Anybody could see that the (90) girl meant no harm.

*sovereign, half-crowns, tuppence (that is, two pence), and ha'pence (or halfpence) are all denominations of British coins.

A sovereign = a pound (100 pence)

Half-crown = 1/8 pound (12.5 pence)

Tuppence = 2 pence

Ha'pence = ½ pence

Adapted from *Pygmalion*, by Shaw

11. What is the flower girl afraid will happen to her?

(1) Her flowers will be stolen
(2) She will be accused of a crime
(3) Her money will be forfeited
(4) Higgins will lose interest in her
(5) The military gentleman will abandon her

12. The bystander can tell that Professor Higgins is not a policeman by

(1) the fact that the military gentleman doesn't know him
(2) the way Higgins speaks
(3) the way Higgins is dressed
(4) the fact that he doesn't want to buy any flowers
(5) the way Higgins takes notes

13. Professor Higgins seems most interested in

(1) possible police involvement in the scene
(2) the girl's flowers
(3) the identity of the military gentleman
(4) the way people speak
(5) when the rain will stop

14. When Liza says "They'll take away my character," (line 45) she means

(1) her name will be changed
(2) her personality will be destroyed
(3) an artistic creation of hers will be lost
(4) no one will recognize her
(5) her reputation will be damaged

15. As indicated by Higgins's and the military gentleman's interactions with Liza, how do they most likely view her?

(1) They are unable to communicate with her
(2) They don't really respect her, and see her as somewhat inferior to them
(3) They are interested in her romantically
(4) They are worried about her welfare
(5) They believe that she is a thief, and are keeping her under surveillance

WHERE IS THIS WOMAN BEING TAKEN?

Because I could not stop for Death,
He kindly stopped for me;
The carriage held but just ourselves
And Immortality.

(5) We slowly drove, he knew no haste,
And I had put away
My labor, and my leisure too,
For his civility.

We passed the school where children played,
(10) Their lessons scarcely done;
We passed the fields of gazing grain,
We passed the setting sun.

We paused before a house that seemed
A swelling of the ground;
(15) The roof was scarcely visible,
The cornice but a mound.

Since then 'tis centuries; but each
Feels shorter than the day
I first surmised the horses' heads
(20) Were toward eternity.

The Chariot, by Dickinson

16. The speaker says she "put away my labor, and my leisure too." This phrase most nearly means that she

    (1)   abandoned her home to move to a new city
    (2)   remembered the birth of her child
    (3)   no longer did the various activities which had comprised her life
    (4)   stored her possessions until a later date
    (5)   had never been able to enjoy herself

17. What is the "house that seemed a swelling of the ground"?

    (1)   The author's childhood home
    (2)   A poor person's dwelling
    (3)   The speaker's grave
    (4)   An underground palace
    (5)   A hospital for accident victims

18. For the speaker of the poem, the image of the school "where children played, their lessons scarcely done" could be best described as being

    (1) comical and hilarious
    (2) strange and incomprehensible
    (3) frightening and eerie
    (4) celebratory and joyous
    (5) nostalgic and melancholy

19. The poet says "Because I could not stop for Death, he kindly stopped for me." The word "kindly" is used ironically, because

    (1) Death was in fact meaner to her than she deserved
    (2) Death mistreated the horses in order to hurry them along
    (3) the poet doesn't understand the meaning of the word
    (4) Death was not treating her any differently than he does anyone else
    (5) the speaker was a cruel person when she was alive

Chapter 6
Reading
Comprehension
Drill Answers

ANSWERS AND EXPLANATIONS

1. **(2)** We need something allowable on Friday, but not Monday through Thursday. It's time to use POE. (1) and (4) are listed as always unacceptable, whereas (3) and (5) are proper on Monday through Thursday as well. (2) is the only one allowable on "casual Friday" only.

2. **(3)** Again, we're going back to the text and eliminating everything that IS there, so what we have left is what IS NOT there. Questions like these are conceptually quite easy—as long as you focus on getting rid of what is in the passage. (1), (2), (4), and (5) are all specified as reasons for "casual Friday attire." (3) is the only one not so indicated.

3. **(4)** Look at the Enforcement section of the dress code: this is an *obvious policy violation*, in that T-shirts are expressly prohibited. The second point says that, under such a circumstance, the employee will be required to go home and change. Eliminate (1). Eliminate (2), since *without pay* doesn't appear in the text. As for (3), evidently all employees have already gotten a copy of the policy, and no one has been asked to sign anything, so get rid of that choice. (5) can go too, since termination occurs only after multiple violations, and nothing indicates that this circumstance is one of several infractions. (4) is the answer best supported by the text.

4. **(2)** For this question, we've got to hunt through the policy looking for any item that it specifically defines. Or, better yet, look at the five answer choices and see which *of them* is so defined. Which is? Not (1), (3), (4), or (5), all of which are simply mentioned and not expanded upon. Skorts, choice (2), however, are particularly described.

5. **(4)** In a sense this is a tricky question, since we can search and search the document without finding any reference to a time limit—or the lack of a time limit—on this policy. However, near the beginning of the document and again near the end, we see that Dubrawsky & Weybright reserves the right to change or nullify the policy at any time. Therefore, (1), (2), (3), and (5) are not supported by the text. (4) is the only answer that accurately reflects what the memo tells us.

6. **(2)** The boy says his father's ship was lost and that the crew drowned. Get rid of what doesn't relate to that. (1), (3), (4), and (5) all refer to other parts of the story, but not to the father's death (or, rather, supposed death).

7. **(4)** There are a variety of clues to indicate that the author is using a mock-ing and unserious tone. First, the boy's name is a compound of "pill" and "garlic"—two things that are *hard to swallow*, just as the revela-tion in this tale is rather *hard to swallow*. Plus—and more obviously—there's the idea that a 6-year-old boy works to support his whole family, a family that includes at least one adult male. And even if you miss all that, there's the moment when the kid pets a "tired ant." Not just any ant, but a *tired* ant. So, lets look for "unserious" and eliminate what doesn't work. (1) *jubilant* means really happy, which doesn't fit. (2) and (5) are both associated with sadness, which isn't the tone we're seeking. And (3) *apathetic* means utterly without interest, so that doesn't match "unseri-ous." "Apathetic" is probably not ever going to be the right answer to a tone question—if the writer didn't care at all, why would he have written the piece?

8. **(1)** In earlier paragraphs, the boy says that he digs wells during the day and does laundry at night. So, his "constant manual exercise" is constant work. Let's POE. (2) doesn't fit, because there's no "school" mentioned in the story. (3) can be eliminated, as it too has no basis in the story. [This is the kind of answer choice there to trap test-takers who just look at the question and answer, and not at the passage itself. Don't be one of those people! Not that you are—the fact that you have this book indi-cates a deeper wisdom residing within you.] Get rid of (4), since the boy had no idea that his father was alive at all, and (5) has nothing to do with the story.

9. **(4)** Although his brother-in-law is presumably an adult (or at least older than George, since he has married the boy's older sister), George supports him along with the rest of the family. Clearly, then, Ann's husband isn't working—or if he is, he's not giving the money to the family. What can we eliminate? (1) is no good, because the happy (and lazy) couple evi-dently still live at home. (2) is no good, because it refers to George's father rather than his brother-in-law. (3) might work, but does George say the man *never* had a job? Just because he doesn't now doesn't mean he never has. Remember, stick with what must be true. (5) can certainly be eliminated, since nothing indicates that the work-averse brother-in-law is on the brink of new employment.

10. **(3)** George says he lives with his mother and 13 siblings, plus his brother-in-law, in a cottage. He works day and night, literally, to support them. So, what can we eliminate? Get rid of (1), since the family is not small (and their happiness is undetermined). (2) describes his father, not the rest of

his family, just as (4) describes George himself and no one else. (5) has no support in the text. So, (3) is the best answer.

11. **(2)** Liza, the flower girl, gets scared when she thinks that Higgins is a policeman. She doesn't want to be *charged* with a crime. So, it's not (1) or (3), which have no support in the passage. Also, get rid of (4) and (5), since neither man is taking any real interest in her as a person anyway. (2) is the best answer.

12. **(3)** The bystander tells the girl that Higgins is a gentleman rather than a policeman, and that one can tell by Higgins's boots that this is so, since those are not the shoes of a policeman. So, it has nothing to do with (1) the military gentleman, nor (2) Higgins's speech, nor (4) his lack of interest in flowers. And even though the girl is upset by (5) Higgins's note-taking, that's not how the bystander deduced his identity.

13. **(4)** When does Higgins become interested in the other characters? When he hears their accents, or when they use some colloquial phrasing like *copper's nark*. Then, out comes his notebook and her starts questioning characters about what their words mean. So, what can we say is wrong? (1) and (2) make absolutely no impact upon the Professor, so we'll get rid of those. In this excerpt he doesn't wonder who the military gentleman is, so lose (3). Nor does he seem to care about the rain (5). (4) best answers the question.

14. **(5)** The expression *take away my character* is not one we hear these days. So, let's try to figure it out from context. What do we know? If Liza is charged with a crime, that would result in her *character* being taken away." And it has something to do with her "talking to gentlemen," which she evidently shouldn't be doing (or she believes that some people don't think she should be doing so). Also, she fears what will happen to her *on the streets* (rather than, say, in court) as a result. Looking at the evidence, *Take away my character* likely has to do with her reputation, and what people will think of her. So, (1) and (3) can definitely be eliminated, since neither has any support in the text. Choice (2) doesn't work either, since we're looking for something about how the public would view the girl, not what's going on inside her own head. And (4), is, if anything, the opposite of what we want: she's afraid too many will recognize her, not that no one will. Thus, (5) best fits what we've put together from what the playwright has told us.

15. **(2)** To answer this question, check out how Higgins and the gentleman speak to Liza, and (even more importantly) whether they listen to her when she speaks. The gentleman tells her to be *a good girl*, as if she were a pet. When she becomes understandably upset, thinking that she's in trouble with the police, Higgins calls her *silly* and tells her to *shut up*. So, the men treat Liza dismissively, as if she is unimportant and not their equal. Let's get rid of what doesn't match that answer. (1) can go, since they are *able* to talk to her. (3) and (4) can definitely be eliminated, since the men are not taking any kind of real interest in her. And (5) isn't right either— that's what the girl fears is going on, but not the reality.

16. **(3)** This question is specific to lines 6–7, but also tests your understanding of the poem's main idea. The speaker of the poem says Death stopped for her, put her into the carriage with him (the poem is old enough that people rode around in horse-drawn carriages), and took her away from her old existence. So, when she says she *put away my labor and my leisure too*, she means, now that she's in Death's carriage, she no longer either works ("labor") or plays ("leisure"). So, let's eliminate what doesn't match the answer we've found in the text. (1) can go, because while she's left her home, it's not to go to a *new* city. [Always be sure to read the FULL answer choice; the whole thing has to be right.] (2) is no good, because it's not the childbirth kind of labor we're dealing with here. We can eliminate (4), since she didn't put anything in storage.

17. **(3)** The speaker of the poem is dead, and arrives at her new house, a house that's like a big lump in the ground. Therefore, what is it? Her grave. Not (1) her *childhood home,* because she's not going back in time. Not (2) a *poor person's dwelling,* which is never mentioned. Certainly not (5) a hospital, since she's past that point of existence. And, while much of it is underground, it's not (4) a palace, since nothing here implies that it's large and spacious.

18. **(5)** This question asks about mood, so what's the mood here? In a poem about death, the mood is, shall we say, rather sad and bleak. As they ride along in Death's carriage, they pass scenes of life, which the speaker makes note of. Even though this poet's style is spare—that is, using very few descriptive words—we can still feel the character's emotion as she is ushered of to her final resting place. So, as she passes by the schoolchildren, what does she feel? She'll never get another chance to play carefree games herself (remember, she "put away" her "leisure"), so she feels regret and sadness for what she has lost. Let's get rid of answers that don't match. Eliminate (1) and (4), because the kids are having fun, but

the speaker of the poem most certainly is not. It's not (2), because that would mean that she didn't understand what was going on. Nor is it (3), since there's nothing scary for her about seeing the children play.

19. **(4)** Irony means that the word used is intended in something other than its literal meaning. So, when the poet says, essentially, "Death was nice enough to take time out of his busy schedule to pick little ol' me up, and escort me to the afterlife." So, is this action really *kind*? No, Death is just doing his job: collecting the people whose time has come, so to speak. So, let's look for something like "Death is just doing his job," and eliminate what doesn't match. It's not (1), since Death does behave in a gentlemanly fashion. (2) and (5) can go, since neither is supported by the text of the poem. Nor is it (3), since the poet is being intentionally ironic, not making an error.

Chapter 7
Social Studies

INTRODUCTION

Although we cannot predict exactly what will be on the GED, we can get you up to speed on all the relevant topics that the GED covers. In this section, you will learn about (or reacquaint yourself with) the following topics:

- Governing systems
- World religions
- United States branches of government
- Political parties
- Economics
- Geography
- History

The first six topics will be covered in Part I, and Part II will cover history (thankfully not ALL of it, but the major high points of United States history).

At the end of each section, you'll find short drills that will test your knowledge on each subject. For the GED Social Studies exams, you'll usually be given a short passage that relates to the question that you need to answer, so feel free to refer to the text if you are unsure of the answer to a particular problem. Also, keep in mind that you have to commit these facts to memory, but be sure that you understand the core concepts. It will help you to ace the GED.

GOVERNING SYSTEMS

First things first: The textbook definition of a government is a political system that is used to manage a nation. There are several different kinds of governments that can be observed in nations today. Some of the more common types are listed below.

Socialism: A political and economic doctrine that envisions the state playing an active part in distributing wealth and caring for its citizens. Began as a working class movement.

Communism: A political and economic ideology according to which society is classless and the nation's economic and productive capital is owned and controlled collectively by the state on behalf of the people.

Fascism: A system of government characterized by authoritarian rule and oppression of dissent for the good of the nation. The polar opposite of liberal democracy.

Representative Democracy: A system in which citizens elect representatives who make the important decisions.

Direct Democracy: A system in which all important decisions are voted on by eligible citizens.

Oligarchy: A system in which a small group of people (who have not been elected by citizens) controls the government.

Monarchy: A system in which a nation is ruled by a king or queen. Power passes from one member of the royal family to the next and from one generation to the next.

Constitutional Monarchy: A system in which a king or queen is the ceremonial head of state, but the decision making is carried out by representatives elected by the citizens.

Dictatorship: A system in which one man or woman controls all decision making without accountability to the country's citizens.

STYLES OF GOVERNMENT—REVIEW

1. A small group of military officers seizes power and declares that it will rule the country as a committee from now on. This is an example of a:

   (1) Direct democracy
   (2) Representative democracy
   (3) Dictatorship
   (4) Oligarchy
   (5) Monarchy

2. Although Queen Elizabeth II is recognized as the head of the United Kingdom, all of the governance is run by a democratically-elected body called the Parliament. The United Kingdom is an example of a:

   (1) Democracy
   (2) Dictatorship
   (3) Oligarchy
   (4) Fascism
   (5) Constitutional monarchy

QUICK TIPS ABOUT WORLD RELIGIONS

There are many religions that exist in the modern world. In terms of deity worship, there are two major categories. Monotheistic religions foster a belief in a singular god (usually capitalized as God) while polytheistic religions believe in numerous gods who co-exist together in what is called a pantheon. Here is a useful chart of the major religions that may by covered during the GED exam:

Major Religion	Theism	Major Scriptures
Christianity	Monotheistic: One god, known as God	Bible, consisting of the Old and New Testament
Judaism	Monotheistic: One god, known as Jehovah or Yahweh	Torah, consisting primarily of the Old Testament
Greco-Roman mythology	Polytheistic: Many gods	Homeric hymns, Theogony
Hinduism	Polytheistic: Many gods	Vedas, Mahabharata, Upanishads, Bhagavad Gita, Ramayana
Buddhism	No denial or acceptance of a creator	Buddhavacana
Islam	Monotheistic: One god, known as Allah	Qur'an

WORLD RELIGIONS—REVIEW

1. The Vedas are sacred texts in which religion?

    (1) Christianity
    (2) Judaism
    (3) Hinduism
    (4) Buddhism
    (5) Islam

BRANCHES OF GOVERNMENT

The United States government consists of three major branches: the **legislative branch** (which creates the laws), the **executive branch** (which enforces the laws), and the **judicial branch** (which interprets the laws). Congress represents the legislative branch. A system of checks and balances are in place to prevent any one branch from gaining power over the other two branches. Let's go into a little bit more detail about the three major branches:

Congress

Congress is divided into two houses: the **House of Representatives** and the **Senate**. It is responsible for the laws of the nation. Congress also serves other functions, such as overseeing the bureaucracy, consensus building, clarifying policy, legitimizing, and expressing diversity. In order for a **bill** (or proposed law) to be passed into law, it must be approved by both the House of Representatives and the Senate.

The House of Representatives is called the lower house, and there are 435 representatives. The number of representatives a state has in the House of Representatives is dependent on the population size of that state.

The Senate is called the upper house, and each state has two senators as representatives regardless of the population size of the state, which adds up to a total of 100 senators. The vice president is the president of the Senate, and when the vice president is absent during Senate sessions, the **president pro tempore** is the presiding officer. The president pro tempore is usually given to the most senior member of the **majority party** (which means the political party with the most members) of the Senate.

Executive Branch

The **president** is responsible for enforcing the laws, handling foreign policy, and serving as the ceremonial head of state. He is also the administrative head of the government. He can force Congress into session, must brief Congress on the "state of the nation," and can veto legislation and grant reprieves and pardons. But regardless of these expansive powers, he must cooperate with Congress because the powers of the presidency are intermingled with the powers of the legislature. The president's appointment of federal judges, Supreme Court justices, ambassadors, and department secretaries all require Senate approval.

The president also serves as commander in chief of the armed forces. But the Framers created a complex institutional situation regarding armed conflict. Only Congress has the power to declare war, but only the president can make war. In a national crisis, the other branches of government and the American people look to the president for leadership.

The **Executive Office of the President** helps carry out the president's administrative responsibilities. It is made up of more than half a dozen agencies involved in the day-to-day operations of the White House and is basically divided into three areas: domestic, foreign, and military affairs. The most important of these positions is The Chief of Staff who works as the top aide to the president. Considered one of the most powerful persons in Washington, the **Chief of Staff** is responsible for managing the Executive Office and can control access to the president, thus potentially controlling the information that the president receives.

The President is also in charge of the **Cabinet**. Cabinet secretaries run their departments and carry out the president's policies. Those who disagree with presidential policy are expected to resign. There are 15 cabinet secretaries. Some of the more familiar cabinet secretaries are the Secretary of State, Secretary of Defense, Secretary of the Treasury, Secretary of Education, and the Attorney General.

Judicial Branch

The judicial branch is made up of all the federal, district, and circuit courts. The **Supreme Court of the United States** is considered the highest court in the land. The Supreme Court's most important power is judicial review: the ability to strike down any state or federal law that is unconstitutional. This power was established in the case of *Marbury v. Madison* in 1803. Unlike Congressmen and the president, Supreme Court judges (known as justices) serve lifetime terms.

BRANCHES OF GOVERNMENT—QUICK REVIEW

1. Although Congress can create and ratify bills into laws, the president has the power to veto any bills that he deems unnecessary or detrimental to the integrity of the United States. This is an example of

   (1) judicial review
   (2) eminent domain
   (3) separation of church and state
   (4) checks and balances
   (5) appointment

2. The executive branch has the power to

   (1) abolish Congress
   (2) appoint judges with the Senate's approval
   (3) appoint senators with the approval of the House of Representatives
   (4) declare laws unconstitutional
   (5) raise money for wars

POLITICAL PARTIES

The United States has two major political parties: **Democrats** and **Republicans**. In the past, there have been several parties that have held control of the U.S. government, including the Federalists, Whigs, and Democratic-Republicans (no relation to our modern day political parties). Although they are not mentioned in the Constitution—in fact, the Framers of the Constitution disliked political parties and hoped to prevent them—political parties became a mainstay of U.S. elections by the year 1800. Below are some important facts about political parties:

- Parties serve as intermediaries between people and the government.
- Parties are made up of grassroots members, activist members, and leadership.
- Parties are organized to raise money, present positions on policy, and get their candidates elected to office.
- Parties were created outside of the Constitution—they are not even mentioned in the document.

POLITICAL PARTIES—QUICK REVIEW

Let's take a look at the chart below that shows the first two-party system of the United States:

The United States' First Two-Party System		
	Federalists	Democratic-Republicans
Leaders	Hamilton, Washington, Adams, Jay, Marshall	Jefferson, Madison
Vision	Economy based on commerce	Economy based on agriculture
Governmental Power	Strong federal government	Stronger state governments
Supporters	Wealthy, Northeast	Yeoman farmers, Southerners
Constitution	Loose construction	Strict construction
National Bank	Believed it was "necessary"	Believed it was merely "desirable"
Foreign Affairs	More sympathetic toward Great Britain	More sympathetic toward France

1. Democratic-Republicans would support all of the following policies EXCEPT

   (1) An agriculture-based economy
   (2) A strict interpretation of the Constitution
   (3) A strong state government
   (4) An alliance with France
   (5) An alliance with Great Britain

2. Which of the following people would most likely be a Federalist?

   (1) A rich New Yorker who is the head of a shipping company
   (2) A South Carolina farmer
   (3) An indentured servant
   (4) A pirate
   (5) A seamstress from Georgia

ECONOMICS

Economics is the study of how to allocate scarce resources among competing ends. Although some people think economics is only about business and money, in truth, the field is as broad as the list of scarce resources and deals with everything from air to concert tickets. Few things have an infinite supply or zero demand, meaning that the need to make choices in response to scarcity—economics—can apply to almost everything and everyone. That brings us to another reason why economics is great; almost any topic is within its domain. Economists are currently studying war, crime, endangered species, marriage, systems of government, child care, legal rules, death, birth—the sky's the limit.

Scarcity occurs because our unlimited desire for goods and services exceeds our limited ability to produce them due to constraints on time and resources. The **resources** used in the production process are sometimes called **factors of production.**

Some key economic terms to keep in mind are:

- **labor**—the physical and mental effort of people
- **human capital**—knowledge and skills acquired through training and experience
- **entrepreneurship**—the ability to identify opportunities and organize production, and the willingness to accept risk in the pursuit of rewards
- **natural resources**—any productive resource existing in nature, including wild plants, mineral deposits, wind, and water
- **capital**—manufactured goods that can be used in the production process, including tools, equipment, buildings, and machinery

Macroeconomics is the branch of economics that deals with the whole economy and issues that affect most of society. These issues include inflation, unemployment, national income, and exchange rates. **Microeconomics** is the branch of economics that looks at decision making at the firm, household, and individual levels and studies behavior in markets for particular goods and services. For example, a household budget that you would draw up could be a case study in microeconomics.

One of the key economic models is **supply and demand**. The **law of demand** states that as the price of a good rises, the quantity of the good demanded by consumers falls. Similarly, as the price of a good falls, the quantity demanded of that good rises. The **law of supply** says that as the price increases, the quantity of a good supplied in a given period will increase, other things being equal.

A **perfectly competitive industry** involves a large number of sellers selling an identical good to a large number of buyers. The key characteristics of a perfect (or pure) competition are:

- many sellers
- standardized (homogeneous) product
- firms are "price takers"
- free entry and exit

Each buyer and seller is too small to have a noticeable effect on the market price or quantity, making the sellers **price takers**—they accept the market price as given and can sell all they want at that price. Also, in a perfectly competitive industry, there are no barriers to entry or exit. Thus, anyone can become a seller in this market at relatively little expense.

A **monopoly** is the sole provider of a unique product. Local monopolies are common. For example, many towns only have one movie theater or bookstore. Utility companies often have a regional monopoly. At the national and international level, absolute monopolies are rare, although individual companies often control large shares of markets, as does DeBeers with diamonds and Microsoft with operating systems.

Some businesses are able to charge different customers different prices that do not reflect differences in production costs. Airlines and car dealers are good examples. This is called **price discrimination.**

An **oligopoly** is an industry with a small number of firms selling a standardized or differentiated product. A **trust** is the collective control of an industry by a small group of separate corporations working together. Many antitrust laws were passed to prevent corporations from artificially driving up prices in order to gain profit to the detriment of consumers.

Inflation happens when the demand for a good is high and the supply is low; during inflation the price of these goods increase. In contrast, **deflation** happens when the demand for a good is low and the supply is high. This drives prices of the good down.

Some final key terms for you to know about: A **recession** is a period of time where employment and economic activity declines. If this period lasts for a longer period of time and becomes more drastic, a recession turns into a **depression** (how sad). When a country **imports** goods, it buys goods another country for the purposes of consumption. When a country **exports** goods, it sells good to another country for consumption in that country.

ECONOMICS—REVIEW

1. Labor, human capital, entrepreneurship, natural resources, and physical capital are all examples of which of the following?

    (1)   Public goods
    (2)   Inferior goods
    (3)   Factors of production
    (4)   Outputs
    (5)   Substitutes in production

2. Which of the following constitute the fundamental questions every economic system must answer?

    I.   What goods and services will be produced?
    II.   How will they be produced?
    III. When will they be produced?
    IV.   For whom will they be produced?
    V.   Where will they be produced?

    (1)   I, III, and V only
    (2)   I, II, and IV only
    (3)   I, II and V only
    (4)   II, IV, and V only
    (5)   II, III, and IV only

GEOGRAPHY

Let's start with the basic question: what is geography? Geography is the study of the earth's physical features.

A **globe** is a three-dimensional representation of the earth. You can also find two-dimensional representations of a globe. A **map** is a visual representation of a region. Take a look at the following globe:

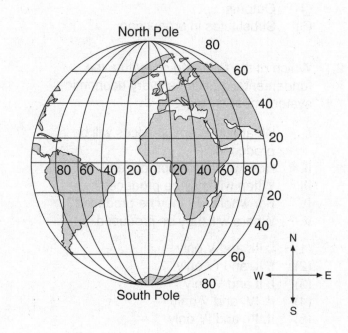

The horizontal lines represent the latitude (the distance a location lies north or south of the equator, which is 0° latitude). The vertical lines represent the longitude (the distance a location lies west or east of the **Prime Meridian**, which is 0° longitude). The **North** and **South Poles** are 90° latitude. Locations that are closer to the equator are warmer than locations that are farther away. The North and South Poles are the coldest regions on the earth.

The **Northern Hemisphere** is the region of the earth above the equator, with the region to the south being called the **Southern Hemisphere** (of course). The Prime Meridian bisects the earth into **Western** and **Eastern Hemispheres**.

Equally important is the concept of **time zones**, which is a roughly 15 degree wide longitudinal zone that has a uniform standard time throughout. Because the sun rises at different times in different regions, we use time zones to help us more accurately measure the amount of daylight we have. If you've ever heard of a television show airing on 7 pm Eastern Time/4 pm Pacific Time, this indicates a change in time zone. The **International Date Line** is a line that runs form the North through the South Pole across the Pacific Ocean that notes the crossing over from one calendar day to the next.

GEOGRAPHY DRILL

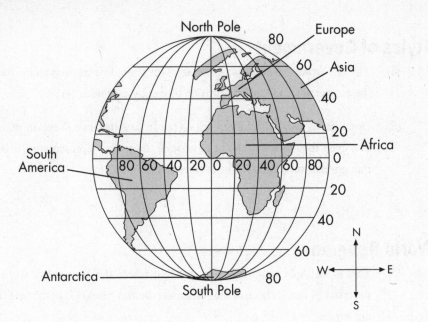

1. The coldest continent shown on this map is

   (1) Europe
   (2) Asia
   (3) Antarctica
   (4) South America
   (5) Africa

2. According to this map, the equator runs through the majority of which continent?

   (1) Europe
   (2) Asia
   (3) Antarctica
   (4) South America
   (5) Africa

ANSWER TO QUICK REVIEW QUESTIONS

Styles of Government

1. **(4)** The key words here is a *small group*. This should be the major clue that the answer you are looking for is an oligarchy, or choice (4).

2. **(5)** Don't be thrown off by the word *queen* in this instance. Keep in mind that even though she is the head of state, there is a representative body that governs the country. The correct answer is (5).

World Religions

1. **(3)** This is a simple comprehension question where the answer lies within the chart. A quick check of the rows and columns reveal (3) as the best fit answer.

Branches of Government

1. **(4)** Let's break down the scenario. In this case, Congress is trying to exercise a right to do something, but the President uses his power to check that exercise because he is worried about the overall health of the nation. See how the word *check* easily fits in? This is a classic example of the system of checks and balances used to prevent abuses of power from any one branch. Choice (4) is obvious.

2. **(2)** This is a comprehension question that can be found within the text itself. But even if you couldn't find it, you can use POE. Since we know that choices (1) and (3) go against the tenets of democracy, we can cross those out immediately. Choice (4) can be ruled out because this is the responsibility of the judicial system. Don't be fooled by choice (5); just because the president can make war doesn't mean that he can raise money to go to war.

Political Parties—Review

1. **(5)** This is a comprehension question that requires you to look at the chart and figure out which viewpoint isn't widely held by Democratic-Republicans. This political group did not support an alliance with Great Britain; they supported an alliance with France. The best choice is (5).

2. **(1)** This question asks you to analyze the data in the chart given to find out which of the five choices would most likely be a Federalist. We know that Northerners favored Federalism, so we can eliminate (2) and (5) since South Carolina and Georgia are in the South. Next, we know that people who are in the trade industry would be more predisposed to Federalism; pirate and servants don't fit the bill, so we can cross off (3) and (4). In case you weren't too sure about choice (1), remember that New York is a northern state.

Economics—Review

1. **(3)** These are all examples of factors of production. They are not public goods because some are excludable and rival in consumption. They are not inferior, which would mean that one would purchase fewer of them as income increased. They are inputs rather than outputs. And they are not substitutes in production, which would mean that one would have to choose which of them to produce using the same resources.

2. **(2)** Here are the fundamental questions for economic systems to answer: What goods and services will be produced? How will they be produced? For whom will they be produced? When and where are lesser concerns not typically discussed among the primary economic questions.

Geography—Review

1. **(3)** For the answer to this question, we have to look for the continent closest to the South Pole. That continent is Antarctica; choice (3) is the correct answer.

2. **(5)** In order to answer this question, we have to first locate the equator, which is at 0° latitude. Then we must figure which land mass passes through the Equator. Europe, Asia and Antarctica do not pass through the equator on this representation, so cross them off. Of the two about 40 longitudinal degrees pass through Africa, in comparison to roughly 25 degrees for South America. The correct answer is (5).

SOCIAL STUDIES PART II: HISTORY

Ah yes, history—the discovery and organization of past events. This is a subject that may hold a great deal of interest for some people and may induce nausea in others. The good news is that you won't be expected to have a running knowledge of all 10,000 years of modern human civilization, or even much about world history. You won't be asked about which case established the idea of Miranda rights, or what year President James Buchanan was elected (by the way, the answers are *Miranda v. Arizona* and 1856 respectively). However, you should have the fundamentals of United States history down in order to help give you a strong context for the questions that you'll be answering. Plus, some of the information in here will be critical in helping you to find the right answer. Besides, this knowledge may help you if you ever play any trivia games or try out for *Jeopardy*.

And now without further ado, how about a little history lesson?

PRE-COLONIAL TIMES IN THE AMERICAS

Commonly, historians refer to the era before Christopher Columbus' arrival in the New World as the **pre-Columbian era**. The most widely accepted theory holds that the first **Native American** people migrated from Asia to North America across a land bridge spanning the Bering Strait that connected the modern-day country Russia to the modern-day U.S. state of Alaska more than ten thousand years ago (the exact number is estimated to be between 20,000 and 40,000 years ago). Many Native American cultures believed in animism (a belief that all human and non-humans are connected through a spiritual force)and held a reverence for nature.

The degree to which Native American cultures flourished depended primarily on their environments. Those in fertile, temperate regions developed complex societies with irrigation systems to aid in **agriculture** (the development and farming of land) and involved religious rituals. Those in more rugged areas necessarily devoted more of their energy to survival and were more **nomadic** (which describes a group of people who travel according to the seasons to search for food and shelter).

In what is now known as southern Mexico, the **Mayan** civilization set up a highly sophisticated empire, with agriculture to sustain thousands of people, a highly organized urban society, a complex writing system, a well-developed calendar, monument architecture and innovative mathematics system. This empire is believed to have reached its peak from 250 AD to 900 AD. The **Inca** people ruled over a vast empire from 1438 to the 1500s which spanned the west coast of South America from modern-day Ecuador, throughout Peru down to the Chilean coastline. The **Aztec** empire (which spanned the fourteenth through the sixteenth centuries) was a more militaristic state, established in modern-day Mexico. Their religious beliefs—that human sacrifice was necessary to appease their gods—meant that they used their prisoners of war as offerings, which did not sit well with the subjugated peoples under their rule.

The Early Explorers

Many people have heard the story of **Christopher Columbus** and his "discovery" of the Americas in 1492, but did you know that there were early European explorers before him? Evidence has shown that Europeans have visited the Americas as early as the year 1000, when the Norse first arrived in modern-day Canada. But unlike Norse predecessors Leif Eriksson and Bjarni Herjolfson, Columbus' journey marked the beginning of the Contact Period.

Spanish Colonialism

Columbus' voyage paved the way for Spanish rule over large parts of the Americas. In 1519 **Hernan Cortes** landed on the coast of Mexico with a small force of 600 men. He arrived at Tenochtitlan, the capital city and heart of the Aztec Empire, on horseback which awed the Aztecs (who had never seen horses before). The ruler **Montezuma** mistook Cortes for a god and sent a gift of gold to appease this false deity. Unfortunately for the Aztecs the offer only whetted the appetite of the Spanish, who came to the New World seeking riches and spices. The Spanish promptly seized Montezuma, who died mysteriously while under Spanish captivity, and began a siege of the beautiful city.

The Spanish also succeeded in destroying the Inca Empire when in 1531, Francisco Pizarro arrived with a small force and conquered the area. The Spanish were aided by their superior weaponry, the instability and social unrest that pre-existed in the empire, and by European diseases like smallpox which were newly introduced to the Native Americans who had no natural resistance. The Spanish taxed the settlers via the *encomienda* system and used first native labor and then imported slave laborer from Africa to mine gold and silver and work on plantations to grow sugar and other cash crops. Keep in mind that you do not need to know all of this information, but you should know that in addition to conquering large parts of South and Central America, the Spanish also established a colony in Florida and were generally brutal rulers.

THE ARRIVAL OF THE ENGLISH

American colonial history as it relates to the United States began in the early 1600s with the first permanent English colony established at **Jamestown, Virginia.** Prior to this, the English first attempted to settle in North America in 1587 when **Sir Walter Raleigh** sponsored a settlement on Roanoke Island (in what is now North Carolina). By 1590, the colony had disappeared, which is why it came to be known as the **Lost Colony.**

The colony of Jamestown was funded by a **joint-stock company**, a group of investors who bought the right to establish New World plantations from the king. This particular company was called the **Virginia Company.** Colony life was initially difficult since the first settlers were ill-suited to the many adjustments life in the New World required of them. In fact, the colony would have perished without the help of a group of local tribes called the **Powhatan Confederacy**, who taught the English what crops to plant and how to plant them. In addition, the cash crop **tobacco** played a huge role in the success of Jamestown. Tobacco was widely desired in England and Virginia's production of it led to a large amount of profits and ensured the survival of the colony.

Many of the early immigrants to the Virginia colony did so for financial reasons. Over-population in England led to widespread famine, disease, and poverty. Chances for improving one's lot during these years were minimal. Thus many were attracted to the New World by the opportunity provided by indentured servitude. In return for free passage, **indentured servants** typically promised seven years of labor in return for their freedom and a small piece of property. Indenture was extremely difficult and nearly half of all servants did not survive their period of servitude.

The second English colony was founded by the **Pilgrims** at **Plymouth, Massachusetts.** These settlers came to the New World to be able to practice their religion freely and without persecution. The Pilgrims are remembered for designing the **Mayflower Compact.** This agreement was drafted to determine what the colony's civil laws would be once the pilgrims landed.

Below is a list of the other English colonies along with the reasons for their founding:

Virginia (1607):	Economic gain
Plymouth (1620):	Religious freedom (Separatist Pilgrims)
Massachusetts (1629):	Religious freedom (Nonseparatist Puritans); later merged with Plymouth
Maryland (1633):	Religious freedom (Catholics)
Connecticut (1636):	Religious differences with Puritans in Massachusetts
Rhode Island (1636):	Religious freedom from Puritans in Massachusetts
New York (1664):	Seized from Dutch
New Jersey (1664):	Seized from Dutch
Delaware (1664):	Seized from Dutch, who took it from Swedes
Pennsylvania (1682):	Religious freedom (Quakers)
Georgia (1732):	Buffer colony and alternative to debtors' prison

FRENCH COLONIZATION

At first glance, the French colonization of North America appears to have a lot in common with Spanish and English colonization. While the English had founded a permanent settlement at Jamestown in 1607, the French colonized what is today Quebec City in 1608. Also like other European colonists, the French were exploring as much land as they could, hoping to find natural resources such as gold, as well as a shortcut to Asia.

Unlike the Spanish and English, the French colonists had a much lighter impact on the Native American population. Few French settlers came to North America, and those who did tended to be single men, some of whom intermarried with women native to the area. They also tended to stay on the move, which made sense since many of the settlers were fur traders.

OTHER EUROPEAN COLONIES

The Dutch Republic established their initial settlement in 1614 near present day Albany, which they called New Netherland. In 1626, they established a fort at the mouth of the Hudson River called New Amsterdam which you may know today as New York City. In 1664, Charles II of England waged a war against the Dutch Republic and sent a naval force to capture New Netherland. Already weakened by previous clashes with local Native Americans, the Dutch governor Peter Stuyvesant, along with 400 civilians, surrendered peacefully. Charles II's brother James, became the Duke of York, and when James became king in 1685, he proclaimed **New York** a royal colony.

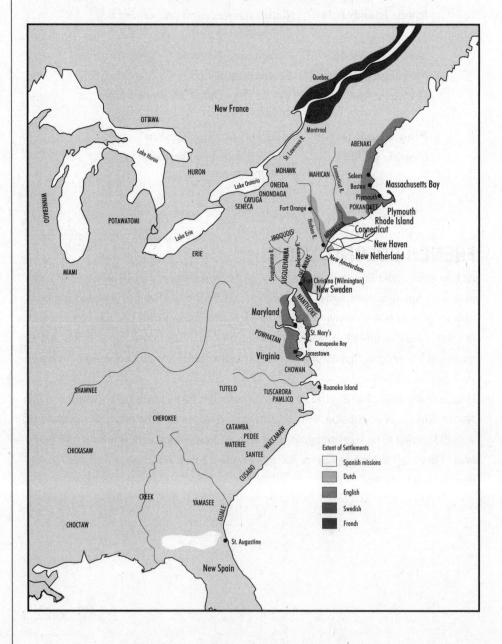

European Settlements in North America, 1650

SLAVERY IN THE EARLY COLONIES

The extensive use of African slaves in the British colonies began when colonists from the Caribbean settled in the Carolinas (now known as North and South Carolina). Until then, indentured servants had satisfied labor requirements. As the farming of cash crops became more widespread, more laborers were needed than indenture could provide. Enslaving Native Americans was difficult; they knew the land so they could easily escape and many Native Americans perished because of European diseases like smallpox. Thus Southerners turned to Africans for slave labor. Unlike Native Americans, African slaves were resistant to European diseases and they did not know the land, which made escaping very difficult. Furthermore, the English considered dark skin a sign of inferiority and used their bias to justify the subjugation of Africans.

The shipping route that brought the slaves to the Americas was called the **Middle Passage** because it was the middle leg of the **triangular trade route** among the colonies, Europe and Africa. Conditions for the Africans aboard were brutally inhumane and many slaves died of sickness or committed suicide throwing themselves overboard. Typically, one-fifth of the Africans died en route to the New World.

Although slavery existed throughout all of the British colonies, the slave trade flourished in the South. Because of the nature of the land and the short growing season, the southern plantation owners bought slaves for the arduous task of farming labor-intensive crops such as tobacco, rice, and indigo. In contrast, most slaves in the North were mostly used as domestic servants.

EARLY EXPLORERS AND EARLY COLONIALISM— REVIEW

1. Colonies were established in the New World for the purpose of gaining each of the following EXCEPT

   (1) religious freedom
   (2) commercial interests
   (3) better trade routes
   (4) military advantage
   (5) manufacturing sites

2. In the seventeenth century the Chesapeake Bay settlement expanded its territorial holdings more quickly than did the Massachusetts Bay settlement primarily because

   (1) Massachusetts settlers were entirely uninterested in expansion
   (2) a high birthrate and healthy environment resulted in a population boom in the Chesapeake region
   (3) no Native Americans lived in the Chesapeake Bay area, and the colonists were free to expand their settlements at will
   (4) farmland in the Chesapeake area was less fertile, and so more of it was needed to support sustenance farming
   (5) farming of the chief Chesapeake export, tobacco, required a great deal of land

3. Which of the following statements about indentured servitude is true?

   (1) Indentured servitude was the means by which most Africans came to the New World.
   (2) Indentured servitude attracted few people because its terms were too harsh.
   (3) Approximately half of all indentured servants died before earning their freedom.
   (4) Indenture was one of several systems used to distinguish house slaves from field slaves.
   (5) Indentured servants were prohibited from practicing religion in any form.

4. The first important cash crop in the American colonies was

   (1) cotton
   (2) corn
   (3) tea
   (4) tobacco
   (5) fresh fruit

THE BIRTH OF THE UNITED STATES

While you may be led to believe that the United States sprang up suddenly in 1776, there were a couple of factors that sowed the seeds of discontent between the colonists and the English.

The Seven Years' War

The **Seven Years' War** (which actually lasted nine years) was a series with Britain and the American colonists on one side and the French and Native American tribes on the other side. It was also called the **French and Indian War**. The war was actually one of several "wars for empire" fought between the British and the French, and the Americans just got stuck in the middle.

When the English settlers started moving into the Ohio Valley, the French tried to halt their progress by building fortified outposts at strategic entry spots. The French wanted to protect their fur trade and assert their control over the region; this military show of strength led to skirmishes in 1754. The English did not officially declare war until 1756. The war dragged on for years before the English finally gained the upper hand. The war concluded in 1763 when the French signed a treaty that gave England control of Canada and virtually everything east of the Mississippi River.

During the Seven Years' War, many Americans served in the English army and, for the first time, came into prolonged contact with English soldiers. The English did not make a good impression, both in how they treated their own soldiers and in how the soldiers behaved themselves. These contacts sowed the first seeds of anti-British sentiment in the colonies, particularly in New England, where much of the fighting took place and where most of the colonial soldiers came from.

A Series of Oppressive Acts

A major result of the Seven Years' War was that in financing the war, the British government had run up a huge debt. The new king George III felt that the colonists should help pay that debt; after all, he reasoned that the colonies had been beneficiaries of the war and the colonists had relatively light tax burdens.

To that end, three acts were passed. The **Sugar Act** of 1764 established a number of duties (or taxes) on sugar in an attempt to discourage molasses smugglers. Another act, the **Currency Act**, forbade the colonies to issue paper money. The **Stamp Act** of 1765 placed a tax on all legal documents and licenses. These acts outraged many colonists and spawned numerous arguments. One of the most famous of thee was the "No taxation without representation" argument, which sated that because the colonists did not elect members to Parliament, they were not obligated to pay taxes.

Rising Tensions

In the 1770s a new English prime minister **Charles Townshend** worked to raise colonial taxes again. Similar protests arose, and this time boycotts and violence accompanied the new taxes. Townshend passed a series of acts; one of these acts involved the stationing of British troops in Boston to help enforce new taxes that were levied on the colonists. This created numerous confrontations, which resulted in the **Boston Massacre**, where five people were killed. The colonists responded with the **Boston Tea Party,** which was not a light gathering. In this famous event, protestors dumped East India tea into Boston Harbor.

We're Having a Revolution!

In 1775, the English crown ordered the newly appointed governor of Massachusetts to go to Concord and to seize guns and ammunition stored there by rebellious colonists. When "minutemen"—so called because they were ready to fight at a minute's notice—met Governor Gage's troops on the road in Lexington, several rebels were killed. Gage continued on to Concord, where they fought with another group of colonists. As word spread about the fighting in **Lexington and Concord**, more and more minutemen moved against the British troops. By the end of the day, nearly 400 British and Americans were dead or wounded. After that kind of bloodshed, there was no going back. The **Revolutionary War** started in earnest, even though a formal declaration of war was not made.

Thomas Paine urged colonists to support the independence movement. He spread his arguments in a pamphlet titled **Common Sense**, which said that the British monarchy encroached on Americans' natural rights and appealed to the colonists to create a better government for themselves. Thousands read Paine's pamphlet, and he helped sway the general public to think that a war for independence should be fought.

Written in 1776, the **Declaration of Independence** asserted the natural rights of colonialists. Despite its limitations, the Declaration is a stunning statement of the relatively new idea of the social contract and the relationship between people and government. The document brought to the forefront the idea that governments derive their just powers from the consent of the governed, and if a government doesn't behave properly, it is the right of the people to alter or abolish it, and to institute new government. The drafters and signers included **Benjamin Franklin, Thomas Jefferson,** and **John Adams.** Along with General George Washington, who led the American troops against the British, these four men were considered the **Founding Fathers of the United States.** Of these four men, three would go onto become President of the United States (Washington, Adams, and Jefferson were the first three presidents, respectively).

One important note to keep in mind is that not all of the colonists supported the American Revolution. These colonists, called **Loyalists**, comprised one-fifth of the population and were government officials, devout members of the Church of England, merchants dependent on trade with the English, and many religious and ethnic minorities who feared persecution at the hands of the rebels.

The war itself lasted from 1775 to 1781 and concluded with the battle of Yorktown when the British surrendered to the Americans. Although the British forces were larger in number, better trained, and supported by the wealth of England, the America colonies had a number of key factors that helped in its victory. First, the colonists were more familiar with the terrain than the British which helped the American army set up better lines of communication as well as access the goods that they needed in order to keep fighting. Second, France was a decisive ally for the Americans, supplying weapons and goods to the revolutionaries in addition to providing a navy. Third, the British had overestimated the support that the revolutionaries had and thus were unprepared for such intense fighting. The **Treaty of Paris** (1783) granted the United States independence and generous territorial rights.

The Creation of a Functioning Government

It is a common misconception that the system of government that we have today has been around since the birth of the United States. Indeed, the first national government was set up by the **Continental Congress** and used the **Articles of the Confederation** (ratified in 1781) as its framework. This document favored strong powers for the individual states and under the Articles, the Continental Congress could not tax or raise funds and each state was allowed to print its own money.

In 1787, after widespread discontent and uprisings including Shays' Rebellion, the nation convened a Constitutional Convention during which the **U.S. Constitution** was written. The Constitution increased the powers of the national government and established the three branches of government that we all know today. Just to refresh your memories from the previous section, the three branches are the legislative branch (Congress), the executive branch (the Presidency) and the judicial branch (the Supreme Court and the judicial courts). A series of **checks and balances** were established so that none of the three branches could gain too much power.

The Constitution was not readily accepted by everyone and a couple of compromises were made in order to cater to all states' interests. One of the most important compromises is the addition of the **Bill of Rights**, the first ten amendments to the Constitution. These rights guaranteed the safety of personal and states' rights. The Constitution was passed in 1789 and the Bill of Rights was added in 1791.

The Bill of Rights in a Nutshell

1. Freedom of religion, speech, press, assembly, and petition
2. Right to bear arms in order to maintain a well-regulated militia
3. No quartering of soldiers in private homes
4. Freedom from unreasonable search and seizure
5. Right to due process of law, freedom from self-incrimination, double jeopardy (being tried twice for the same crime)
6. Rights of accused persons; for example, the right to a speedy and public trial
7. Right of trial by jury in civil cases
8. Freedom from excessive bail, cruel and unusual punishment
9. Rights not listed are kept by the people
10. Powers not listed are kept by the states or the people

THE BIRTH OF THE UNITED STATES—REVIEW

1. The Sugar Act of 1764 represented a major shift in British policy toward the colonies in that, for the first time, the British

    (1) allowed all proceeds from a tax to stay in the colonial economy
    (2) attempted to control colonial exports
    (3) offered the colonists the opportunity to address Parliament with grievances
    (4) required the colonies to import English goods exclusively
    (5) levied taxes aimed at raising revenue rather than regulating trade

2. During the Revolutionary War, the Loyalists

    (1) were few in number and had little, if any, significance
    (2) made up approximately 20–30 percent of the population
    (3) were mostly former indentured servants who felt obligated to the crown
    (4) were mostly from the royal colony of Virginia and felt loyal to the crown
    (5) had their largest following in New England, where the benefits of the mercantilist system were most visible

WESTWARD HO!

While George Washington and John Adams spent their presidential terms helping to establish the United States as a nation and promote neutrality, Thomas Jefferson promoted a different strategy. His policies began an era of American expansion. Jefferson believed that farming was the noblest and most democratic aspect of life and he sought to add territory to help citizens achieve their agricultural goals. Jefferson is famous for the **Louisiana Purchase** (1803), which virtually doubled the size of the land. France sold the Louisiana Territory to the United States because the French political leader **Napoleon Bonaparte** needed funds to establish an empire in Europe. The purchase gave the United States control over the Mississippi River and the port of New Orleans, invaluable trade routes for the Ohio Valley and western territory.

The **Lewis and Clark Expedition** (1804–1806) was funded by Congress soon after the Louisiana Purchase. These explorers, aided by Native American guides, traveled from St. Louis to the Pacific Ocean in a year and a half. Their expedition helped establish U.S. claims to the disputed Oregon territory.

During the 1840s, Presidents **John Tyler** and **James K. Polk** were huge advocates of westward expansion and supporters of the idea of **Manifest Destiny**, a belief that America's destiny was to stretch beyond its current boundaries until it governed the entire North American continent. Polk in particular had won on a campaign of re-annexing **Texas** and re-occupying **Oregon**. This slogan glossed over the fact that Texas was, at the time claimed by Mexico, and the Oregon territory was jointly held with Great Britain. Soon after Polk's election in 1845, Texas (newly freed from Mexico) requested annexation as a U.S. slave state. This pressured the U.S. Congress to resolve the ownership of Oregon and admit it as a free state. Ultimately, Texas was allowed in the Union and the U.S. and Great Britain agreed to divide the Oregon territory at the 49th parallel.

Two other expansions that you should keep in mind are the acquisition of the Southwest, which was gained through the **Mexican-American War** (1846–1848) and the addition of **Alaska** which was gained through the actions of **William H. Seward**, who engineered the purchase from Russia. This purchase was known as **Seward's Folly** because the Alaska territory, located in the far northern part of the Americas was considered worthless (later on, Alaska became a treasure with the discovery of oil in the region).

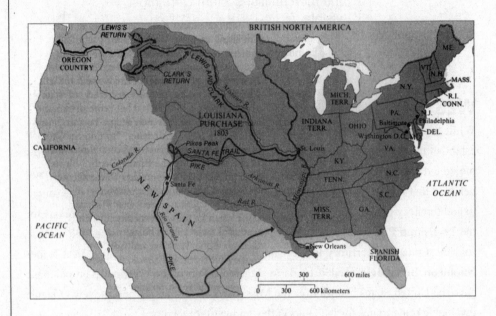

The United States After the Louisiana Purchase

NATIVE AMERICAN RESISTANCE TO WESTWARD EXPANSION

Because of the economic reliance on agriculture and the expanding population, the United States had increasingly looked westward to Native American territories. Land was acquired in two ways, either by making treaties or by forcibly taking it. Congress wanted to take the land honorably, through treaties and "just and lawful wars." However, settlers along the frontier didn't care about the government's concern for expansion with honor. Individual states frequently made treaties and fought tribes for land without federal approval. And even the few treaties that were made with Congress were seldom upheld and enforced.

WESTWARD HO! AND NATIVE AMERICAN RESISTANCE—REVIEW

1. The controversy surrounding the admission of Texas to the United States arose from

   (1) a border dispute with the newly created Republic of Mexico
   (2) the creation of a large, pro-slavery state
   (3) the violation of a long-standing treaty with Spain
   (4) the displacement of large numbers of Native American inhabitants of Texas
   (5) the inclusion of Spanish-speaking people in the Texas state government

2. By what means did the United States take possession of the Oregon Territory?

   (1) The United States was granted the territory in a postwar treaty with France.
   (2) The United States bought it from the Native Americans who lived there.
   (3) U.S. Settlers were the first to arrive in the region; they claimed it for their country.
   (4) Great Britain ceded it to the United States as part of a negotiated treaty.
   (5) The French sold it to the United States as part of the Louisiana Purchase.

3. Manifest Destiny is the belief that

    (1) the colonists were destined to leave the British empire because of the distance between the New World and England
    (2) women are biologically predestined to lives of child rearing and domestic labor
    (3) America's expansion to the West Coast was inevitable and divinely sanctioned
    (4) the abolition of slavery in the United States was certain to come about, because slavery was immoral
    (5) American entry into World War I was unavoidable and was in America's long-term interests

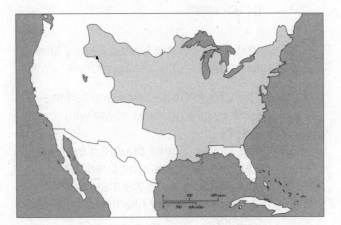

4. The shaded region on the map above shows the land held by the United States immediately following the

    (1) American Revolution
    (2) passage of the Northwest Ordinance
    (3) negotiation of the Treaty of Greenville
    (4) Louisiana Purchase
    (5) War of 1812

INDUSTRIALIZATION

The Industrial Revolution was a period that lasted throughout the 1800s where many new machines and other technological advancements changed many aspects of life. The mass production of textiles (clothing), steel, electricity, plastics and other durable goods helped to make people's lives easier and to greatly aid in making transportation more efficient. Also, because these new factories and means of production needed labor, industrialization gave rise to a **middle-class** and a **working class**. The middle class was made up of tradesmen, brokers, and other professionals, while the working class comprised factory workers and low-paying craftsmen.

Industrialization had the strongest foothold in the Northern states. New factories cropped up in places like New York City and Boston, using new methods of production such as interchangeable parts (parts made to a standard so that they could be replaced easily). Railroad networks were built throughout the North, which helped to transport goods and people more easily. In addition, the use of the telegraph helped people to communicate faster over longer distances.

Cities had numerous pluses. First, cities meant jobs. Many Northern farmers, unable to compete with cheaper produce carted in from the West and South, moved to the cities work in the new factories. Craftsmen (like tailors, cobblers, and blacksmiths) also found it easier to make a living in cities. Second, cities offered more opportunities for social advancement. The development of public schooling and labor unions was an important advancement that helped to improve the lives of city dwellers.

But, living in cities had it drawbacks. Modern waste disposal, plumbing, sewers, and incineration had not been developed yet and cities were notorious for being smelly and rampant with diseases. In addition, people lived very close together which made living situations uncomfortable and privacy virtually impossible.

SECTIONAL STRIFE

As we discussed previously, the North became a center for industrialization and commerce. While there was a large disparity in the distribution of wealth (meaning that the rich made far more money than the poor), social advancement was possible with many working-class families rising to the middle class.

In contrast, the South maintained its original economic structure: the plantation system. With almost no major cities, the South also lacked centers of commerce and the population density was low (meaning that people lived spread out and in near isolation from each other). Similar to the North, the South had a great disparity in the distribution of wealth, but unlike the North social advancement was next to impossible. Wealthy plantation owners were a very small group, but they controlled Southern society politically, socially, and economically. Below this class were yeomen farmers, who could grow just enough to feed their families and afford only the most basic comforts. Less fortunate were landless whites. Unlike the North, slavery became very institutionalized. Slaves lived in a state of subsistence poverty, with two families housed in one room cabins. The conditions were poor and unsanitary.

In contrast to both the North and South, the West offered the most opportunities for advancement and freedom. Events such as the California Gold Rush in 1848 and jobs such as fur trading gave Americans a chance to get rich and advance socially. Also, because of the flatness of the land, the West was seen as very suitable to farming and many cattle ranchers moved there as well. Frontier life was quite rugged and settlers had to battle rough climates and hostile Native American tribes.

These cultural differences led to conflicts and cultural disagreements between the three regions. Unfortunately these differences would soon lead to bloodshed.

INDUSTRIALIZATION AND SECTIONAL STRIFE— REVIEW

1. All of the following contributed to the growth of manufacturing during the middle of the nineteenth century EXCEPT

    (1) the completion of the transcontinental railroad
    (2) the development of labor-saving machines
    (3) the perfection of the assembly line
    (4) an increase in the discovery and use of natural resources
    (5) increased production made possible by the economies of scale available to large companies

2. Which of the following best describes the difference in economy between the Northern states and the Southern states before the outbreak of the Civil War?

   (1) The North relied upon manual labor while the South did not.
   (2) Northern factories had better working conditions than Southern factories.
   (3) The South was primarily agricultural while the North relied upon industry.
   (4) The standard of living in the South was higher than that in the North.
   (5) The North offered more employment opportunities to blacks than did the South.

3. By the first decade of the nineteenth century, American manufacturing had been revolutionized by the advent of

   (1) interchangeable machine parts
   (2) the electric engine
   (3) transcontinental railroads
   (4) labor unions
   (5) mail-order catalogues

THE ABOLITION MOVEMENT

Before the 1830s, few whites fought aggressively for the liberation of the slaves. The Quakers believed slavery to be morally wrong and argued for its end. The movement was also primarily supported by freed blacks, with abolition associations formed in every large black community to assist fugitive slaves and publicize the struggle against slavery. The movement began to gain ground in the 1830s with white abolitionists divided into two groups. Moderates wanted emancipation to take place slowly and with the cooperation of slave owners. Immediatists, as their name implies, wanted emancipation to happen all at once.

In the 1840s, **Frederick Douglass**, a former slave, began publishing his influential newspaper *The North Star,* and was renowned as a gifted writer and an intelligent advocate of freedom and equality. His book *Narrative of the Life of Frederick Douglass* is one of the great American autobiographies. Other prominent black abolitionists include **Harriet Tubman**, who escaped slavery and then returned south repeatedly to help more than 300 slaves escape via the underground railroad (a network of hiding places and "safe trails"); and **Sojourner Truth,** a charismatic speaker who campaigned for emancipation and women's rights.

SECESSION FROM THE UNION AND CIVIL WAR

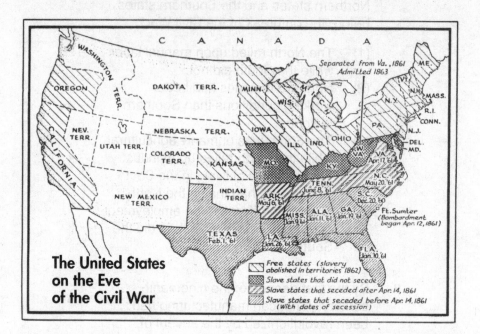

The United States on the Eve of the Civil War

In the mid-1850s, many skirmishes and compromises were being made about the allowance of slavery in certain regions. The westward expansion added new territories but the North and South became increasingly concerned over whether these new territories would be pro-slavery or anti-slavery.

Abraham Lincoln became a rising star for the anti-slavery Republicans in 1858 when he debated with Democratic Senator **Stephen Douglas**. Lincoln famously delivered his "House Divided" speech (where he said "this nation cannot exist permanently half slave and half free") which garnered support, whereas Douglas's political career was destroyed with his ambiguous stance on popular sovereignty.

When Lincoln was elected in 1860, South Carolina proclaimed that its interests would not be represented by the new government and seceded from the Union. Soon after, Alabama, Florida, Georgia, Louisiana, Mississippi, and Texas also withdrew. These states formed the **Confederate States of America** and elected **Jefferson Davis** as their president. Although some abolitionists cheered the departure of the Southern states, most Northerners wanted to preserve the Union.

As president, Lincoln declared the secession illegal. He sent munitions to Fort Sumter and the Union's military leaders announced to the Confederates that they would have to acknowledge the authority of the federal government. The **American Civil War** officially began when the Confederacy responded by attacking Fort Sumter in April

1861. Once the Civil War began in earnest, Virginia, North Carolina, Tennessee, and Arkansas left the Union as well. The war lasted from 1861 to 1865 and both sides suffered many casualties. **General Ulysses S. Grant** and **William T. Sherman** were instrumental in helping to end the war in favor of the North. **General Robert E. Lee** was the most prominent of the Southern military leaders and had achieved major victories for the South but he was ultimately led to surrender to Grant at **Appomattox** in April 1865, which officially ended the war.

Although slavery was a major issue, the Civil War was fought to keep the Union together and not to free the slaves. Indeed, Missouri, Kentucky, Maryland, and Delaware (known as the **Border States**) were slave states that fought for the Union. Still, the power of the Emancipation Proclamation should be acknowledged. Lincoln's declaration freed the slaves in the Confederate states and upon its announcement, half a million slaves fled the plantations and went to the North.

RECONSTRUCTION

The Reconstruction era took place between 1865 and 1877. During this era, the Southern states were re-integrated back into the Union, the Union army withdrew from the South and three amendments were passed. The **Thirteenth Amendment** prohibited slavery throughout the United States. The **Fourteenth Amendment** granted African Americans the right to vote. Finally the **Fifteenth Amendment** gave African Americans citizenship and equal treatment before the law.

Unfortunately, white Southerners reacted to the reforms by passing **Black Codes**, which restricted African Americans from many rights of citizenship. They also used methods to dissuade African Americans from exercising the right to vote, including violence and intimidation from groups like the **Ku Klan Klan**, a literacy test (that many African Americans could not pass because they had been denied an education under slavery), a poll tax (that many African Americans could not afford to pay), prohibitive property requirements, and a grandfather clause that permitted any man to vote whose grandfather had voted. With the **grandfather clause**, uneducated or poor Caucasians could vote, whereas many African Americans whose grandfathers were slaves could not.

CIVIL WAR AND ABOLITION—REVIEW

1. The Congressional Reconstruction Acts, enacted after the Civil War, had which of the following effects on the Southern States?

    (1) Former Slaves were all given 40 acres of land and a work animal.
    (2) Constitutional voting laws were changed to enfranchise former slaves as citizens.
    (3) Segregation of public institutions was mandated to appease white constituents.
    (4) Northern citizens were given tax subsidies as an incentive to migrate to the South to help in the rebuilding efforts.
    (5) Radical white supremacist groups, such as the Ku Klux Klan, were outlawed.

2. The Emancipation Proclamation was designed to accomplish all of the following EXCEPT

    (1) give Southern slaves an incentive to take up arms against their Confederate masters
    (2) expand the southern boundaries of the Union
    (3) gain the support of European powers in the battle against the Confederates
    (4) increase public support for abolition in the Northern states
    (5) impose a penalty on secessionist states

THE RISE OF BIG BUSINESS AND THE PROGRESSIVE ERA

The Rise of Big Business

Following the Civil War, many factors led to a large rise in industrialization and manufacturing. Between the abundant natural resources, the large labor supply (provided by ex-soldiers, freed slaves, immigrants, women and children), and improved transportation (via the railroad system), the United States was well on its way to become one of the world's biggest industrial giants.

The period between the Civil War and World War I is known as the Gilded Age, because there was a small group of wealthy businessman, but their wealth was made off of factory laborers who were underpaid and suffering from terrible working conditions.

The term "**big business**" refers to the large corporations that first developed as a result of industrialization. While it was generally believed that that competition in the marketplace produced fair prices for consumers, corporations were interested in maximizing their profits (which translated to maintaining unfair prices) and saw competition as hurtful to them. So, to reduce competition with other big businesses, these owners would get together and set prices for the industry, forming monopolies or trusts.

The key difference between a **monopoly** and a **trust** is that in a monopoly, one corporation owns all of the means of production and in a trust, a small collection of corporations work together to control the prices of the products. A handy way to remember this is that the prefix mono- means one, which tells you that only one corporation is in control. However a small group of people need to *trust* each other, which reminds you that a trust is made up of a small cabal of separate corporations (for a more expanded definition, you can check out the Economics section). Many big business owners believed in the laissez-faire theory, which is the idea that government has no right to interfere with private enterprise.

Many of these super-rich business owners were called the "captains of industry" by their fans and "robber barons" by their detractors. You may recognize some of the last names of these owners: John D. Rockefeller (oil industry), Leland Stanford (railroads), Cornelius Vanderbilt (also railroads) and J.P. Morgan (banks). Some businessmen like Andrew Carnegie believed that rich entrepreneurs had a responsibility to give large donations to charity. This was known as the Gospel of Wealth.

In order to limit the power of these corporations, antitrust laws were passed. The most famous of these was the **Sherman Antitrust Act**, which worked to break up monopolies. Another factor in reducing the power of big business was the rise of **labor unions**.

These unions represented the interest of the downtrodden workers and bargained for higher wages, better working conditions and shorter hours (since workers were typically working 12 to 14 hour days), and child labor laws (which prevented children below a certain age from working without their parent's consent). Some influential unions were the **Knights of Labor,** the **American Federation of Labor** (AFL), and the **Industrial Workers of the World.**

The Progressive Era

The **Progressive Era** occurred as a reaction to the political scandals and big business corruption of the late 1800s and lasted from 1900 to 1920. Presidents Theodore Roosevelt, William Howard Taft, and Woodrow Wilson were very powerful in directing this reform movement.

During this time period, the women's suffrage movement really started to take hold. Although a constitutional amendment extending voting rights to women was sent to Congress in the 1880s, the **Nineteenth Amendment** wasn't ratified until 1920). Susan B. Anthony and Elizabeth Cady Stanton were important feminists and major champions in the women's rights movement. During this era, increasing numbers of women began to work outside the home and, in some cases, to pursue higher education.

In addition, the foundations for the advancement of the rights of African Americans were being laid out as well. Because of the Ku Klux Klan and intimidation tactics, many African Americans were unable to use their civil rights. Racial segregation was legalized and standardized through the use of **Jim Crow laws**. And a famous Supreme Court decision, *Plessy v. Ferguson,* ruled that laws requiring separate but equal facilities for each race were constitutional. The facilities that were justified under this ruling were separate, but they were anything but equal. In response to these injustices, many strong African American leaders emerged. The **National Association for the Advancement of Colored People (NAACP)** and the **National Urban League** were multiracial groups founded to combat racial discrimination.

Also, between 1880 and 1920, America experienced its largest ever influx of immigrants. Twenty-four million people, mostly from southern and eastern Europe, moved to the United States. The new immigrants settled in cities and dramatically changed the social, cultural, and economic landscape of the areas in which they lived.

THE RISE OF BIG BUSINESS AND THE PROGRESSIVE ERA—REVIEW

1. Which of the following best describes the philosophy of Progressive reformers in the early 1900s?

   (1) Individuals and their families are solely responsible for their own well-being
   (2) Government action should be used to remedy poor social conditions and unfair business practices
   (3) Religiously based, nonprofit groups should be prohibited from providing community welfare
   (4) Corporations should be encouraged to support arts and education through philanthropy
   (5) State and local governments should cede authority to federal programs in the provisions of social welfare

2. Which of the following was sought by reformers during the Progressive era?

   (1) Laws against racial discrimination
   (2) The creation of the Securities Exchange Commission
   (3) The creation of industrial trusts
   (4) More frequent use of referendums
   (5) The rejection of the Nineteenth Amendment

Year	Total in Thousands	Rate[1]
1881–1890	5,247	9.2
1891–1900	3,688	5.3
1901–1910	8,795	10.4
1911–1920	5,736	5.7

[1]Annual rate per 1,000 U.S. population. Rates computed by dividing the sum of annual immigration totals by the sum of annual United States population totals for the same number of years.

3. Which of the following can be inferred from the above table?

   (1) More immigrants arrived in the United States between 1911 and 1920 than during any other period from 1881 to 1920.
   (2) The period between 1891 and 1900 marked the lowest rate of immigration between 1881 and 1920.
   (3) Political persecution in Europe led to a rise in immigration to the United States between 1881 and 1920.
   (4) World economic factors led to a rise in immigration from East to West.
   (5) During the years between 1881 and 1920, the U.S. government provided incentives to draw immigrants to the United States.

4. Laissez-faire capitalism was most strongly endorsed by

   (1) moderate socialists
   (2) mercantilists
   (3) free-market industrialists
   (4) abolitionists
   (5) labor unions

WORLD WAR I

You may be familiar with the phrase "the war to end all wars"; this phrase was used to describe World War I. Unfortunately, there was another war after this that was even more devastating, but at the time World War I was the first war to take place on a global scale and roughly 15 million people were killed with another 20 million wounded.

Thankfully you don't need to know about the exact causes of the war, but you should be aware that a variety of complicated secret alliances drew most of the European powers into conflict with each other. The catalyst was the assassination of Archduke Franz Ferdinand, the ruler of Austria-Hungary. From there, Austria-Hungary and its allies Germany and the Ottoman Empire (known as the **Central Powers**) declared war on the **Allies** (Great Britain, France, and Russia). U.S. president Woodrow Wilson desperately wanted to stay out of the war and maintained a stance of **neutrality**. Although Wilson tried to mediate between the Allies and the Central Powers with a call of peace without victory, no one in Europe was willing to listen.

American sentiment leaned toward the Allies, a tendency further exaggerated by the German policies of submarine warfare. Basically, Germany felt that it could destroy any ship within the naval war zones whereas the United Sates felt that under international law, neutral and merchant ships should not be attacked. The 1915 sinking of the **Lusitania**, a luxury passenger liner which killed 1,198 people (128 of them Americans), turned public opinion against Germany and the Central Powers. In early 1917, Germany torpedoed five American merchant ships, killing all aboard. The Zimmerman Telegram (1917), was the last straw for the United States. Soon after, the U.S. joined the Allied Nations and declared war on Germany. In 1918, the war was won in favor of the Allies.

PEACE TALKS

One of the major benefits of the American victory was that it helped to establish the United States as a superpower. President Wilson outlined a Fourteen Point plan, which called for a peaceful settlement and the creation of a League of Nations that would work to help nations cooperate with each other. The French and British instead sought to punish Germany and signed the **Treaty of Versailles**, which abolished Austria-Hungary and the Ottoman Empire and levied severe financial punishment on the Central Powers. The United States did not sign the treaty because the nation did not want to be drawn into another major European war. Unfortunately the harsh terms of the treaty coupled with a large economic depression caused a situation ripe for the rise of Adolf Hitler in the 1930s.

WORLD WAR I AND PEACE TALKS—REVIEW

1.   Which of the following correctly states Woodrow Wilson's position on Germany's use of submarine warfare during World War I?

(1)   Wilson demanded that all submarine attacks be stopped because he believed they violated international law.

(2)   Wilson opposed the use of submarine warfare only against British ships.

(3)   Wilson supported the submarine attacks, because their primary targets were British ships.

(4)   Because the submarines were built by American manufacturers, Wilson actively campaigned for their use.

(5)   Because the submarines traveled underwater, their existence was secret and Wilson did not learn of them until after the war ended.

2.   Which of the following statements about the Treaty of Versailles is true?

(1)   The United States Senate rejected it because it treated Germany too leniently.

(2)   The United States Senate rejected it because it required increased American involvement in European affairs,

(3)   The United States Senate approved it, with reservations concerning the division of Eastern Europe.

(4)   The United States Senate approved it without reservations.

(5)   It was never voted on by the United States Senate.

THE ROARING TWENTIES

After World War I, the American economy grew rapidly and by 1922 America was hitting new peaks of prosperity. The invention of the practical electric motor, the automobile and the radio greatly enhanced the lives of many upper- and middle-class citizens. In addition, there was a prevailing attitude that businesses and people should be able to do what they wished without government interference.

The loosening social structure led to many new freedoms for women, who had gained the right to vote during this period. A new image of American women developed and became a symbol of the Roaring Twenties—the **flapper**. These women discarded the corset and long dark dresses favored by their Victorian grandmothers in favor of waistless dresses worn above the knee (scandalous!), little hats, ruby-red lips and wrists full of bracelets. Many flappers smoked cigarettes, drank in public, and danced provocative (for its time) dances like the tango and the lindy.

Black Americans also gained some social respect as they returned from military service in World War I and gained some economic advantages from relatively high-paying jobs in the northern war industries. During the war, tens of thousands of African Americans moved to the North to seek better-paying jobs. A movement of black nationalism began under the leadership of Marcus Garvey, who believed in worldwide black unity. Also the **Harlem Renaissance** took place in New York City, where jazz music became popular and black poets and writers emerged as great cultural figures.

The postwar period brought many restrictions as well. Afraid of an impending human flood washing over the United States following the destruction in Europe during the war, Congress instituted **immigration quotas** that allowed only a small fraction of people to enter the United States from Europe. And as we mentioned before, the Ku Klux Klan was a powerful influence in squelching the rights of non-whites.

In addition, the passing of the **Eighteenth Amendment** outlawed drinking as well as the manufacturing of alcohol and ushered in the institution of **Prohibition**. Many people resented the government's intrusion on drinking and speakeasies were opened that sold alcohol illegally. During this period, organized crime rose in power as they produced and sold most of the liquor consumed by rebels of the Prohibition Act. Prohibition was finally repealed in 1933.

THE GREAT DEPRESSION

In 1928 the Republicans elected Herbert Hoover, who parlayed a strong economy into an easy victory. Hoover believed that the day would soon come when no American would live in poverty. Who knew he'd be proven so wrong?

On October 29, 1929 (a day known as **Black Tuesday**) the stock market collapsed and about $30 billion worth of stocks was wiped out. This was the major catalyst that led to the nation's plunge into economic depression but it was not the only factor. Manufacturers and farmers had been overproducing for years, creating large inventories. This led factories to lay off workers and made the farmers' crops worth much less on the market. Furthermore, production of new consumer goods outstripped the public's ability to buy them. Supply had exceeded demand for so many goods that it led to deflation (or devaluing of goods and services). Finally, the government laxity in regulating large businesses led to the concentration of wealth and power in the hands of a very few businessmen. When their businesses failed, many people lost their jobs.

Franklin Delano Roosevelt (known by the initials FDR) became president in 1932 and ushered in an unprecedented era of reform in order to get the United States back on its economic feet. He worked to reform banks and other economic institutions to make them more stable. His banking reforms included the creation of the **Federal Deposit Insurance Corporation** (FDIC) to insure personal bank deposits and the **Securities and Exchange Commission** (SEC) to regulate the trading of stocks and bonds. His administration also passed the first laws guaranteeing minimum wage, unemployment insurance, and Social Security (which provided funded to the elderly, the poor, and widows and fatherless children). Furthermore, he projected strong leadership and instilled in the country a new confidence.

During the 1930s and 1940s, FDR established numerous economic programs; some failed while others succeeded. A few of the important ones are contained in the following chart:

Program		Function
CCC	Civilian Conservation Corps	Provided work for unemployed young men
NIRA/ **NRA**	National Industrial Recovery Act (National Recovery Administration)	Established rules for fair competition; the idea was to keep prices down and employment up
WPA **PWA**	Works Project Administration Public Works Administration	Both programs gave people jobs; some went to writers and artists, some for building roads and hospitals
AAA	Agricultural Adjustment Act	Paid farmers to reduce their production, hoping this would bring higher prices for farm goods
TVA	Tennessee Valley Authority	A government-owned business that helped produce and distribute electrical power services to a large number of people

ROARING TWENTIES AND THE GREAT DEPRESSION—REVIEW

1. The efforts of the United States government to rectify the problems of the Great Depression led to increases in all of the following EXCEPT

   (1) the role of government in managing the economy
   (2) the role of government in supporting the arts
   (3) the regulation of the banking industry
   (4) the use of presidential power in creating government agencies
   (5) the abolition of the sale or manufacture of alcohol

2. The Social Security Act of 1935

   (1) protected workers from unfair dismissal
   (2) led to the establishment of the Tennessee valley Authority
   (3) insured depositors against bank failures
   (4) created public works projects for unemployed workers
   (5) provided insurance for retired persons over 65

3. The Agricultural Adjustment Act of 1933 sought to lessen the effects of the Depression by

   (1) paying farmers to cut production and, in some cases, destroy crops
   (2) purchasing farms and turning them into government collectives
   (3) instituting and early retirement program for farmers over the age of 50
   (4) encouraging farmers to increase production
   (5) subsidizing food processing plants in order to lower food prices

WORLD WAR II

In the late 1930s, the situation in Europe looked pretty bleak. Having been hit hard by both the **Great Depression** (which had affected Europe as well as the United States) and severe poverty due to the after effects of the Treaty of Versailles, Germany fell under the control of **Adolf Hitler** and the fascist **Nazi Party**. In Italy, **Benito Mussolini** set up his own fascist regime. The **Allied Powers** (consisting of France, Great Britain and Poland, with the Soviet Union, or USSR, joining the Allies after a surprise attack by Germany in 1941) feared another world war and many compromises and negotiations took place while Germany and Italy (who were later joined by Japan in 1940 into an alliance known as the **Axis Powers**) committed acts of aggression against their neighbors. Only after Germany violated the terms of the **Munich Conference of 1938** by invading Poland did Great Britain and France declare war on the Axis Powers. As the war went on, Hitler carried out a policy of genocide, directed at Jews, Gypsies, homosexuals and political enemies of the **Third Reich** of Germany. This decimation was known as the **Holocaust**.

The United States first stressed a policy of isolationism, where American troops would not get involved in the war. Congress passed a series of Neutrality Acts to forbid the sale of weapons and the issuing of loans to the warring nations, and prohibited U.S. citizens from traveling on the ships of countries at war. Later, in 1939, the act was revised to allow weapon sales on a "cash and carry" basis, meaning that friendly nations could come to the United States and buy supplies as long as they shipped the weapons themselves. This avoided placing American ships at risk. As public opinion turned toward helping the Allies win while also staying out of the war, Congress passed the **Lend Lease Act** which expanded the power of the president to lend, lease, sell, exchange or do whatever he wanted to get arms and supplies to the Allied Forces.

The United States was successful in avoiding war until the Japanese bombed **Pearl Harbor** in Hawaii on December 7, 1941. FDR called it a "date which will live in infamy." The attack claimed about 2,500 American lives and the shocked FDR administration had no choice but to declare war on the Axis Powers.

Once the government declared war, nearly everyone supported the war effort. A few noteworthy events occurred: rationing and price-fixing were accepted for meat, sugar, gasoline, and other staples; women went to work at war factories by the thousands doing jobs that had previously been considered men's work (inspiring the **Rosie the Riveter** posters); and the sale of war bonds and a large-scale revision of tax laws were instituted to finance the war. In 1945, **Harry S. Truman** became president after FDR died in office.

One of the most tragic black marks on the United States was the **internment of Japanese Americans** from 1942 until the end of the war. Fearful that the Japanese might serve as enemy agents within U.S. borders, the government imprisoned more than 110,000 Japanese Americans, over two-third of whom had been born in the United States and thus were U.S. citizens. None of the interred were ever charged with a crime, and none of them were traitors. The government placed these people in desolate prison camps far from the West Coast. Most lost their homes and possessions as a result of the internment. Unfortunately, it wasn't until 1988 that a government apology was made and reparations of about $1.6 million were disbursed to surviving internees and their heirs.

The war in Europe ended in May 1945 when Allied troops marched into Berlin from both sides (the U.S. and Great Britain from the west and the Soviet Union from the east). Hitler supposedly committed suicide upon hearing of his imminent defeat. After issuing an ultimatum to Japan to surrender unconditionally, the United States dropped an atomic bomb on **Hiroshima** and an atomic bomb on **Nagasaki** in August 1945. Japan surrender soon after the cities were obliterated and nearly a quarter of a million people perished.

THE END OF WAR, THE BEGINNING OF PEACE TALKS

At the war's conclusion, the Allied Powers occupied German, Italian and Japanese territories. The Allies set about prosecuting war criminals and establishing peace treaties. Germany was split into West Germany (a nation that was connected to the Western Allies) and East Germany (which was a communist nation) during this time period and American General Douglas MacArthur ruled the occupied nation of Japan until a U.S.-Japan peace treaty was signed in the early 1950s. A positive result of the peace conferences and negotiations was the formation of the **United Nations**, an organization established to help facilitate cooperation among countries, in 1946.

WORLD WAR II—REVIEW

1. Which of the following is a complete and accurate list of the Axis Powers in World War II?

   (1) The United States, France, and Italy
   (2) The United States, Britain, and the Soviet Union
   (3) The United States, Britain, and Japan
   (4) The United States, Germany, and Italy
   (5) Germany, Italy, and Japan

2. During World War II, the availability of consumer goods to civilians

   (1) increased greatly, because the war invigorated the economy
   (2) increased slightly, because some citizens were overseas serving in the armed forces
   (3) remained at the same level it had been at prior to the war
   (4) decreased slightly, causing prices to rise; only the poor were substantially affected
   (5) decreased greatly, to the point that the government had to ration most necessities

3. Which of the following was LEAST likely a factor in the decision to drop atomic bombs on Hiroshima and Nagasaki?

   (1) Hope that a quick victory in the Pacific would hasten an allied victory in Europe
   (2) Fear that the Soviet Union would soon enter the war with Japan
   (3) Concern that a land war in Japan would result in massive American casualties
   (4) Awareness that Japanese forces were numerous and spread throughout Asia
   (5) Desire to demonstrate to other world powers the potency of America's new weapon

4. Which of the following is true about the internment of those Japanese living in the United States during World War II?

(1) The majority of those confined were native-born Americans.
(2) Many of those relocated were known dissidents.
(3) Only 2,000 Japanese Americans were relocated.
(4) Congress passed a law requiring the relocation of all aliens during the war.
(5) Those who were relocated eventually recovered their homes and possessions.

POSTWAR AND THE COLD WAR

Immediately following the world war, tensions between the Western Allies and the Soviet Union deepened and two **superpowers** emerged: the United States and the Soviet Union (or USSR). The power struggle between the superpowers was called the **Cold War**, because there was no actual combat as there is in a "hot war." The new presence of atomic weapons kept the Cold War pretty chilled because a war could mean worldwide nuclear annihilation.

President Truman adopted a policy of **containment**, where the U.S. would halt the spread of communism around the world and enacted the **Marshall Plan** to help Europe rebuild after World War II. Another show of Western strength was the formation of **NATO (North Atlantic Treaty Organization)**, which declared that the ten nations of Western Europe and the U.S. and Canada would stand together in an attack on any one of them. The communist Eastern European nations countered with the formation of a similar coalition known as the **Warsaw Pact**.

Anti-communist sentiment took hold within the United States and Senator Joseph McCarthy spearheaded a crusade to rid the government of communists, suspected communists, and communist sympathizers. He ultimately affixed these labels to anyone who disagreed with him. His tactics, known as **McCarthyism**, were ruthless and his claims were often unfounded. McCarthyism's demise came about when his bullying tactics were televised as part of a Senate investigation of Army spies; this caused popular opinion to sharply turn against him.

The **Korean War** became one of the earliest stages where Cold War hostilities played out. After World War II, Korea had been divided into North Korea (under Soviet control) and South Korea (under American occupation). Once the Soviet and U.S. troops withdrew from the Korean peninsula, North Korea attacked South Korea without provocation to unify the country under a communist regime. Led by America, the United Nations Security Council sent a force led by General MacArthur to Korea which pushed the North Korea force back towards the Korean-Chinese border. This prompted the involvement of newly communist China, who pushed the U.S./UN forces back to the 38th parallel. After that, armistice talks began but they dragged on for two extra years before the border was established at that parallel.

Other major skirmishes include the **Bay of Pigs invasion** (a failed attempt by the United States government to overthrow the communist ruler of Cuba, Fidel Castro); **the space race** (a race between the U.S. and USSR to see which superpower could reach outer space first—the USSR won this battle by launching *Sputnik,* the first man-made satellite to reach space, but the U.S. formed NASA, or the National Aeronautics and Space Administration, and was the first country to send a man to the moon); the erection of the **Berlin Wall** (to separate communist East Berlin from the Western-aligned West Berlin) and the **Cuban missile crisis** (where the U.S. and the USSR most nearly came to open conflict with the result of Soviet missiles aimed at the United States being removed from Cuba peacefully).

However the most important battle you should know about is the **Vietnam War**. While the war is basically a story of communists versus anti-communists, the different players in this war are a little bit more complex. On one side was communist controlled **North Vietnam** (led by **Ho Chi Minh**) and on the other side was the anticommunist **South Vietnam**. Another player was the **Viet Cong** who had the support of North Vietnam and were entrenched in South Vietnam.

In the early 1960s North Vietnam and the Viet Cong led raids on Saigon, the capital of South Vietnam, in an attempt to unify the country. President **John F. Kennedy**, at the request of South Vietnam, sent U.S. military support. He was motivated by the **domino theory**, which held that once one country "fell" to communism, others in the region would also swiftly fall.

American hopes for a swift end to the war were crushed by the **Tet Offensive of 1968**, which soundly defeat the anticommunist troops. The American army's mixed success on the battlefield coupled with moral outrage led Americans to believe that their own country was the aggressor and not the liberator. Thus public support became strongly against the war. Under President Richard Nixon, the war officially ended in favor of North Vietnam but American troops finally withdrew in 1975. Ultimately, the Vietnam War lasted more than 12 years and became a symbol of the lack of clear goals in our foreign policy and relationships with communist nations.

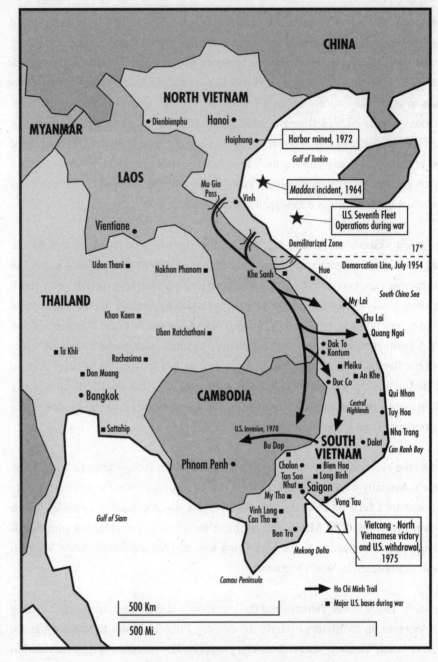

Southeast Asia During the Vietnam War

POSTWAR AND COLD WAR—REVIEW

1. According to the map of Southeast Asia during the Vietnam War on page 258, how many years after the *Maddox* incident did the United States withdraw from Vietnam?

   (1) 8 years
   (2) 11 years
   (3) 14 years
   (4) 20 years
   (5) 22 years

2. Which of the following conflicts did not occur during the Cold War?

   (1) Vietnam War
   (2) Korean War
   (3) The space race
   (4) The Persian Gulf War
   (5) Cuban missile crisis

3. Senator Joseph McCarthy gained national prominence with his accusation that

   (1) American meat packers disregarded fundamental rules of sanitation
   (2) the Federal Bureau of Investigation was violating many innocent citizens' right to privacy
   (3) some congressmen were taking bribes in return for pro-business votes
   (4) massive voter fraud was common throughout the Southwest
   (5) the State Department had been infiltrated by communist spies

4. The difference between a "cold war" and a "hot war" is that, during a "cold war"

    (1) neither side publicly acknowledges its animosity toward its enemy
    (2) United Nations armed forces are used to maintain treaties
    (3) the opponents differ over religious, rather than political, ideals
    (4) the opposing sides are military superpowers
    (5) the opposing sides do not engage in military combat

5. The United States' primary reason for participating in the war in Vietnam was

    (1) to fight under the terms of its military alliance with Japan
    (2) to provide military aid and assistance to Vietnamese leader Ho Chi Minh
    (3) to promote Asian autonomy and anticolonialism
    (4) because American foreign policy experts believed that, without intervention, communism would spread from Vietnam throughout Southeast Asia
    (5) because the government felt obligated to protect the United States' considerable business interests in Vietnam

RICHARD NIXON AND THE WATERGATE SCANDAL

We mentioned **Richard Nixon** earlier as the president who brought an end to the war between the United States and North Vietnam. He is best known for his policy of **détente** in foreign relations, meaning a policy of decreased tensions between the United States and the Soviet Union. This policy allowed him to reach trade agreements with China and begin a period of arms negotiations with the Soviet Union.

Nixon's downfall came with the **Watergate scandal** which occurred during his second term. Men connected to the president and his reelection campaign were caught breaking into the Democratic National Headquarters at the Watergate Hotel in Washington D.C. The subsequent scandal and cover-up became national news. In 1974, Nixon resigned his office (the first and only president in history to do so) rather than face impeachment.

THE CIVIL RIGHTS AND EQUALITY MOVEMENTS

In the 1950s, the civil rights movement came into full force as African Americans demanded equal treatment and the repeal of Jim Crow and segregation laws. In additions, feminists began bringing the issue of women's rights to the forefront and an infant environmental movement began.

A major victory in African American civil rights was the landmark *Brown v. Board of Education* case in 1954, where the Supreme Court ruled that separate but equal institutions (such as public schools and bathroom facilities) were unconstitutional. Furthermore, President Dwight D. Eisenhower supported the Civil Rights Acts of 1957 and 1960, which sought to remove the voting barriers that many Southern states had put into practice and also to help minimize violence directed toward African Americans. Another notable act passed was the **Twenty-fourth Amendment** (1964), which prohibited the use of poll taxes to deny people the right to vote.

Two major African American civil rights leaders emerged during the Civil Rights Era: **Dr. Martin Luther King Jr.** and **Malcolm X. King** was an advocate of using non-violent methods of protest such as sit-ins, bus boycotts and mass marches and is most famous for his **"I Have A Dream"** speech which called for racial equality. Speaking of bus boycotts, a notable figure was **Rosa Parks** who famously refused to give up her seat to a white person in 1955. She is seen by many as the "first lady of civil rights." Malcolm X urged African Americans to claim their rights "by any means necessary" and pushed for more aggressive tactics. Unfortunately, both men were assassinated (X was shot in 1965 while King was shot in 1968), but thanks to their efforts, many reforms were made to get rid of racist laws and institutions.

In the 1960s women became frustrated with being treated as second-class citizens and started their own political groups. In 1966 **Betty Friedan** helped to found the **National Organization of Women (NOW)** as an advocacy group that fought for legislative changes including the Equal Rights Amendment, which stated that men and women should have equal rights under the law (this amendment unfortunately did not pass). Friedan is also famous for her book *The Feminine Mystique,* which challenged many people's assumptions about women's place in society. **Gloria Steinem** became the media spokesperson for feminism and is famous for co-founding **Ms. Magazine.** Another major victory for feminists was the 1973 landmark case *Roe v. Wade,* which enabled women to obtain abortions in all 50 states within the first trimester.

In addition, the modern movement for gay rights began to solidify in the 1960s, with the first **Gay Pride parades** happening on November 2, 1969. The first Pride parade occurred on the anniversary of the **Stonewall riots**, an event at which gays fought back against the police in New York City.

WATERGATE SCANDAL; CIVIL RIGHTS AND EQUALITY RIGHTS MOVEMENTS—REVIEW

1. Which of the following statements about Watergate is true?

    (1) It was the first time a president had been involved in a scandal while in office.
    (2) It was of little interest to the American people.
    (3) It led to the resignation of President Richard Nixon.
    (4) It led to the impeachment of President Richard Nixon.
    (5) It bolstered the popularity of the Republican Party.

2. The 1956 boycott of the Montgomery bus system

(1) was led by Malcolm X
(2) started because the city doubled bus fares
(3) was instigated by the arrest of Rosa Parks
(4) lasted for three weeks and failed to achieve its goal
(5) resulted from the assassination of Martin Luther King, Jr.

3. In which decision did the Supreme Court invalidate the practice of "separate but equal" facilities for blacks and whites?

(1) *Marbury v. Madison*
(2) *Bradwell v. Illinois*
(3) *Plessy v. Ferguson*
(4) *Brown v. Board of Education of Topeka, Kansas*
(5) *Holden v. Hardy*

4. Which book was a major impetus in the growth of the women's movement in the 1960s?

(1) Betty Friedan's *The Feminine Mystique*
(2) Rachel Carson's *Silent Spring*
(3) Pearl S. Buck's *The Good Earth*
(4) Lorraine Hansbury's *A Raisin in the Sun*
(5) Harriet Beecher Stowe's *Uncle Tom's Cabin*

5. During the 1950s, many black and white activists fought against the persistence of Jim Crow laws throughout the South by all of the following means EXCEPT

   (1) bringing lawsuits in federal courts
   (2) using violence to intimidate local politicians
   (3) boycotting local businesses that supported segregation
   (4) staging sit-ins in segregated public places and facilities
   (5) forging a coalition between Southern black churches and civil rights advocates

THE THAWING OF THE COLD WAR AND THE MODERN AGE

The Modern Age is rarely tested on the GED, primarily because this part of history is too recent in everyone's memories and it is very hard for historians to decide what is really important. Nevertheless, it's still good information for you to have.

Nixon's resignation led to Gerald Ford assuming the presidency, and after Ford the Democrat Jimmy Carter assumed the Presidency. Both men's presidencies were plagued by a troubled economy and an energy crisis, caused by the Arab nations refusal to ship oil to any Western countries.

Republican President Ronald Reagan began a legacy of conservatism in politics and economics. He is well-known for his **supply-side economic plan** advocated cutting taxes on the rich so that their subsequent investments will trickle down to the poorer classes.

As the Cold War waned, nuclear armaments around the world began to be dismantled. Mikhail Gorbachev's leadership of the USSR led to better American-Soviet relations. He is best remembered for his 1980 economic reform policy of *perestroika* and his social reform policy known as *glasnost*. Reagan and Gorbachev met frequently and negotiated a successful withdrawal of nuclear warheads from Europe.

In the early 1990s, two major events ended the Soviet Union's reign as a superpower. In 1990, the Berlin Wall was deconstructed and East and West Germany were reunited. And in 1991, the USSR was disintegrated into Russia and 15 sovereign states.

President **George H. W. Bush** is known for his slogan "Read my lips; no new taxes" and for leading the international community in the **Persian Gulf War** of 1990, which turned back an invasion of Kuwait by Iraq. **Bill Clinton's** presidency (1993–2001) marked a switch from a Republican in office to a Democrat in office. His presidency was well received for his overhaul of the nation's welfare system, his securing the rights of workers to maintain health care provisions after changing jobs, and increasing the minimum wage. His career was unfortunately marred when his extramarital affair with a White House intern came to light. He was impeached because Congress determined that he lied about the affair, but he was acquitted of all charges.

The 2000 Election was a major event where Republican George W. Bush was pitted against Democrat Al Gore. In this election, although the popular vote claimed that Gore won the presidency, the election resulted in Bush winning. After many debates and vote recounts, the **Supreme Court** validated Bush's victory.

On **September 11, 2001,** four commercial airliners were hijacked and used as weapons of destruction. Two planes were flown into the World Trade Center, destroying the twin towers ; another plane was flown into the Pentagon and caused extensive damage; a fourth plane crashed in a field in Sharpsburg, Pennsylvania. More than 2,800 people were killed. The attacks, attributed to **Osama bin Laden** and a radical Muslim terrorist group called **al Qaeda,** sparked a War on Terrorism. Osama bin Laden was killed by U.S. forces in May 2011.

Most famously, the precedent of having white male Presidents was finally shattered when **Barack Obama** became the first African American to be elected president of the United States in 2008.

ANSWERS AND EXPLANATIONS

Early Explorers and Colonialism—Review

1. **(5)** Answer this EXCEPT question using "Yes" or "No" for each choice. If you remember any colony established for this reason, it's a "Yes" and should be eliminated. Religious freedom (1), commercial interests (2), and trade routes (3) are clearly common reasons for establishing colonies; military advantages were also important, especially given the ongoing tensions among the British, the French, and the Spanish. Manufacturing (5), normally associated with the nineteenth century, is the anti-era choice and the right answer.

2. **(5)** Area Native Americans introduced the Chesapeake settlers to tobacco, and its export to England proved an immediate success. Tobacco farming requires abundant acreage, because the crop drains nutrients from the soil and therefore cannot be grown repeatedly in the same fields. Accordingly, Chesapeake area settlers sought and received large land grants until there was no more land to acquire. The other answers to this question are wrong. (1): Massachusetts settlers certainly were interested in expansion, but at a slower rate. Unlike Chesapeake settlers, Massachusetts colonists built permanent, sturdy houses and settled in towns. (2): The birthrate and life expectancy were higher in the Massachusetts Bay colony; the Chesapeake region was more conducive to epidemic, and the English settlers, used to more temperate weather, found its climate inhospitable. Furthermore, whereas many Massachusetts settlers arrived with their entire families intact, most Chesapeake settlers arrived alone. Men greatly outnumbered women in the Chesapeake region, and so marriage and family life were less common there than in Massachusetts. (3): Both areas were populated by Native Americans when the colonists arrived; indeed each group would have starved to death had it not been for the Native Americans' assistance. (4): Land in the Chesapeake region was more fertile, not less, than land in the Massachusetts Bar region.

3. **(3)** Indentured servitude promised freedom and a parcel of land to those who survived its seven-year term of service. Fewer than half did; most indentured servants worked in the fields performing grueling labor, and many died as a result. Indentured servitude was available only to the English, and nearly 100,000 took advantage of it.

4. **(4)** Virginia, one of the earliest colonies, developed around the tobacco trade; tobacco was the colonies' first important cash crop. You should have eliminated (5) by using common sense; fresh fruit would hardly have remained fresh during the long sea journey from the colonies back to England. Cotton (1) did not become a major export until the early nineteenth century, when the invention of the cotton gin made large-scale cotton farming practical.

The Birth of the United States—Review

1. **(5)** English taxes and levies on the colonists prior to the Sugar Act were proposed and accepted as acts of mercantilist protectionism. The Sugar Act was something different. England had accrued a large war debt during the French and Indian War. England felt that since the war was fought to protect the colonists, the colonists should share in its expense. Revenues from the Sugar Act were earmarked toward repaying that debt. The colonists saw things differently, however. Many argued that people could not be taxed without their consent, and that since the colonists had no representatives in Parliament, they simply could not be taxed. The Sugar Act is often regarded as a major catalyst in the chain of events that led to the Revolutionary War.

2. **(2)** Many historians believed that the Loyalists were made up of about 20 percent of the population.

Westward Ho! and Native American Resistance—Review

1. **(2)** For this question, any of the answer choices seem reasonable, but if you think of the era of the question, it is easy to identify (2) as the right answer. A major issue in adding new states to the United States prior to the Civil War was whether the new state would be "slave" or "free." From 1800 to 1865, new states were only admitted if they could be balanced to maintain the uneasy compromise on the question of slavery. The annexation of Texas, especially as a large state, threatened to disrupt that balance. Any questions on this subject should instantly ring a bell on the question of slavery. In this case, Oregon was admitted as a "free state" to the United States a few months later via a treaty with Great Britain.

2. **(4)** The United States almost fought a war over the Oregon Territory, which consisted of present-day Oregon, Washington, and parts of Montana and Idaho. Originally, American expansionists and settlers demanded all the territory up to the 54 40' boundary, and were willing to fight the British (who held it as part of their Canadian territories) to get it. Contemporaneous conflicts near Mexico caused President James Polk to reconsider war with Great Britain; he feared that two wars would spread forces dangerously thin, as well as damage his popularity with voters. Therefore, Polk decided to negotiate a settlement with the British—the United States accepted a boundary at the 49th parallel—and directed his military activities southward. The United States subsequently entered a war with Mexico, which netted it much of the territory that makes up the Southwestern States.

3. **(3)** The idea of Manifest Destiny was originally advanced by a newspaper editor in the 1840s, and it quickly became a part of the public's and government's vocabulary. Part and parcel with the doctrine of Manifest Destiny was the notion that Europeans, especially English-speaking Europeans, were culturally and morally superior to those whom they supplanted, and so were entitled to the land even if others were already living on it. Manifest Destiny was later invoked as a justification for the Spanish-American War.

4. **(4)** A little historical background: In 1802 Spain ceded New Orleans to the French. This caused considerable unease in the Jefferson administration; while Spain had never taken advantage of New Orleans' strategic location (it controls access to the Mississippi River from the Gulf of Mexico, and vice versa), France seemed much more likely to exploit the advantage. Jefferson sent James Monroe to France to offer to buy New Orleans for $2 million. What the Americans did not know, however, was that Napoleon had decided to withdraw from the New World entirely in order to deploy his troops in Europe, which he hoped to conquer. Thus, Monroe received a pleasant surprise when he arrived in Paris: The French offered to sell the entire territory for $15 million.

Industrialization and Sectional Strife—Review

1. **(3)**   In this question, the answer choices should be connected to the era. Ask yourself: Was this a nineteenth-century development or not? Choices (1), (2), (4), and (5) seem reasonably set in the nineteenth century, but choice (3), assembly-line technique, should jump out as a later innovation. Remember: Henry Ford's company was one of the first to use assembly lines to build Model T's in 1910.

2. **(3)**   The primary difference between Northern and Southern economies prior to the Civil War is that the North was more industrialized and the South was more agricultural (3). Both the North and the South relied on manual labor, and their factory conditions were similar (although there were few factories in the South), thus eliminating choices (1) and (2). It is difficult to compare the different standards of living or employment opportunities, because the types of labor and wages cannot be compared, thus eliminating choices (4) and (5).

3   **(1)**   In 1798 Eli Whitney patented a process for manufacturing interchangeable parts. Previously, manufacturers had custom-fitted parts, so guns, machines, etc., could only be assembled from their own, specifically fitted parts. Whitney's innovation brought about the end of cottage industries and gave rise to an American Industrial Revolution so successful that, by 1850, Europe was sending delegations to the United States to study its manufacturing systems.

Civil War and Reconstruction—Review

1. **(2)**   One of the effects of the Reconstruction acts was to change voting laws so that freed slaves could vote, or be enfranchised (2). These changes spurred the creation of white supremacist groups and local laws to hinder the voting process for African Americans, such as the poll tax and literacy requirements. Use the era, and your knowledge that Congressional Republicans wanted to punish rather than appease the South right after the Civil War, to lead you to the best answer. Choice (3) can be eliminated. Choice (1), providing 40 acres and a mule to freed slaves, was discussed in Congress, but never enacted.

2. **(2)**   The answer to this EXCEPT question is choice (2). The Emancipation Proclamation promoted the freeing of all slaves in the seceding states in order to mobilize Union support and draw clear sides on the issue of slavery for the new Union.

Rise of Big Business and the Progressive Era— Review

1. **(2)** During the Progressive Era of the early 1900s, reformers demanded more accountability from businesses and more action from local, state and national government on social issues. A core tenet of their philosophy was that government regulation could better protect and help citizens, making (2) the best choice.

2. **(4)** If you didn't know what a referendum is (which is a direct vote where a body is asked to accept or reject a particular proposal in a method to enact new laws), you can use POE here to knock out all the incorrect choices. Choice (3) is pro-business and therefore does not fit. Choices (1) and (2) were issues focused on in the years after the Progressive era. And choice (5) is never mentioned at all.

3. **(2)** You only need to apply the information from the chart to answer this question—the rate of 5.3 from 1891–1900 is the lowest, making choice (2) the correct choice.

4. **(3)** "Laissez-faire" is a term associated with free market economies. Choice (3) fits best. But if you were unfamiliar with that term, you could use the concept of capitalism in the question to eliminate wrong choices (1), (4), and (5). As for choice (2), mercantilists were more associated with colonial economic structures.

World War I—Review

1. **(1)** As part of its World War I strategy, Germany used its submarines to attack ships providing supplies to its enemies (the attacks were meant to counter a British blockade of trade to Germany). According to international law at the time, an attacker had to warn civilian ships before attacking. Submarines could not do this, because doing so would eliminate their main advantage (i.e., the enemy doesn't know where they are). To address this legal issue, Germany issued a blanket announcement stating it would attack any ship it believed to be carrying military supplies to the enemy. President Wilson was not satisfied, demanding a specific warning before each and every such attack. Choice (1) is the correct answer here.

2. **(2)** Many Americans supported the U.S. war effort only grudgingly, and then only after German (and, to a lesser extent, British) interference with American Shipping had provoked the United States to action. President Woodrow Wilson negotiated the Treaty of Versailles (the peace treaty following World War I) for the United States, which included provisions for the League of Nations (which Wilson had fought hard for) and contained a clause that could have been interpreted as committing the American military to the defense of European borders. Wilson, a Democrat, tried to sell this treaty to the Republican Senate, but could not muster the two-thirds majority required for ratification, and so the treaty was never approved by the United States.

Roaring Twenties and the Great Depression—Review

1. **(5)** Cross out the EXCEPT and treat each choice as a "Yes" or "No" question: Would the U.S. government do this to aid the economy during the Depression? Also think of the era: The Great Depression started roughly from the Crash of 1929 through the 1930s. You should know that, following Franklin D. Roosevelt's election in 1932, the U.S. government took an activist role in the economy by increasing regulation of market forces and launching public works projects to create jobs. Choices (1), (2), (3), and (4) each reflect this or should at least rank as a "maybe" as you read it. Choice (5) is about the restriction of alcohol, which is known as Prohibition. Nationally enacted by the Eighteenth Amendment in 1919, Prohibition predates the Great Depression of the 1930s. So (5) is the anti-era choice and the correct answer. The Twenty-first Amendment, which repealed Prohibition, was enacted in 1933.

2. **(5)** As you may remember from the text, The Social Security Act of 1935 was one of the most popular and enduring of the New Deal programs, providing retirement insurance or pensions to persons over age 65. Choice (5) is the correct answer.

3. **(1)** As he began his first term, President Franklin D. Roosevelt was faced with an agricultural market in which the bottom had dropped out; farmers had so overproduced that their crops were worth virtually nothing. Roosevelt's solution, the AAA, provided payments to farmers in return for their agreement to cut production by up to one-half. The money to cover this program came from increased taxes on meat packers, millers and other food processors. The program stabilized agricultural prices and increased American income from imports.

World War II—Review

1. **(5)** For this question, it helps to know who was on which side in World War II and then use what you know to eliminate wrong choices. Germany was clearly one of the enemies and so was Japan. Only answer choice (5) reflects that alliance. The United States was part of the Allied forces, so you can use that to eliminate answer choices as well.

2. **(5)** For obvious reasons, the U.S. government declared the war effort the nation's chief priority. As part of the effort, the economy was retooled to support the war. Manufacturers and producers of raw materials gave top priority to military shipments, resulting in a sharp decline in consumer goods for those at home. The situation grew so bad that the government had to ration such items as gasoline and meat.

3. **(1)** The Axis powers in Europe had surrendered months before the bombing of Hiroshima and Nagasaki, so speeding the end of war in Europe could not have been a consideration. The United States was primarily concerned with the difficulty of defeating the Japanese forces; they were both powerful and tenacious. Earlier land battles with the Japanese had resulted in heavy casualties for both sides. But the United States was also concerned about the Soviet Union; with the war in Europe over, the Cold War was beginning. President Harry Truman was anxious to finish the war in Japan before the USSR could enter the fray and establish a greater presence in the region. He also hoped that, by demonstrating the power of the atomic bomb, he could intimidate the Soviets and other potential enemies.

4 **(1)** More than 110,000 Japanese Americans were relocated during World War II. Most lost their homes and possessions, to the tune of an estimated $40 million. The relocation was mandated by presidential order; Congress was compliant in that it never acted to stop it, but that was the extent of congressional participation. There were not 100,000 Japanese American dissidents in the United States before the war, nor even half that many, making answer choice (2) incorrect.

Postwar and the Cold War—Review

1. **(2)** This is a map interpretation question that is asking you to do a little bit of Math. As you can see on the map, the Maddox incident occurred in 1964. The U.S. withdrew from Vietnam in 1975. Subtract these two numbers and you will get 11 years, or choice (2).

2. **(4)** This is an era question. You may recall that the space race, the Vietnam War, the Korean War, and the Cuban missile crisis all occurred during the Cold War Era. The Persian Gulf War is the only incident that did not happen then (this war took place in 1990, by the way).

3. **(5)** Senator McCarthy leapt into the national scene when he stated that he was aware of known Communists in the State Department. The charges gained immediate national attention, and McCarthy had discovered a potent political issues: America's widespread fear of communism, heightened by the Chinese Revolution and the USSR's successful detonation of an atomic bomb. In the years to come he would preside over numerous investigative hearings, but he would never uncover any communist spies.

4. **(5)** A "cold war" is one in which the two countries do not engage in military battles but are nonetheless clearly enemies. During a cold war, the prospect of military engagement is never far off. During the Cold War, the United States and the Soviet Union battled in every way except on the battlefield. They plotted against each other politically, denounced each other repeatedly, and poured billions into weapons research and development in an effort to gain the upper hand on the other.

5. **(4)** Answer choice (4) sums up the "domino theory," first articulated by President Dwight D. Eisenhower. In a speech explaining America's interest in Vietnam, Eisenhower said, "You have a row of dominoes set up; you knock over the first one, and what will happen to the last one is that it will go over very quickly." Some of the incorrect answers are noteworthy. Ho Chi Minh was the leader of the North Vietnamese, who were Communists; Ho had been a U.S. ally during World War II and had even received CIA assistance, but ultimately the United States opposed him for political reasons. The United States first came to assist France, the colonial power in Vietnam, so U.S. policy was hardly anti-colonial. Finally, the United States had few business interests in the area at the time, although the government was interested in the Vietnamese rice market, which fed America's strongest ally in the region, Japan.

Watergate Scandal; Civil Rights and Equality Rights Movements—Review

1. **(3)** President Nixon resigned in 1974 to avoid impeachment proceedings over accusations of obstruction of justice regarding the Watergate affair.

2. **(3)** Rosa Parks was arrested after she refused to give up her seat on a bus to a white man; a Montgomery ordinance required blacks to sit in the back of the bus and to give up their seats to whites if asked to do so. Outrage over the arrest, coupled with long-term resentment to Jim Crow laws, provided the impetus for the year-long boycott. The boycott also brought Martin Luther King, Jr. to national prominence.

3. **(4)** In 1954 the Supreme Court ruled invalid the "separate but equal" standard approved by the court in *Plessy v. Ferguson* (1896). In a 9-to-0 decision, the court ruled that "separate educational facilities are inherently unequal." The suit was brought on behalf of Linda Brown, a black school-age child, by the NAACP. About the other cases mentioned here, in case you are curious: *Marbury v. Madison* is the case that established the principle of judicial review. *Bradwell v. Illinois* is an 1873 decision in which the court upheld the state of Illinois' right to deny a female attorney the right to practice law simply on the basis of gender. That case represented a setback for both women's rights and the Fourteenth Amendment. In *Holden v. Hardy,* the Court ruled that states could pass laws regulating safety conditions in privately owned workplaces.

4. **(1)** Betty Friedan's 1963 book, *The Feminine Mystique,* helped spark the feminist movement. Friedan, a Smith graduate, chronicled the lives of affluent wives and mothers living out the American Dream, yet finding themselves unfulfilled and unhappy.

5. **(2)** All of the other choices were ways that activists used in the struggle for equal rights. However, neither black nor white activists in the 1950s used violent intimidation tactics to persuade politicians to repeal any laws.

SOCIAL STUDIES DRILL

Questions 1–3 are based on the following passage about World War I and the League of Nations

At the end of World War I in 1918, the Allied Nations (United States, Great Britain, France, and formerly Russia) were victorious against the Central Powers (Germany, Austria-Hungary, and the Ottoman Empire). U.S. President Woodrow Wilson forwarded a plan that he proclaimed "the only possible program" for maintaining peace in Europe after the war. It was called the Fourteen Points Plan. Many of the points dealt with reduced armaments, freedom of the seas, and other aspects of international relations. The fourteenth point (arguably the most important point) called for a "general association of nations" that would work to assure the political independence of all nations.

The association came to be known as the League of Nations. Wilson had trouble selling this plan not only to the nationalistic Allies, but also to the strongly Republican U.S. Congress; the Senate was especially peeved because they felt he wrote his plan without due consultation with them. In the end a League of Nations was established which included most of the Allied nations, but it excluded the Central Powers and Communist Russia. The United States also did not join the League of Nations; ultimately the Republicans in Congress feared that the League would obligate the United States to enter another world war.

1. Which of these countries was a Central Power?

   (1) Ottoman Empire
   (2) Great Britain
   (3) United States
   (4) Russia
   (5) Canada

2. The word "league" in this instance most nearly means:

   (1) Country
   (2) Confederation
   (3) Unit of length
   (4) Presidency
   (5) Senate

3. Which of the following best describes a rationale for the failure of the United States to join the League of Nations after World War I?

   (1) Communist-controlled Russia would have a central role in the League of Nations.
   (2) The Allies wanted to continue fighting the war against the Central Powers.
   (3) Republicans in the Senate were concerned that involvement in the League of Nations would curtail the United States' ability to act in its own best interests.
   (4) President Woodrow Wilson was not wholly supportive of U.S. admission to the League of Nations.
   (5) Great Britain and France refused to join the League of Nations

4. There are two types of money. Commodity money has value beyond its usefulness as money. Examples include coins made of precious metals, cigarettes used as money in prisons, and shells and arrowheads used as money in the past. Today, most of our money is fiat money, meaning that it has no intrinsic value. Currency made of paper and inexpensive metals has value as money only because it is deemed to have such value by government order or "fiat."

Which of the following would be an example of fiat money?

(1) Cigarettes used as money in prisons
(2) Dollar bills
(3) Gold coins
(4) Arrowheads used as a medium of exchange
(5) Chickens used for bartering

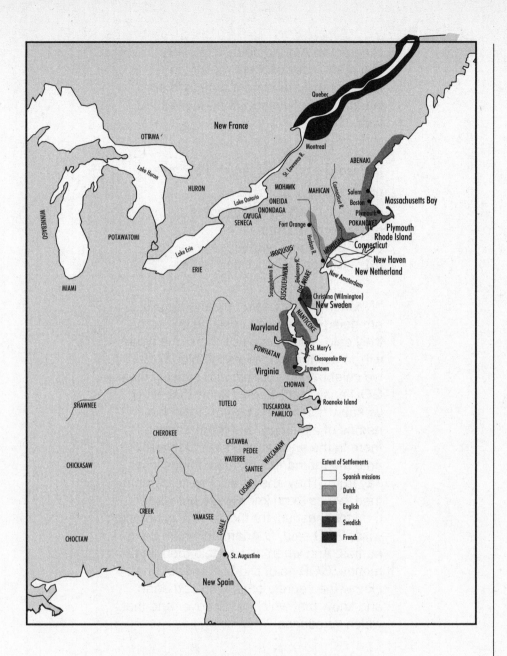

European Settlements in North America, 1650

5. According to the map above, it can be
    inferred that the sites of colonial cities
    were chosen primarily on the basis of their
    proximity to

    (1) gold mines
    (2) coal reserves
    (3) wild game
    (4) mountains
    (5) waterways

6. Nineteenth Amendment (1920)—A landmark victory for suffragists, the Nineteenth Amendment promised all women in the United States the right to vote.

The word "suffragist" most likely means

(1) Woman
(2) Advocate of voting rights
(3) Congressman
(4) Supreme Court judge
(5) Citizen of the United States

7. "When thy LORD said unto the angels, I am going to place a substitute on earth; they said, Wilt thou place there one who will do evil therein, and shed blood? But we celebrate thy praise, and sanctify thee. GOD answered, Verily I know that which ye know not; and he taught Adam the names of all things, and then proposed them to the angels, and said, Declare unto me the names of these things if ye say truth. They answered, Praise be unto thee; we have no knowledge but what thou teachest us, for thou art knowing and wise. GOD said, O Adam, tell them their names. And when he had told them their names, GOD said, Did I not tell you that I know the secrets of heaven and earth, and know that which ye discover and that which ye conceal?"

The text above is a selection from the holy book of the

(1) Greeks
(2) Hindus
(3) Babylonians
(4) Buddhists
(5) Muslims

Questions 8–9 refer to the following paragraph

During the Progressive Era of the early 1900s, many African American leaders emerged. But within the African American community, opinion was widely divided over which path to take in the pursuit of equal rights. Booker T. Washington advocated that African Americans should refrain from "agitating" the white majority, and instead strive to achieve economic equality through job training and diligent work. He believed that once economic parity was achieved, political and social rights would follow. In contrast, W. E. B. DuBois argued that, while job training was beneficial, African Americans should aggressively demand political social and economic rights immediately.

8. The difference between the positions of Booker T. Washington and W. E. B. DuBois can be best summed up as the difference between

   (1) despair and optimism
   (2) violence and pacifism
   (3) religiosity and atheism
   (4) democratic and totalitarian ideals
   (5) confrontation and accommodation

9. Which of the following ideas would Booker T. Washington and W. E. B. DuBois most likely agree to be beneficial to the advancement of African Americans in society?

   (1) Political rights should be demanded immediately.
   (2) Social reform is a slow and gradual process.
   (3) The talented tenth of the African American community should spearhead the equality movement.
   (4) Job training is a necessity to help African Americans advance.
   (5) African Americans should use nonviolent methods as a way of achieving equal rights.

Cold War Europe

10. According to the map, which two countries would most likely have the largest difference in political ideologies?

    (1) Romania and Bulgaria
    (2) Great Britain and Italy
    (3) Switzerland and Sweden
    (4) Spain and Poland
    (5) Soviet Union and East Germany

Questions 11–12 refer to the following paragraph

Directly after World War II, President Harry S Truman responded to the threat of the Soviet Union with a policy of "containment" that became known as the Truman Doctrine. This policy set the tone for the Cold War and pledged U.S. economic and military support to help "free peoples" resist Soviet "aggression." Soon after, Truman's Secretary of State, George C. Marshall, argued that the best way to "protect" nations from succumbing to communism was to help them become economically and politically strong. The Marshall Plan provided grants and loans to war-torn European nations. It was targeted against "hunger, poverty, desperation, and chaos." Soon, this economic support helped bring Western Europe to a strong postwar recovery and aided its stiff opposition to communist expansion.

11. One result of the Marshall Plan of 1948 was

   (1) the shipment of food, raw material, and machinery to postwar Europe
   (2) the airlift of vital supplies to blockaded West Berlin after the Second World War
   (3) the division of Germany into four administrative zones
   (4) the withdrawal of the United States from foreign affairs
   (5) the admission of China to the United Nations

12. The Marshall Plan was significant because it

   (1) involved the United States in the rehabilitation of post-World War II Europe
   (2) contradicted the Cold War doctrine of President Truman
   (3) enabled the Allies to win World War II earlier than expected
   (4) compelled the Soviet Union to withdraw from East Germany
   (5) was the first time the United States intervened in European affairs

13. "Television has been far more influential than even Gutenberg's printing press. Books, magazines, and radio have all been described as mass media, but none can compare to the size and shape of television; it is massive. Audiences are drawn from every social class and every demographic. Television focuses and directs these disparate individuals by engaging them in a purely homogenous activity."

The above statement made by a media critic most likely refers to

(1) the impact of television as a mass-communication technology on the general public
(2) the results of government censorship in the mass media
(3) the difficulties faced by traditional media publishers with the rise of television viewing
(4) the lack of information available to the average television viewer
(5) the influence wielded by the media on political affairs

14. Andrew Jackson, waging a fierce campaign, was elected president by a landslide in 1828 with John C. Calhoun as his vice president. While in office, Jackson surrounded himself with friends and supporters and advocated what was known as the spoils system, as in "to the victor go the spoils." This meant that the winning political party should get all the political jobs in Washington.

The "spoils system" favored by President Andrew Jackson led to

(1) the establishment of the Food and Drug Administration
(2) the development of negative campaign tactics still in use today
(3) the distribution of government jobs to members of the president's party
(4) the increase in legal discrimination based on race
(5) the defeat of American troops in the War of 1812

15. A historian wanting to analyze quantitative data concerning how Americans earned their livings during the 1880s would probably find the most useful information in which of the following sources?

(1) The diary of a man who worked several jobs during the decade
(2) U.S. census reports
(3) Employment advertisements in a large city newspaper
(4) Letters from a mid-level government bureaucrat to a friend overseas
(5) Lyrics to popular songs from that era

16. The rapid growth of the textile industry in the early 1800s resulted in a shortage of labor in New England. Consequently, textile manufacturers had to "sweeten the pot" to entice laborers (almost all of whom were women from nearby farms) to their factories. The most famous worker-enticement program was called the "Lowell System," which guaranteed employees housing in respectable, chaperoned boardinghouses; cash wages; and participation in cultural and social events organized by the mill.

The Lowell System of early nineteenth-century textile manufacturing was noteworthy for its

(1) practice of hiring only adult males at a time when textiles was considered "women's work"
(2) commitment, in the face of the Industrial Revolution, to maintaining the old, "by-hand" method of manufacture
(3) efforts to minimize the dehumanizing effects of industrial labor
(4) pioneering advocacy of such issues as parental leave, vacation time, and health insurance for employees
(5) particularly harsh treatment of employees

17. The following table summarizes the characteristics of the major market structures.

	Perfect Competition	Monopolistic Competition	Oligopoly	Monopoly
Firms	very many	many	few	one
Barriers	none	low	high	prohibitive
Market Power	none	some	substantial	complete
Product	homogenous	differentiated	homogenous or differentiated	unique
Long-Run Economic Profit	zero	zero	positive or zero	positive or zero

In the long run, a monopolistically competitive firm

(1) earns zero economic profit
(2) earns positive economic profit
(3) earns negative economic profit
(4) earns a slightly positive economic profit
(5) earns a slightly negative economic profit

18. "If I could save the Union by freeing all the slaves, I would do it...What I do about slavery, and the colored race, I do because I believe it helps to save the Union."

The above statement was made by which of the following people?

(1) Horace Greeley
(2) Abraham Lincoln
(3) Stephen Douglas
(4) James Buchanan
(5) Ulysses S. Grant

19. Signs such as the one shown in the photograph represent

(1) the philosophy of Radical Reconstructionists
(2) the reforms of the Fourteenth Amendment to the Constitution
(3) the enforcement of the Taft-Hartley Act
(4) desegregation efforts by southerners
(5) the prevalence of Jim Crow laws

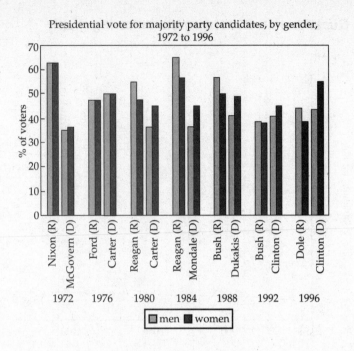

Presidential vote for majority party candidates, by gender, 1972 to 1996

Source: *New York Times*/CBS exit polls

20. The graph above supports which of the following conclusions about presidential elections?

(1) If only men had voted in the 1980 election, Jimmy Carter would have won.

(2) There is little difference in the level of support that the Republican Party receives from men and women.

(3) The gender gap was more prominent in the 1980s and 1990s than it was in the 1970s.

(4) In order for a Republican candidate to win, he or she must receive more votes from women than from men.

(5) The 1976 election was the closest in history.

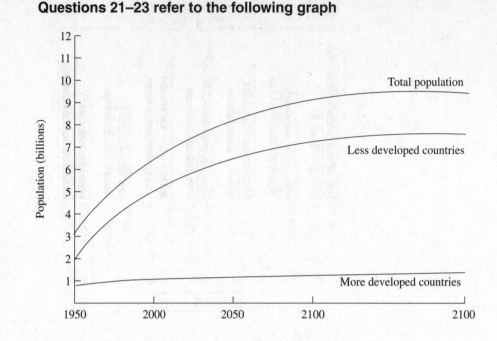

21. Which of the answers below best describes the change in the population of less developed countries between the years 1950 and 2050?

(1) There will be an increase of approximately 1 billion.
(2) There will be an increase of approximately 4 billion.
(3) There will be an increase of approximately 10 billion.
(4) There will be a decline of 1 billion.
(5) There will be a decline of 6 billion.

22. According to the graph, the total population of the world is most likely to increase due to which of the following?

(1) The rise in populations of developed countries
(2) The continued emigration of people
(3) The use of more fossil fuels
(4) The rise in populations of developing countries
(5) An increase in the amount of food produced in less arable land

23. According to the graph, in the year 2000 the less developed countries had a population that was how many times bigger than the developed countries?

    (1) 12 times
    (2) 8 times
    (3) 4 times
    (4) 1.5 times
    (5) 0.5 times

24. In 1896 the United States Supreme Court in the case *Plessy v. Ferguson* resolved that public schools and other institutions were legally segregated under the doctrine of "separate but equal." In 1954 the Supreme Court in the case *Brown v. Board of Education of Topeka* unanimously reversed this decision and declared this policy unconstitutional. Chief Justice Earl Warren's decision stated that "separate educational facilities are inherently unequal" and ordered that all public schools desegregate

    All of the following statements are true except

    (1) Since 1954, segregating a public school is illegal.
    (2) Before 1954, it was legal for schools to be segregated.
    (3) The doctrine of "separate but equal" applied to segregated schools.
    (4) Some of the members of the 1954 Supreme Court voted against reversing *Plessy v. Ferguson*.
    (5) The Chief Justice at the time of *Brown v. Board of Education of Topeka* was Earl Warren.

25. During the Progressive Era in the United States (1900–1920), a group of journalists and writers known as muckrakers went about exposing all the nasty abuses of power and money that went on during the end of the nineteenth century. They stirred up public opinion and helped win public support for various social reforms.

Which of the following is true about muckrakers?

(1) They blindly supported politicians.
(2) They committed abuses of power and money.
(3) They came about in the late twentieth century.
(4) They may have had something to do with some social reform.
(5) They received bribes by Congress in order to not print negative stories.

26. Which sources of information would be most useful in studying the activity of the Underground Railroad?

(1) Personal accounts and recorded oral histories taken from the "passengers" and "conductors" involved
(2) North to South timetables of the Union Pacific, dated 1860
(3) Treaties for the transcontinental railroad
(4) Letters and diaries belonging to Confederate soldiers
(5) Public speeches of abolitionists

27. The recovery programs instituted by President Franklin Roosevelt during the Great Depression were significant because

(1) they encouraged government participation in the economic development of the nation

(2) they received little cooperation from industrialists and businessmen hurt by the stock market crash

(3) they required the involvement of foreign governments in rebuilding the U.S. economy

(4) they were important to the success of British and French forces during World War II

(5) they caused Roosevelt's political opponents to gain popularity

28. The stock market crash of 1929 was not the only cause of the Great Depression. Historians do not agree on all of the details, but they do agree on some key contributors to the downfall of the American economy

- The vast expenses of World War I
- The sharp decline in trade after 1930
- The rise of borrowing on credit
- The constriction of the money by the Federal Reserve System and other nations
- The excesses of business and the creation of an economic "bubble"
- Over-speculation of land in Florida

Which of the following contributed LEAST to the economic factors that resulted in the Great Depression?

(1) Technological advances that allowed farmers and manufacturers to overproduce, resulting in large inventories.

(2) Concentration of wealth in too few hands, guaranteeing that business failures would have widespread ramifications.

(3) A steadily widening gap between the cost of consumer goods and the buying power of the average consumer.

(4) Wild speculation by stock investors, producing an unstable and volatile stock market.

(5) Interventionist economic policies from the federal government, resulting in overly conservative behavior on the part of private investors.

Chapter 8
Social Studies
Drill Answers

ANSWERS AND EXPLANATIONS

1. **(1)**   This is a matter of checking the paragraph to find the instance where the Central Powers were mentioned. Only choice (1) is mentioned in the parentheses that cover which nations were part of the Central Powers.

2. **(2)**   This is a comprehension question that is asking you to gather clues from the context. The easiest way to solve this question is by replacing each choice with the word "league" in the sentence *The association came to be known as the League of Nations*. Even if you didn't know what the word *confederation* means, you can eliminate (1) and (3) for sounding ridiculous (what would a country of nations even look like?) and (4) and (5) are simply two specific types of governing bodies. Choice (2) is the best answer.

3. **(3)**   As we read in the paragraph, Woodrow Wilson championed the League of Nations, but he could not get Republicans in the Senate to support U.S. involvement in the organization because they were concerned that an alliance with European nations could lead the country into another war. Using this information, you can safely pick choice (3).

4. **(2)**   According to the passage, fiat money has no intrinsic value, and its value in exchange comes as the result of government order or "fiat." Cigarettes, gold, arrowheads, and chickens all have value beyond their usefulness as money, so they cannot be considered fiat money. A dollar bill, on the other hand, is a piece of paper that has value as money only because the government says it does.

5. **(5)**   The question tests both your map observation skills and a basic principle of geography. Cities are nearly always located near a major source of water. At the time colonial cities were established, waterways provided the best means of long-distance travel. Cities also needed water for drinking and bathing, and to power whatever manufacturing plants they might have. In short, to build a successful city, you've got to have plenty of water.

6. **(2)**   This question is a little bit tricky because you aren't given much information to use. However, we can figure out the context and use POE to find the correct answer. We can eliminate (3) and (4) right off the bat because the passage of voting rights to women would not affect Congress or the Supreme Court. We can also get rid of (1) and (5) because judging from the term, we are probably looking for a more specific category than women or citizens. In general, the word *suffrage* mean the right or privilege of voting.

7. **(5)** This quotation is from the Qur'an, the holy book of Muslims. The mention of God and Adam suggests the Bible, but Christianity is not one of the answer choices. We know from history Islam and Christianity spring from a shared mythology and that the Qur'an draws upon many of the stories that appear in the Christian Bible. The ancient Greeks (1) did not have a holy book in the same sense as the Muslims. Hinduism and Buddhism (choices (2) and (4) respectively) have a collection of holy texts, but not a single holy book. Also bear in mind that Babylonian religion (3), Hinduism, Buddhism, and Greek mythology are polytheistic religions that are inconsistent with the use of "God" in the quotation. (5) is the best possible choice.

8. **(5)** This is a simple question of interpreting the paragraph. Because Booker T. Washington did not demand an immediate end to legal discrimination, we can infer that his statement would be seen as accommodationist. In contrast, W.E.B. DuBois more aggressive approach would be viewed as confrontational. Thus, (5) is the correct choice here.

9. **(4)** This question can be easily answered by looking back at the paragraph and seeing which of the five choices overlaps with DuBois's and Washington's views. Only choice (4), job training, was advocated for by both DuBois and Washington.

10. **(4)** For this question you are basically looking for which pair of countries are shaded differently, since this will indicate their political ideologies. In this instance Spain is affiliated with NATO and Poland is affiliated with the Warsaw Pact. You may recall that the Warsaw Pact is pro-communist, and NATO was a Western-based alliance. Thus, choice (4) is the correct answer.

11. **(1)** According to the paragraph, by connecting to the post-World War II era, indicated by the 1948 date, you should be able to eliminate choices (4) and (5) as anti-era. Choices (2) and (3) are accurate, making them decent guesses, but they were not part of the Marshall Plan.

12. **(1)** The Marshall Plan provided postwar Europe with the means to rebuild, provided that those countries side with the United States in its anticipated Cold War with the Soviet Union. The program sent more than $12 billion to Europe to help it revitalize its cities and economy, in part because the United States believed that countries with recovering economies would find communism less attractive. Although the Marshall Plan was offered to Eastern Europe, no countries in the Soviet sphere participated in the program. As a result, the Marshall Plan benefitted only Western European Nations.

13. **(1)** Key parts of this quote are that television is "more influential than Gutenberg's printing press" and that it has a mass audience of viewers, making (1) the best choice. Don't read anything into the quote that is not explicitly stated. There is nothing in the quote about the political ramifications of television or the level of information it brings, eliminating choices (2), (4), and (5). Choice (3) also goes beyond the scope of the quote.

14. **(3)** The term "spoils system" comes from the phrase "to the victor go the spoils." Choices (2) and (5) are from the correct period of time, but are not related to the quoted phrase. Choices (1) and (4) are anti-era, because they refer to political issues of the twentieth century.

15. **(2)** This question asks you to assess the usefulness of various historical documents. Note that the question asks you to focus specifically on quantitative data about all American labor during the 1880s. This should help you eliminate answer choice (1), which would provide anecdotal evidence about a single individual only; (3), which provides information about one city only and, therefore, might not provide a representative sample for the entire nation; (4), which like (1), is anecdotal and would provide information about too small a group of works; and (5), which provides no quantitative data whatsoever. In fact, none of the incorrect answers would likely provide any useful quantitative data, meaning that (2) must be the correct answer by process of elimination.

16. **(3)** In order to solve this question, take a look at the paragraph. The paragraph talks about how textile manufacturers had to convince workers to come and work in their factories. The enticement program involved setting up decent wages and offering boarding-houses. These offers helped to make factory life more humanizing and bearable, so choice (3) is your best answer. Don't be fooled by choice (4); the paragraph does not mention parental leave or vacation time.

17. **(1)** This is a matter of referring to the chart for the answer. On the chart itself, in the row that is marked "Long Run Economic Profit", you can see that the box in the column called "Monopolistic Competition" says zero. Thus the correct answer is (1).

18. **(2)** Abraham Lincoln wrote this in an 1862 letter to anti-slavery editor Horace Greeley, identifying the preservation of the Union rather than the emancipation of the slaves as his primary reason for going to war.

19. **(5)** Jim Crow laws, passed by many Southern states in the era following Reconstruction, mandated forced racial segregation in the South. The Supreme Court essentially endorsed the laws by ruling that the Fourteenth Amendment did not protect African Americans from discriminatory state laws, and that blacks would have to seek equal protection from the states, not from the federal government. By accepting the "separate but equal" principle in the infamous *Plessy v. Ferguson* decision, the Court ensured more than a half-century of legal segregation in the South.

Radical Reconstructionists (1) sought to integrate the South quickly after the Civil War; the Fourteenth Amendment (2) was designed specifically to guarantee the rights of African Americans; and the Taft-Hartley Act (3) was passed after World War II and was intended to curb the growing power of labor unions. Choice (4) is the opposite of what the picture shows—forced segregation.

20. **(3)** The chart shows little difference between the presidential votes of men and women in both the 1972 and the 1976 elections. Starting with the 1980 election, however, a clear gender gap can be seen, with women consistently giving greater support to the Democratic candidate than men do.

21. **(2)** This is a question about graph interpretation. In 1950, the developing countries had a population of approximately 2 billion people. In 2050, the population is expected to be about 6 billion people. The difference of 4 billion is the correct answer.

22. **(4)** This graph interpretation question asks you to observe what contributes most to the rise in world populations. The developed nations' overall population rises very slowly. On the other hand, in developing countries, there is a rapid rise in the number of people. This would contribute to most of the total population.

23. **(3)** In the year 2000, the less developed countries had a population of approximately 4 billion people. During that same year, the developed countries collectively contained approximately 1 billion people. The best answer is (C).

24. **(4)** This is an EXCEPT question, so you are looking for the answer that is not stated in the passage. D is the answer because the court voted unanimously.

25. **(4)** POE is your friend here. There is no mention of politicians or Congress in the passage so eliminate choices (1) and (5). They exposed abuses of power and money, so get rid of (2). They came about in the end of the nineteenth century so cross out (3). (4) is the correct answer.

26. **(1)** The Underground Railroad was the secret system used to help runaway slaves escape to free states, territories, or countries. It was really a network of people working together, although the system often employed the language of the railroad, including such terms as "passengers" and "conductors." It was not an actual railroad or a type of transportation, eliminating choices like (2) and (3). Also, because it was secret, you would not be able to find references about it in public speeches, eliminating choice (5). Choice (1) is the best choice; personal accounts, handed down through families, or oral histories from the actual participants would be needed to identify routes, locations, and strategies used in the Underground Railroad system. Even thought the participants would now be deceased, information might be obtained from family records or from recorded or written accounts taken early in the twentieth century.

27. **(1)** Prior to the New Deal, the role of the federal government in economic development and social welfare was very different from its role today. Franklin Roosevelt's recovery programs marked a new era of government involvement in economic monitoring of productivity and wealth, job creation and protection, large-scale public works programs, and many other characteristics of government today (1). Choice (2), even if true, would not rank as significant. Choice (5) is completely wrong; Roosevelt was a very popular president, earning four terms in office. Choice (4) is appropriate to the era of the question, but the recovery programs were not directly connected to the war efforts when they were instituted in the early to mid-1930s.

28. **(5)** For this problem, you simply have to look at the bullet points. As you can see the government's interventionist economic policies were not a factor in the Great Depression. Choice (5) is clearly the best choice.

Chapter 9
Science

INTRODUCTION

As we said before, the GED Science test does not require any specific knowledge of high-level science but you should still be familiar with the basic concepts necessary to pass the GED exam.

SCIENTIFIC METHOD

The job of scientists is to answer questions. To find the answers to their questions, scientists design and perform experiments where they collect data and then analyze it to see if the data help them answer their questions.

Some of the test questions on the GED may give you information that scientists have collected. The information might be organized in a table or a graph. It might be a picture of what happened during an experiment. You need to be able to make conclusions from the information. That means you need to be able to figure out what the information tells you.

A conclusion is something that you can say because the data tell you it is true. You can only make a conclusion from the information given to you, so it is not a guess. It can't be about other information you might have learned somewhere else. A conclusion can start, "The information tells me that..."

If you were told that Mercury is 35,991,000 miles from the sun, and that the earth is 92,976,000 miles from the sun, what conclusion could you make? Well, you could conclude that Mercury is closer to the sun. You could also conclude that the earth is a little more than two and a half times farther from the sun than Mercury. You could not conclude that the earth was a nicer place to live, because the data don't tell you that.

The science test may ask you about the control group in an experiment, or ask you to identify assumptions. These are precise terms, but they too just follow common sense in good scientific design. Let's see what they're looking for.

A **control** is anything in an experiment that is held constant or left alone. For example, if a researcher wants to test the effectiveness of various organic pesticides on a tomato, she will likely leave one tomato untreated. This will allow her to see what effects the different pesticides have on the treated tomato, because she can compare its growth to that of the untreated tomato. The untreated tomato is the *control* group.

An **assumption** is anything that the researchers think will not affect their experiments. That is, if the researcher above treats the tomato by injecting the pesticide, she will likely assume that poking it with a needle does not by itself affect the health of the tomato.

SCIENTIFIC METHOD—REVIEW

1. Below is a table giving information from three earthquake detection stations. The map under the table shows where these stations are located. Use the map and the table below to answer the following question.

Station	Distance of Station from Earthquake Epicenter
1	140 miles
2	70 miles
3	170 miles

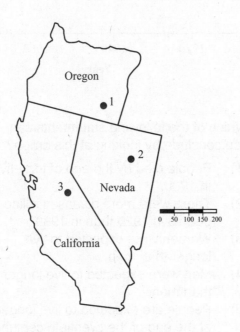

What is a valid conclusion from the information in the table and map?

(1) Most earthquakes happen in California.

(2) The epicenter was probably inside the borders of Nevada.

(3) The epicenter was on the border between Oregon and California.

(4) The earthquake happened closest to station 3.

(5) The earthquake happened in northern Oregon.

2. Scientists collected information about how long people lived during the twentieth century. Their results are in the graph below:

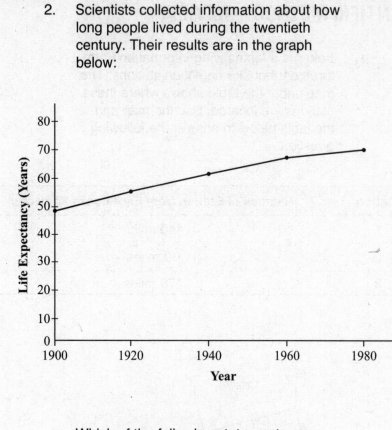

Which of the following statements can you conclude by looking at this graph?

(1) People died by the age of forty-five in 1900.

(2) There were more diseases killing people in 1920 than in 1980.

(3) Women were expected to live longer than men.

(4) Men were expected to live longer than men.

(5) People are expected to live longer at the end of the twentieth century than at the beginning.

3. The table below gives information about how much energy children are recommended to eat in their food each day. Use the data to help you answer the question below.

Age	Average Weight (lbs.)	Average Height (in.)	Average Calories/Day
0.5–1	20	28	850
4–6	44	44	1,800
7–10	62	52	2,000
15–18 (boys)	145	69	3,000
15–18 (girls)	120	64	2,200

Which of the following is a valid conclusion from this table?

(1) Children grow fastest when they are less than one year old.
(2) Young children need calcium to build bones.
(3) Children that exercise more eat more calories.
(4) A sixteen-year old girl needs to consume fewer calories per day than a sixteen-year-old boy.
(5) Children who play video games eat fewer calories.

ELEMENTS

Although organisms exist in many diverse forms, they all have one thing in common. They are all made up of **matter**. Matter is made up of **elements**. Elements, by definition, are substances that cannot be broken down into simpler substances by chemical means. Below is a periodic table of all the elements. You don't have to memorize it (what a relief), but you should be familiar with what this chart looks like.

PERIODIC CHART OF THE ELEMENTS

1 H 1.0																	2 He 4.0
3 Li 6.9	4 Be 9.0											5 B 10.8	6 C 12.0	7 N 14.0	8 O 16.0	9 F 19.0	10 Ne 20.2
11 Na 23.0	12 Mg 24.3											13 Al 27.0	14 Si 28.1	15 P 31.0	16 S 32.1	17 Cl 35.5	18 Ar 39.9
19 K 39.1	20 Ca 40.1	21 Sc 45.0	22 Ti 47.9	23 V 50.9	24 Cr 52.0	25 Mn 54.9	26 Fe 55.8	27 Co 58.9	28 Ni 58.7	29 Cu 63.5	30 Zn 65.4	31 Ga 69.7	32 Ge 72.6	33 As 74.9	34 Se 79.0	35 Br 79.9	36 Kr 83.8
37 Rb 85.5	38 Sr 87.6	39 Y 88.9	40 Zr 91.2	41 Nb 92.9	42 Mo 95.9	43 Tc (98)	44 Ru 101.1	45 Rh 102.9	46 Pd 106.4	47 Ag 107.9	48 Cd 112.4	49 In 114.8	50 Sn 118.7	51 Sb 121.8	52 Te 127.6	53 I 126.9	54 Xe 131.3
55 Cs 132.9	56 Ba 137.3	57 La 138.9	72 Hf 178.5	73 Ta 180.9	74 W 183.9	75 Re 186.2	76 Os 190.2	77 Ir 192.2	78 Pt 195.1	79 Au 197.0	80 Hg 200.6	81 Tl 204.4	82 Pb 207.2	83 Bi 209.0	84 Po 209.0	85 At 210.0	86 Rn 222.0
87 Fr 223.0	88 Ra 226.0	89 Ac 227.0															

	58 Ce 140.1	59 Pr 140.9	60 Nd 144.2	61 Pm 145.0	62 Sm 150.4	63 Eu 152.0	64 Gd 157.3	65 Tb 158.9	66 Dy 162.5	67 Ho 164.9	68 Er 167.3	69 Tm 168.9	70 Yb 173.0	71 Lu 175.0
Lanthanum Series														
Actinium Series	90 Th 232.0	91 Pa 231.0	92 U 238.0	93 Np 237.0	94 Pu (244)	95 Am (243)	96 Cm (247)	97 Bk (247)	98 Cf (251)	99 Es (252)	100 Fm (258)	101 Md (258)	102 No (259)	103 Lr (260)

If you break down an element into smaller pieces, you'll eventually come to the **atom**. An atom is the smallest unit of an element that retains its characteristic properties. In essence, atoms are the building blocks of the physical world. You can further break apart atoms into smaller subatomic particles called protons, neutrons, and electrons. Let's take a look at a typical atom:

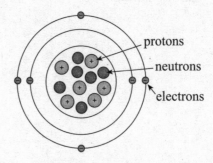

Protons and **neutrons** are packed together in the core of an atom called the nucleus. You'll notice that protons are positively charged (+) particles, whereas neutrons are uncharged particles.

Electrons, on the other hand, are negatively charged (–) particles that spin around the nucleus. Electrons are very small compared to protons and neutrons. In fact, for our purposes, electrons are considered massless. Most atoms have the same number of protons and electrons, making them electrically neutral. Some atoms have the same number of protons but differ in the number of neutrons in the nucleus. These atoms are called isotopes.

When two or more different types of atoms are combined in a fixed ration, they form a chemical compound. You'll sometimes find that a compound has different properties from those of its elements. For instance, hydrogen and oxygen exist in nature as gases. Yet when they combined to make water, they often become a liquid. When hydrogen atoms get together with oxygen atoms to form water, we've got a chemical reaction:

$$2H_2 \ (g) + O_2 \ (g) \rightarrow 2H_2O \ (l)$$

The atoms of a compound are held together by chemical bonds. The two most important bonds to be aware of are ionic bonds and covalent bonds.

An **ionic bond** is formed between two atoms when one or more electrons are transferred from one atom to the other. In this reaction, one atom loses electrons and becomes positively charged and the other atom gains electrons and becomes negatively charged. The charged forms of the atoms are called ions. For example, when Na reacts with Cl, charged ions, Na^+ and Cl^- are formed.

A **covalent bond** is formed when electrons are shared between atoms. If the electrons are shared equally between the atoms, the bond is called nonpolar covalent. If the electrons are shared unequally, the bond is called polar covalent. When one pair of electrons is shared between two atoms, the result is a single covalent bond. When two pairs of electrons are shared, the result is a double covalent bond.

WATER: THE VERSATILE MOLECULE

One of the most important substances in nature is water. Did you know that more than 60 percent of your body weight consists of water? Water is considered a unique molecule because it plays an important role in chemical reactions.

Let's take a look at one of the properties of water. Water has two hydrogen atoms joined to an oxygen atom:

In water molecules, the hydrogen atoms have a partial positive charge and the oxygen atom has a partial negative charge. Molecules that have partially positive and partially negative charges are said to be polar. Water is therefore a polar molecule. Because of this, water can dissolve many polar substances (including table salt and sugar).

At room temperature, water is a liquid. The solid state of water is called **ice**, and this occurs when the temperature of water is at 0 degrees Celsius (or 32 degrees Fahrenheit). The temperature at which water turns into ice is known as the **freezing point**. The gas form of water is known as steam, or **water vapor**. This occurs when the temperature of water is at 100 degrees Celsius (or 212 degrees Fahrenheit). This point is known as the boiling point.

ACIDS AND BASES

You have probably encountered acids and bases in your regular life. Lemon juice and cola drinks (like ginger ale or diet soda) are examples of acids. Conversely if you've ever used laundry bleach or ammonia cleaning solution, you've been close to a base.

The definition of an **acid** is a substance that releases hydrogen ions when it is dissolved in water. Acids usually have a sour taste. A **base** is a substance that does not release hydrogen ions, but instead releases hydroxide ions (which are noted as OH^-).

You can measure the strength of a base or acid by using a **pH scale**. The pH scale ranges from 1 to 14. The midpoint, 7, is considered neutral pH. Distilled water is a 7. If a solution is acidic, it will have a pH lower than 7; if a solution is basic it will have a pH higher than a 7. You'll notice from the scale that stronger acids have lower pHs and stronger bases have higher pHs.

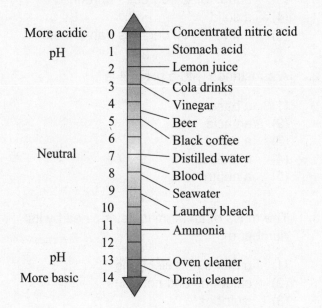

More acidic 0 — Concentrated nitric acid
pH   1 — Stomach acid
             2 — Lemon juice
             3 — Cola drinks
             4 — Vinegar
             5 — Beer
             6 — Black coffee
Neutral   7 — Distilled water
             8 — Blood
             9 — Seawater
            10 — Laundry bleach
            11 — Ammonia
            12
pH   13 — Oven cleaner
More basic 14 — Drain cleaner

ELEMENTS, WATER, ACIDS, AND BASES—REVIEW

1. Water that is 100 degrees Celsius is

    (1) at the boiling point
    (2) at the freezing point
    (3) equal to 32 degrees Fahrenheit
    (4) a solid
    (5) equal to 100 degrees Fahrenheit

2. A substance with a pH of 4 is

    (1) a base
    (2) an acid
    (3) a metal
    (4) a molecule
    (5) a neutron

3. The mass of an atom is determined by its number of

    (1) protons and electrons
    (2) electrons and neutrons
    (3) isotopes
    (4) protons and neutrons
    (5) positrons and electrons

4. Which of the following is closest in mass to a proton?

    (1) Helium molecule
    (2) Hydrogen gas
    (3) Neutron
    (4) Electron
    (5) Table salt

NITROGEN, CARBON, AND WATER CYCLES

Earth is like a big recycling machine. Certain resources get used and changed and used again so that we don't run out of these important materials. Here are the three things that go through cycles of use in nature.

- Water
- Carbon
- Nitrogen

Every living thing needs all three of these resources. Let's review how each of these resources gets reused. It's important to know not only because you live on Earth, but also because you'll have to know it for the GED.

THE WATER CYCLE

The surface of our planet is about 71 percent water. There is water in the oceans, rivers, lakes, and frozen ice caps. There is also water underground called ground water. That's what plants use, and that's where we get our well water. There is even water in the air and in the clouds. Clouds are made up of tiny water droplets.

The water cycle keeps water moving between the ground, air, oceans, lakes, and rivers. The sun creates the energy to keep the cycle going. Look at the picture of the water cycle on the next page to see how this works.

Evaporation is when the sun's energy changes water from liquid on the surface to gas in the air. **Condensation** is when water in the air forms droplets to make clouds. **Precipitation**, such as rain or snow, is when water from clouds falls to the ground. These three processes form a cycle. Water goes up, forms clouds, and then comes back down.

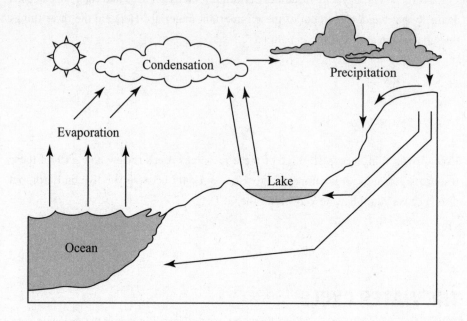

Water Cycle

A drop of water can go through this cycle millions of times. Think about where a drop of water goes during the water cycle. Maybe it evaporates from a pond in Cleveland and forms a cloud. The drop might not fall down to the surface as precipitation until it is over China!

THE CARBON CYCLE

All living things need carbon. Plants get carbon in the form of **carbon dioxide** during **photosynthesis**. Animals get carbon from the plants and animals they eat. Carbon goes back and forth between animals and plants. Below is a picture of the carbon cycle.

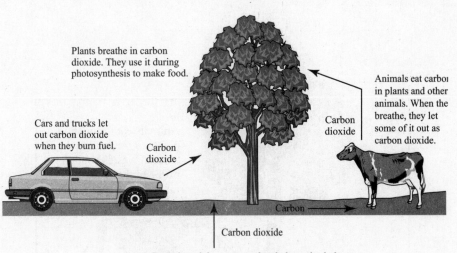

Plants breathe in carbon dioxide. They use it during photosynthesis to make food.

Animals eat carbon in plants and other animals. When the breathe, they let some of it out as carbon dioxide.

Cars and trucks let out carbon dioxide when they burn fuel.

Carbon dioxide

Carbon dioxide

Carbon

Carbon dioxide

Bacteria and decomposers break down dead plants and animals. They change the carbon in the dead organisms into carbon dioxide.

When humans cut down trees to make lumber and paper, it affects the carbon cycle. Trees use the carbon dioxide in the air. If we get rid of trees, there will be too much carbon dioxide in the air.

Carbon dioxide has another important job on Earth. In the air, it traps heat from the earth. Without carbon dioxide in our air, the earth would get very cold. This heat trapping is called the **greenhouse effect**. When humans change the carbon dioxide in the air, we change the greenhouse effect. If more people drive cars, what will happen? More cars would mean more carbon dioxide in the air. More carbon dioxide in the air would lead to more heat being trapped. Earth will get warmer.

THE NITROGEN CYCLE

All living things need nitrogen to build protein. There is a lot of nitrogen in the air, but we can't use that nitrogen. Bacteria must first change the nitrogen to a substance we can use. The way that nitrogen moves between the air, soil, plants, and animals is called the nitrogen cycle. Look at the diagram below.

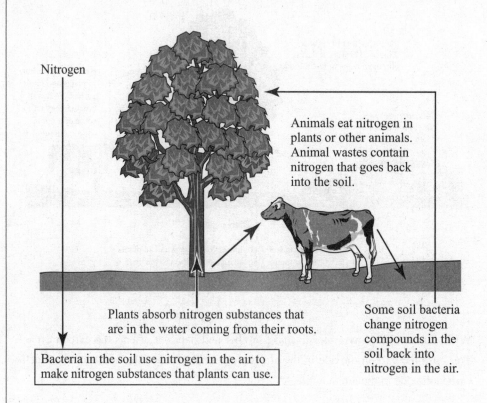

Nitrogen

Animals eat nitrogen in plants or other animals. Animal wastes contain nitrogen that goes back into the soil.

Plants absorb nitrogen substances that are in the water coming from their roots.

Some soil bacteria change nitrogen compounds in the soil back into nitrogen in the air.

Bacteria in the soil use nitrogen in the air to make nitrogen substances that plants can use.

Bacteria have very important jobs in the nitrogen cycle. They help get the nitrogen out of the air so plants can use it. They also recycle some nitrogen back up into the air. Without plants to get the nitrogen from the soil, animals would be in trouble. Animals can only get nitrogen from plants, or from other animals that have eaten plants. So organisms are really depending on each other to keep the nitrogen-recycling path going.

NITROGEN, CARBON, AND WATER CYCLES—REVIEW

1. In the carbon cycle, plants use sunlight to make carbon compounds for food. Where do plants get the carbon from to make this food?

   (1) rainwater
   (2) soil
   (3) air
   (4) bacteria in soil
   (5) the sun

2. Carbon dioxide in the atmosphere traps heat coming up from the earth's surface and keeps the heat from escaping into space. This is called the greenhouse effect. When cars burn gasoline, how does that affect the greenhouse effect process?

   (1) Car engines make more carbon dioxide in the air, increasing the greenhouse effect.
   (2) Cars use carbon dioxide to burn gasoline, reducing the greenhouse effect.
   (3) Car engines release water vapor in the air, which increases the greenhouse effect.
   (4) Soot from car exhaust reacts with carbon dioxide and stops it from trapping heat.
   (5) Heat from car engines destroys carbon dioxide, reducing the greenhouse effect.

3. Evaporation is one step of the water cycle. Which of these provides the energy for evaporation?

   (1) waves
   (2) sunlight
   (3) decomposers
   (4) bacteria
   (5) animals

4. Plants get nitrogen from the soil, which helps them to grow. Animals can get nitrogen by eating the plants, or by eating other animals that eat plants. How does nitrogen get recycled back into the soil for more plants to use?

(1) Rain washes nitrogen back into the soil.
(2) Sunlight breaks down the air into nitrogen that seeps into the soil.
(3) Plants breathe in nitrogen from the air and bring it to the soil.
(4) Nitrogen from underground rocks moves up into the soil.
(5) Animal wastes return nitrogen to the soil.

CELLS

The **cell** is the basic building block of all life. Every living organism—from plants to animals—is made up of cells. Organisms that are made up of only one cell, like bacteria and green algae, are called unicellular and tend to be smaller than the human eye can see. Organisms with many cells are called multicellular and tend to be larger. Humans, for example, are made up of billions of cells. All cells contain **DNA** (deoxyribonucleic acid), which contains the genes (or blueprints) of the cell. Cells also have RNA (ribonucleic acid) which is important for protein synthesis. Cells come in two types: animal cells and plant cells. Below is a picture of a typical animal cell:

Animal Cell

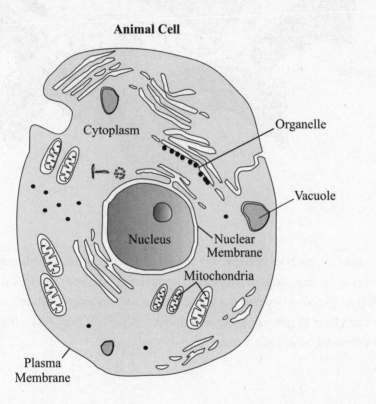

All animal cells have a **cell membrane** which protects the innards of the cell. This membrane is called a **permeable membrane**, which means that it allows only certain molecules to cross its barrier.

Now let's look at a picture of a plant cell:

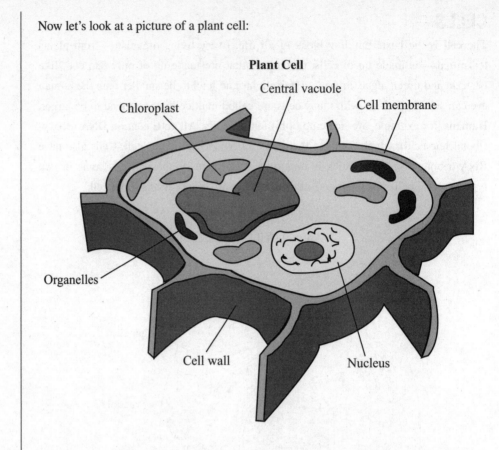

Plant Cell

Chloroplast

Central vacuole

Cell membrane

Organelles

Cell wall

Nucleus

You will notice that plant cells are very similar in structure to animal cells but there are a few key differences. In addition to a cell membrane, plants cells also have a **cell wall**, which is a rigid outer covering that surrounds the cell membrane. The cell wall serves as an extra layer of protection and helps to prevent the cell from becoming oversaturated with water, which would cause the cell to break apart.

THE CELL CYCLE

As you read this text, thousands of cells are dying in your body right now. However, your body is making new cells as quickly as the old ones die out. In fact, your skin cells die off so fast that you have an entirely new skin every few weeks. The body produces all these new cells through a process called **mitosis** (or cell division).

Mitosis allows our body to replace the aging cells with fresh new ones. There are two periods in a cell's life span: interphase and mitosis.

Interphase

Interphase is the time period after the cell's birth and before it undergoes mitosis, when it copies itself. During interphase the cell is carrying out its normal functions. Before interphase ends, the cell makes a copy of all its chromosomes. The duplicated chromosome is connected to the original chromosome by the centromere. Each individual chromosome is called a chromatid.

When interphase is over, all 46 of the original chromosomes have duplicated. The cell now has 46 chromosomes with 2 chromatids each. The cell is now ready for mitosis.

Mitosis

Mitosis is the process a cell goes through when it divides. There are four stages to mitosis, with the end result being a new cell.

Stage 1: Prophase: During prophase the nuclear membrane begins to break up. The chromosomes thicken and form coils. The centrioles move away from each other and form a system of microtubules called spindle fibers. The Spindle fibers attach to the chromosomes and help them move around.

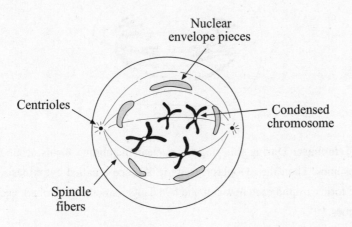

Nuclear envelope pieces

Centrioles

Condensed chromosome

Spindle fibers

Stage 2: Metaphase: Now that the spindle fibers are attached to the chromosomes, they help them line up in the middle of the cell. That area of the cell is called the metaphase plate.

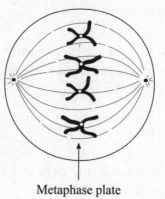

Metaphase plate

Stage 3: Anaphase: During this stage, the spindle fibers pull the chromatids apart. The separated chromatids are pulled to opposite poles.

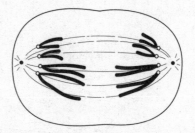

Stage 4: Telophase: During this stage, a nuclear membrane forms around each set of chromosomes. Then the cytoplasm splits in a process called cytokinesis. The cell membrane forms around each new cell and two daughter cells are formed, each with 46 chromosomes.

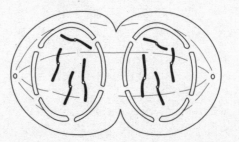

Once the daughter cells are formed, they enter interphase and the whole process starts up again.

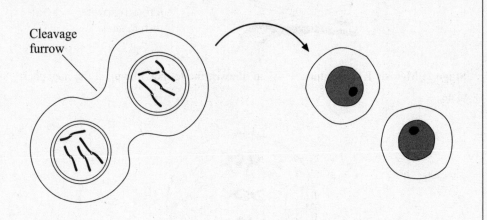

Cleavage furrow

Meiosis

Meiosis is a special form of cell division; it is the process by which sex cells are made. Many multicellular organisms, including plants, dogs, and humans have cells which undergo meiosis. Meiosis occurs only in sex organs called gonads. In males, the sex organs are the testes; in females they're the ovaries. Sex cells are the cells that combine to create a new cell, called a zygote, that will grow into a multicellular organism. In a normal human cell, there are two sets of chromosomes. The number of chromosomes in this cell is known as the diploid cell. At the end of meiosis, only one set of chromosomes will be present. This number is known as the haploid number. Meiosis, unlike mitosis, takes place in two rounds. Let's take a look at what happens during meiosis.

Stage 1: Meiosis I, Prophase I: The nuclear membrane disappears and the centrioles move to opposite ends of the cell (similar to mitosis). However, in meiosis, the chromosomes line up side-by-side with their counterparts and two sets of chromosomes combine to form a tetrad. This event is called synapsis.

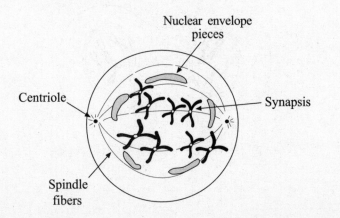

Nuclear envelope pieces

Centriole

Synapsis

Spindle fibers

Once synapsis has occurred, the four chromatids exchange segments in a process called crossing-over.

Crossing over
at two sites

Stage 2: Meiosis I, Metaphase I: As in mitosis, the tetrads line up at the metaphase plate.

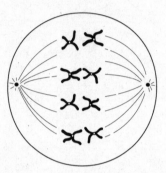

Stage 3: Meiosis I, Anaphase I: The tetrads separate and move to the opposite poles.

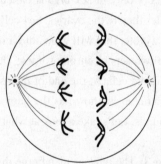

Stage 4: Meiosis I, Telophase I: The nuclear membrane forms around each set of chromosomes and two daughter cells form as a result. Not that the cell still has two sets of chromosomes.

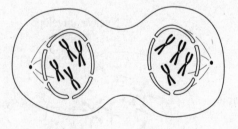

Stages 5–8: Meiosis II: After a brief period, the two daughter cells divide again. The cells will undergo prophase, metaphase, anaphase, and telophase and the result will be four cells with half the number of chromosomes.

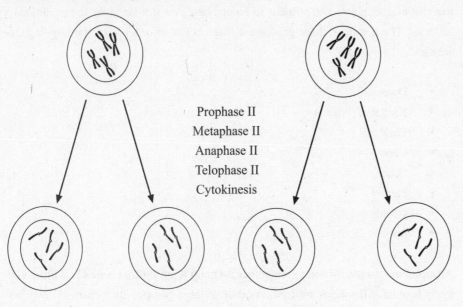

Prophase II
Metaphase II
Anaphase II
Telophase II
Cytokinesis

CELLS AND THE CELL CYCLE—REVIEW

1. A cell that has both sets of chromosomes is a diploid cell. If a cell has only one set of chromosomes, it is called a haploid cell. Haploid cells are very important for sexual reproduction.

    If the diploid number for an organism is 24, the haploid number is

    (1)   6
    (2)   12
    (3)   18
    (4)   24
    (5)   48

CLASSIFICATION

Since the beginning of human civilization, scientists have worked to understand how living organisms are related to each other. To do this, they created a classification system that assigns plants and animals to groups based on similar traits and evolutionary histories. The names of these groups are listed below in order from the largest to the smallest:

- Domain
- Kingdom
- Phylum
- Class
- Order
- Family
- Genus
- Species

A helpful mnemonic for you to remember is **D**umb **K**ing **P**hilip **C**ame **O**ver **F**rom **G**ermany **S**oaked. All species are first classified in large groups which narrows down into groups with more and more traits in common. So, two organisms from the same family have more in common than two organisms from the same phylum.

You won't be expected to know all of the phyla, class, and orders (whew!) but you do want to be familiar with the six major kingdoms. This helpful chart below will give you the basics:

Kingdom	Characteristics	Examples
Eubacteria	Have a cell wall, lack nuclei, asexual reproduction	*E. coli*, cyanobacteria
Archaebacteria	Have a cell wall, lack nuclei, can live in extreme environments like salt-rich ponds and hot springs	Halobacteria
Protists	Have a nucleus, two-part life cycle, membrane-bound organelles	Algae, amoeba, slime molds
Plants	Multi-cellular, have a cell wall, has chlorophyll, asexual and sexual reproduction	Trees, grass, roses, corn, bushes
Fungi	Multi-cellular, have a cell wall, asexual and sexual reproduction	Mushrooms, penicillium
Animals	Multi-cellular, sexual reproduction, lack a cell wall, have some form of symmetry	Dogs, humans, squid, birds, snakes

Viruses are a special case of organisms. Scientists don't really believe that viruses are really alive since they are not true cells. By this, we mean that it doesn't live or reproduce independently. Viruses consist of a coat made of proteins and a viral chromosome, which can be either DNA or RNA.

The reproductive process of a virus works like this:

- A virus attaches to a host cell.
- Once acid the virus injects its genes into the host cell.
- The virus's nucleic acid forces its host to use its metabolic machinery to synthesize viruses
- The viruses are released and the host cell is destroyed

EVOLUTION

While you won't need to know much about evolution for this exam, you should have a rough idea of how and why it takes place, so let's run through that now. Evolution is the change in a population's genetic composition over time. Speciation is the process by which new species are formed.

Strictly speaking, a species is defined as a group of organisms that are capable of breeding with one another-and incapable of breeding with other species. As you may recall, individual organisms that are better adapted for their environment will live and reproduce, ensuring that their genes are part of their population's next generation. This is what Charles Darwin meant by evolutionary fitness.

HOW EVOLUTION WORKS

When a habitat (an organism's physical surroundings) selects certain organisms to live and reproduce and others to die, that population is said to be undergoing natural selection. In natural selection, beneficial characteristics that can be inherited are passed down to the next generation, and unfavorable characteristics that can be inherited become less common in the population. It is important to remember that natural selection acts upon a whole population, not on an individual organism during its lifetime. What changes during evolution is the total genetic makeup of the population, or gene pool, and natural selection is one of the mechanisms by which evolution operates.

The other way evolution operates is genetic drift. Genetic drift is the accumulation of changes in the frequency of alleles (versions of a gene) over time due to sampling errors—changes that occur as a result of random chance. For example, in a population of owls there may be an equal chance of a newly born owlet having long talons of short talons, but due to random breeding variances a slightly larger number of long-taloned owlets are born. Over many generations, this slight variance can develop into a larger trend, until the majority of owls in that population have long talons. These breeding variances could be a result of a chance event—such as an earthquake that drastically reduces the size of the nesting population one year. Small populations are more sensitive to the effects of genetic drift than large, diverse populations.

Just as new species are formed by natural selection and genetic drift, other species may become extinct. Extinction occurs when a species cannot adapt quickly enough to environmental change and all members of the species die.

CLASSIFICATION AND EVOLUTION—REVIEW

Questions 1 and 2 refer to the following flow chart.

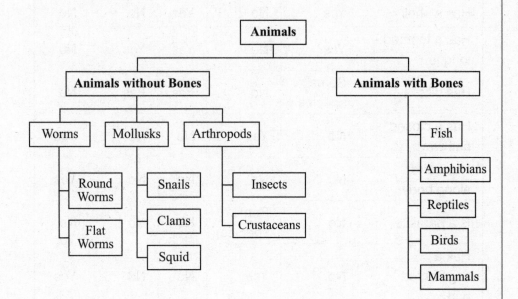

1. According to the chart, which of the following animals have bones?

    (1) crustaceans
    (2) amphibians
    (3) insects
    (4) squid
    (5) round worms

2. Which of the following animals is most likely to be similar to a clam?

    (1) octopus
    (2) frog
    (3) turtle
    (4) spider
    (5) earthworm

Questions 3 and 4 refer to the following chart.

Trait	Snail	Leech	Clam	Octopus	Earth-worm
Has a shell	Yes	No	Yes	No	No
Has a toothed tongue	Yes	No	Yes	Yes	No
Has gills	Some species	No	Yes	Yes	No
Has a closed pathway	No	Yes	No	No	Yes
Has hairs along body	No	No	No	No	Yes
Is a parasite	No	Some species	No	No	No
Has a segmented body	No	Yes	No	No	Yes
Has eyes	Yes	No	No	Yes	No
Lives in the water	Some species	Some species	Yes	Yes	No

3. An unknown vertebrate lives in the water, has no shell, and has a toothed tongue. What else must be true about this animal?

   (1) It has a closed blood pathway
   (2) It has bristles along its body.
   (3) It has gills.
   (4) It has a segmented body.
   (5) It is a parasite.

4. Biodiversity is a direct result of which of the following?

   (1) Deforestation
   (2) Sanitization
   (3) Respiration
   (4) Erosion
   (5) Evolution

PLANTS

As we discussed in the Classification section, plants are organisms that get their energy from the sun. Just like animals, plants struggle to survive. They both need food, water, air, and protection. Most plants have the same basic parts to help them survive. Almost all plants have leaves, stem, and roots.

Leaves perform a couple of very important jobs for plants. They collect energy from sunlight and turn the energy into food using photosynthesis and they have tiny holes that let air in and out of the plant, allowing it to breathe.

Roots help plants stay in the soil. They also collect water from the soil. Water travels up from the roots to the rest of the plant. For most plants, the stem is the highway that water and nutrients travel along to move around the plant. **Stems** also keep the plants standing tall and help them grow toward the sun.

Plants need to reproduce for their species to survive. Some plants make spores and others make seeds. Spores are tiny plants that are spread to make more plants. Seeds contain the baby plant as well as some food for the baby plant.

There are many examples of adaptations in plants. Some adaptations help plants catch sunlight or collect water better. Some help them reproduce better. Different plants have different traits depending on their ecosystem.

In order to grow healthily, plants need **soil** with plenty of nutrients. Soil has bits of rock in it, but it also has something called **humus**. Humus is the decaying material from dead animals or plants. Soil forms when water or wind breaks up the top layer of rock. Humus then gets added to the bits of rock, creating soil. The humus gives the soil nutrients for plants to use. Below is a drawing of how soil forms on flat, sheltered rock.

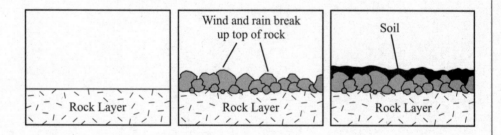

If an area is very windy, it's hard for soil to form. The broken-up rock and humus get blown away before they can become soil. Soil doesn't form well on steep hills, either. Rain washes the bits of rock and humus down the hill.

ECOSYSTEMS AND FOOD CHAINS

An **ecosystem** is a place where many organisms live and depend on other organisms for survival. For example, grass uses the energy of the sun to grow, a rabbit eats the grass, a hawk eats the rabbit. Every animal is eating something else to get energy, except for the grass, which gets its energy from sunlight through photosynthesis.

To balance an ecosystem, all of the different organisms, including plants and animals, have certain jobs. Let's look at the different roles that plants and animals have in an ecosystem.

Plants get energy from the sun to make food. Plants are **producers** because they make (produce) their own food. Animals, unlike plants, need to eat to get energy. Animals are **consumers** because they must eat (consume) other living things for food. Primary consumers only eat producers. Rabbits and cows are examples of primary consumers because they only eat plants. A consumer that eats another consumer is called a secondary consumer. Frogs are secondary consumers because they eat flies, grasshoppers, and other consumers.

All primary consumers eat plants, and the scientific term for these consumers is **herbivores**. Secondary consumers that only eat animals and not any plants are called **carnivores**. Many consumers eat both plants and animals, depending on what is available. These consumers are called omnivores.

There are other organisms in an ecosystem besides producers and consumers. These organisms, like earthworms, bacteria and fungi, eat dead organisms and return nutrients back to the soil for plants to use. These organisms are called **decomposers** because they break down other organisms to get energy.

Food Chains

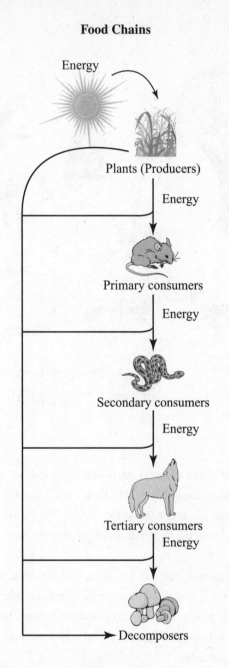

Energy

Plants (Producers)

Energy

Primary consumers

Energy

Secondary consumers

Energy

Tertiary consumers

Energy

Decomposers

The picture that represents the recycling of energy is called a **food chain**. In food chains, the arrows depict the transfer of energy through the levels. Thus the arrow pointing from the mouse to the snake (for example) means that when the snake eats the mouse, it will gain energy. A food web is a more complicated version of a food chain. **Food webs** are used to show the many different kinds of consumers. See the following picture:

Food Web

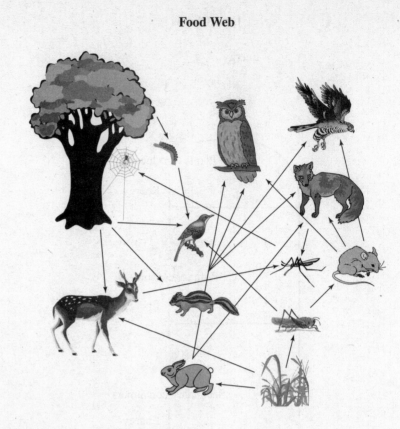

Not all relationships between animals are predatory. Some are **mutualistic**, meaning that both organisms in a relationship benefit from each other. For example, insects that eat nectar from a flower are also helping the flower. The flower's pollen sticks to the insects as they eat, and then the pollen drops off as they fly into another flower.

Some are **parasitic**, meaning that one organism benefits while another organism suffers. Think about fleas on a dog. The fleas bite the dog to get energy from its blood and in return, the poor dog gets itchy welts and possible diseases. In this kind of relationship, the flea is called a parasite and the dog is called a host. Tapeworms, ticks, and lice are other examples of parasites.

Some exhibit **commensalism**, meaning that one organism is helped while the other organism is neither helped nor harmed. A great example of commensalism is the relationship between a remora and a whale. The remora has a sucker on the top of its head that attaches to the whale's top, mouth or underside. Through this attachment, the remora can travel around more easily and eat any debris that falls from the whale. The whale is left unharmed.

PLANTS, ECOSYSTEMS, AND FOOD CHAINS—REVIEW

1. Lampreys attach to the skin of lake trout
    and absorb nutrients from the lake trout's
    body. This relationship is an example of

    (1) commensalism
    (2) parasitism
    (3) mutualism
    (4) gravitropism
    (5) competition

2. A food web in an ecosystem is shown
    below:

    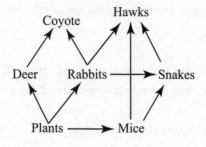

    What do snakes and hawks have in
    common?
    (1) They both are food for mice
    (2) They are herbivores
    (3) They receive their energy from the
         sun
    (4) They both use mice as a food
         source
    (5) They are both herbivores

3. Plants make their own food through

    (1) photosynthesis
    (2) meiosis
    (3) cell division
    (4) respiration
    (5) excretion

EARTH SCIENCE

Earth science is the study of the earth and the universe around it. It encompasses geology, oceanography, meteorology, and astronomy. Let's start by looking back in time.

Geology is the study of the origin, history, and structure of the earth. Geologists look inside the earth for clues about what is was like thousands and even millions of years ago. The surface of the earth is always changing due to erosion, volcanic eruptions, earthquakes, and climatic conditions. These changes are recorded in the earth's layers, and geologists have created a geologic time scale to track them. There are four geologic time periods, also called eras. They are:

Precambrian Era: This era began at the formation of the earth, approximately 4.6 billion years ago, and ended about 570 million years ago. It is by far the longest era. There are very few fossils from this time period. Those found tend to be bacteria and algae, but a few fossils of primitive sponges, worms, and corals from the end of the era have also been found.

Paleozoic Era: The next era, the Paleozoic, lasted about 325 million years. A wide variety of fossils of plants and animals have been found from this era.

Mesozoic Era: This era started about 245 million years ago and ended about 65 million years ago. Fossils from this time period show a variety of lizards, turtles, snakes, and dinosaurs. Toward the end of this era, the mass extinction of numerous species occurred, including all dinosaurs.

Cenozoic Era: This era started 65 million years ago and continues today. During this period, a wide range of mammals have flourished, including humans.

The structure of Earth is made up of three layers. The crust is the outermost layer and consists of a thin, rigid layer of rock. Beneath the crust is the mantle which is made of mostly solid rock, although it has an area of slowly flowing rock called the asthenosphere. At the center of the earth is the core. The core has two parts, a molten outer core, and a solid inner core, composed of mostly nickel and iron. The inner core is solid due to the tremendous pressures at the center of the earth.

Earth's Layers

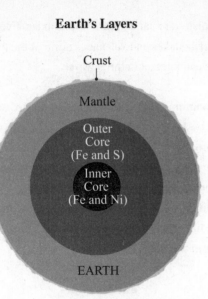

Volcanoes are mountains formed by magma from the interior of the earth. Volcanoes that have erupted within recorded history or are currently erupting are called **active volcanoes. Dormant volcanoes** are those which have not been known to erupt, and **extinct volcanoes** are those which it is believed will never erupt again. Volcanoes form where tectonic plates meet. At these plate boundaries, magma flows out of breaks in the earth's crust. If there is no outlet for the magma as the plates push together, pressure will build up until an explosion occurs—known as a **volcanic eruption**.

The edges of tectonic plates are called **plate boundaries**. Events like sea floor spreading, along with most earthquakes and volcanoes occur at the locations where two plates meet. Plate boundaries can interact in three ways.

- **Convergent boundary:** Two plates moving toward each other. One of the plates will be pushed below the other and down into the mantle.
- **Divergent boundary:** Two plates moving away from each other, causing a gap between them. Magma (molten rock) will often fill the gap and cool to form new crust.
- **Transform fault boundary:** Two plates sliding from side to side relative to each other, like when you rub your hands back and forth. They are also called transform boundaries.

Earth's Plates

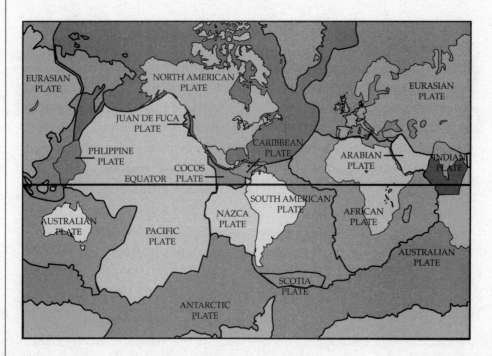

EARTH SCIENCE—REVIEW

1. The movement of sections of the earth's crust is known as

   (1) mass depletion
   (2) plate tectonics
   (3) background extinction
   (4) migration
   (5) emigration

2. The motion of tectonic plates accounts for most of the earth's

   (1) carbon dioxide emissions
   (2) formation of rivers
   (3) change of seasons
   (4) volcanic activity
   (5) oil formations

3. Which of the following choices gives the geologic eras in the correct sequence, from the oldest to the most recent?

   (1) Cenozoic—Mesozoic—Paleozoic—Precambrian
   (2) Precambrian—Paleozoic—Mesozoic—Cenozoic
   (3) Paleozoic—Precambrian—Cenozoic—Mesozoic
   (4) Paleozoic—Cenozoic—Precambrian—Mesozoic
   (5) Mesozoic—Paleozoic—Precambrian—Cenozoic

4. The rock cycle is a process by which old rocks are recycled into new rocks. In the rock cycle, time pressure, and the earth's heat interact to create three types of rocks. Sedimentary rocks are formed as sediment (eroded rocks and the remains of plants and animals) build up and is compressed. Metamorphic rock is formed as a great deal of pressure and heat is applied to rock. Igneous rock results when rock is melted by and pressure below the earth's crust into a liquid and then resolidifies.

Which of the following rock types would contain the greatest number of fossils?

(1) Igneous rock only
(2) Metamorphic rock only
(3) Sedimentary rock only
(4) Igneous and metamorphic rock
(5) Sedimentary and igneous rock

ASTRONOMY

Astronomy is the study of the universe beyond the earth. Astronomers study the moon, planets, solar system, galaxy, and everything farther away. It is one of the oldest branches of science, dating back to ancient times. In fact, some scientists theorize that the pyramids in Egypt were actually used for astronomical purposes. Thankfully, you won't be asked to know everything about the deepest reaches of space, but here are the basics of the universe.

Earth and the Solar System

We currently live on **Earth**, the third-closest planet to the **sun**. Earth is a part of the solar system, which in turn is part of the **Milky Way Galaxy**. All solar systems are made up of a sun and the objects revolving around it. For a long time, scientists believed that the earth was the center of the solar system. **Nicolaus Copernicus**, a Polish astronomer, was the first to introduce the idea of a heliocentric, or sun-centered, model of the solar system in the sixteenth century. It has since been proven that our solar system is indeed heliocentric. The following is a model of our solar system (not to scale):

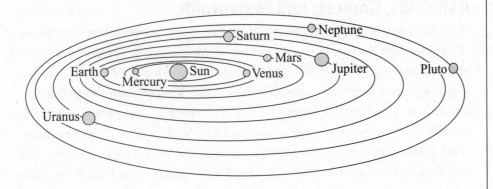

Inner Planets

The four planets closest to the sun—Mercury, Venus, Earth, and Mars—are called the inner planets. They consist mainly of rock with metal cores. They notably do not have rings. Earth and Mars are the only inner planets that have moons; Earth only has one moon and Mars has two (called Phobos and Deimos).

Outer Planets

The four planets farthest from the sun—Jupiter, Saturn, Uranus, and Neptune—are called the outer planets. They are also sometimes called the Jovian planets because their structure is similar to that of Jupiter. These planets are the largest in the solar system (with Jupiter being the largest of them all) and are gas giants (meaning that they are not primarily made up of rock or solid matter. They all have numerous moons, ranging from 8 to approximately 20. Also, all of these planets have rings, with Saturn's rings being the most notable and plentiful.

Pluto Demoted

Pluto, the outermost major body in the solar system, has been controversial since its discovery in 1930. Although it was once considered the smallest of the planets, in 2006 the International Astronomical Union (IAU) formally downgraded Pluto to a dwarf planet. It has a moon roughly half its size (called Charon) and its elliptical orbit sometimes brings it closer to the sun than Neptune.

Asteroids, Comets, and Meteoroids

The solar system also contains millions of smaller objects. **Asteroids** are large pieces of rock that orbit the sun, just as the planets do. Most asteroids are located between Mars and Jupiter in an area that is called the asteroid belt. **Meteoroids** are small pieces of rock and metal. Sometimes meteoroids enter the earth's atmosphere. When that happens, they are called meteors. Usually the meteor will burn up when passing through the atmosphere. However, on rare occasions they hit the earth and are then called meteorites. **Comets** are made up of rock, dust, methane, and ice. Like asteroids, they also orbit the sun. The Kuiper Belt is a disk-shaped region past the orbit of Neptune that is thought to be the source of the short-period comets.

The Earth's Orbit

Did you know that the earth is moving, even as you read this book? Right now, the earth is traveling around the sun at an average speed of about 106,000 km per hour. The earth's revolution, or trip around the sun, takes 365 days (approximately one year). As the earth revolves around the sun, it is also spinning on its axis. This spinning is called rotation. It takes the earth 24 hours (or one day) to make one complete rotation.

The Sun

Ah the sun, the center of the solar system. There are two major facts you should know about the sun: The sun is very hot and very large. The outer layer (known as the corona) averages 2,000,000 degrees Celsius and the core (or center) is 15,000,000 degrees Celsius! The sun is about 109 times more massive than the earth, and it accounts for 99 percent of the total mass of the solar system.

Eclipses

An **eclipse** occurs when a planet or moon passes through the shadow of another. There are two types of eclipses that occur on Earth: solar eclipses and lunar eclipses. During a solar eclipse, the moon moves between the sun and the earth. The moon blocks the light of the sun and casts a shadow over a certain part of the Earth. During a lunar eclipse, the earth moves between the sun and the moon. When this happens, the earth blocks the sunlight and casts a shadow on the moon.

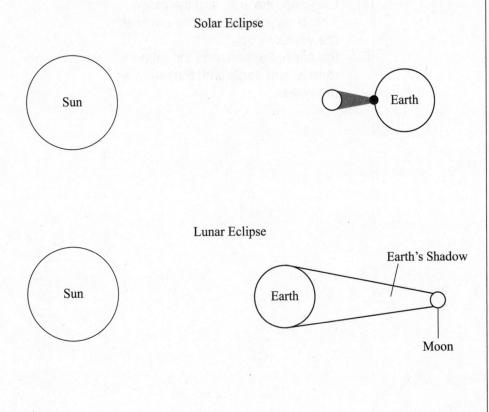

Solar Eclipse

Lunar Eclipse

ASTRONOMY—REVIEW

1. What is the largest planet in the solar system?

   (1) Jupiter
   (2) Mercury
   (3) Mars
   (4) Saturn
   (5) Venus

2. During a solar eclipse

   (1) the earth passes directly between the moon and the sun
   (2) the moon passes directly between the earth and the sun
   (3) the sun passes directly between the earth and the moon
   (4) the earth, the sun, and the moon form a right angle with the earth as the vertex
   (5) the earth, the sun, and the moon form a right angle with the moon as the vertex

ANSWERS TO REVIEW QUESTIONS

Scientific Method—Review

1. **(2)** Answering this question involves being able to understand both the map and the table. According to the table, Station 2 was the closest to the epicenter of the earthquake. Now if you look at the corresponding map, you can see that Station 2 is located in the eastern part of Nevada. By doing a quick comparison with the scale provided, you can see that the epicenter would most likely be located inside Nevada. Thus choice (2) is best answer.

2. **(5)** Remember that your answer must fit with the information that you've seen on the graph. You can immediately get rid of choice (1) because the dot on the graph looks to be higher than 45. Choices (2), (3), and (4) are statement that may or may not be true but since the graph does not give you any information on diseases or gender, you can safely cross off all of them. Choice (5) is the most accurate conclusion.

3. **(4)** While many of the answer choices might be true, we have to use the table to see if these conclusions can be drawn from the table. Of all the choices, only (4) can be proven. A sixteen-year girl needs to consume about 2,200 calories whereas a sixteen-year-old boy needs to consume about 3,000 calories per day. Since 2,200 is less than 3,000, we can assume that sixteen-year-old girls need to consume fewer calories per day than sixteen-year-old boys.

Elements, Water, Acids, and Bases—Review

1. **(1)** Recall that at 100 degrees, water will turn from a liquid state to a gas state. In other words, it will boil over. The corrected answer is that 100 degree Celsius is the boiling point. You can also use Process of Elimination if you remember other facts about water. 100 degrees Celsius is too hot to be the freezing point, and since water becomes a solid at the freezing point, you can eliminate (2) and (4). 32 degrees Fahrenheit is the freezing point of water so you can eliminate (4). And finally the Celsius to Fahrenheit conversion rate is not a 1 to 1 ratio so choice (5) is incorrect. Just in case you are curious the equation to convert Celsius to Fahrenheit is $\left(\dfrac{9}{5}\right)C + 32 = F$.

2. **(2)** First off, you can eliminate choices (3), (4), and (5) since we are dealing with the pH scale in this case. Anything below 7 on the pH scale is an acid. Anything above 7 on the pH scale is a base. Thus the correct answer here is 2.

3. **(4)** Protons and neutrons both have a weight of approximately 1 atomic mass unit. By adding them together you get the mass of the atom. Electrons have practically no mass.

4. **(3)** The mass of a proton is approximately the same as the mass of a neutron. An electron is much lighter than a proton. All the other molecules weigh much more than a proton.

Nitrogen, Carbon, and Water Cycles—Review

1. **(3)** We can use Process of Elimination for this question. We know that plants need both sunlight and water in addition to carbon, but there is no carbon in either of those things so you can eliminate (1) and (5). We also know that the soil contains nitrogen, which the bacteria produces, so you can eliminate (2) and (4). Because animals breathe out carbon dioxide that the plant uses for its carbon, you can safely guess that plants get their carbon from the air. Choice (3) is the best answer.

2. **(1)** Use Process of Elimination to ferret out the incorrect answers. Water vapor is never mentioned in the statement, so you can get rid of choice (3). Choice (2) is incorrect because cars use oxygen and not carbon dioxide to burn gasoline. Choice (5) does not make sense; the heat from a car engine is not hot enough to destroy carbon dioxide. Choice (4) also doesn't make sense; soot is equal to carbon-filled impure air. Would sooty air and carbon dioxide combine to create something to reduce the greenhouse effect? Probably not. The correct answer is (1).

3. **(2)** This question requires an understanding of the water cycle coupled with a little vocabulary. The process of evaporation involves turning a liquid into a gaseous state using heat. Because heat is necessary for evaporation, the answer that best fits the definition is sunlight.

4. **(5)** For this question, you should have an understanding of the nitrogen cycle. The question is asking for the final step in the cycle that gets nitrogen from animals to the plants. Only choice (5) closes the loop and directly involves animals in the process. All the other choices do not involve animals as directly and some of the choices are scientifically implausible, namely choices (2) and (4).

Cells and the Cell Cycle—Review

1. **(2)** This question is basically asking you to use your math skills to get the required result. Since the diploid number is 24, you have to divide by 2 to get the haploid number, which is choice (2), 12.

Classification and Evolution—Review

1. **(2)** To best answer this question, look at the chart and follow the lines to see which one is attached to the "Animals with bones" branch of the chart. Only amphibians are attached. Thus the correct answer here is (2).

2. **(1)** All similar organisms are located close to each other in the flow chart. Start at the top of the chart and work your way down the path to "clams." Then follow the paths of the answer choices. The answer choice whose path closely mirrors the one of the clam is the squid. Since an octopus is located in the squid family, the best choice here is (1).

3. **(3)** First let's look at the chart to figure out what the unknown vertebrate could be. We know that the unknown animal lives in the water so we know that it's not the earthworm. Next, the animal does not have a shell so cross clam and snail off the list. Finally the animal has a tooth tongue. This leaves you with the octopus. Now that we know that we are dealing with the octopus, go through the answer choices and see what matches up with the traits of the octopus. The correct answer is choice (3).

4. **(5)** This is a trickier question that relies more heavily on your vocabulary skills in addition to your science skills. We see that the word "biodiversity" has the word diversity in it, meaning that this means a wide variety. "Bio-" is a prefix that means life. So you are looking for which term means a wide variety of life. Deforestation, respiration, sanitation, and erosion do not increase the variety. Only evolution does; choice (5) is the best answer.

Plants, Ecosystems, and Food Chains—Review

1. **(2)** This relationship is an example of parasitism. Parasitism is a form of symbiosis in which one organism benefits and the other is harmed.

2. **(4)** Look at hawks and snakes on the food web and look at the arrows coming and going from them. Use Process of Elimination to cross out answer choices that are not true about both types of animals. Both types of animals eat mice (and are not food for them) and are carnivores. The correct answer is (4).

3. **(1)** Photosynthesis is the process by which plants convert water, carbon dioxide, and sunlight into food.

Earth Science—Review

1. **(2)** The movement of tectonic plates in the earth's crust occurs because these plates are floating on the semi-liquid magma underneath them. (1) and (3) both deal with the loss of species, and (4) and (5) deal with the movement of populations.

2. **(4)** When two of these massive rock plates collide, often one slips under the other; this process is called subduction. The collision of two plates causes the rock layer of the crust to crack. At these sites, magma may rise from the molten interior of the earth, and a volcano is formed. (1) is a human activity; (2) can be caused by many geological processes; (3) is an effect of the relationship between the earth and the sun; and (5) is a biological process.

3. **(2)** You will not be expected to memorize every eon, era, period and epoch of the geological time scale, but you should be familiar with the most recent era, and the most talked-about ones. (2) correctly starts with the earliest era, the Precambrian (600 million years ago), then the Paleozoic (500 to 250 million years ago), then the Mesozoic (250 to 65 million years ago), and finally, the Cenozoic (65 million years ago to today).

4. **(3)** Since sedimentary rock is made of the remains of dead organisms, it would contain the greatest number of fossils. (5) is not correct because the melting and cooling process the forms igneous rock would destroy fossils, which are usually quite fragile.

Astronomy—Review

1. **(1)** Jupiter is the largest planet in the solar system, with a diameter of 88,700 miles. Jupiter's diameter is roughly 11 times that of the earth.

2. **(2)** During a solar eclipse, the moon passes between the earth and the sun, blocking out the light from the sun to Earth. Choice (1) describes a lunar eclipse, where the earth passes between the sun and the moon, blocking the sun's light to the moon, and making the moon invisible in the night sky. Choices (3), (4), and (5) are scientifically impossible (although they would be cool to watch).

SCIENCE DRILL

Questions 1–3 refer to the following passage and graph.

A scientist placed 100 fish eggs into each of
seven solutions with different pH values. The
definition of a pH value is the measure of the
number of hydrogen ions in a solution. The lower
the pH value, the more acidic the solution is. After
96 hours the number of survivors was counted
and converted into a percent. The percent
surviving is given in the graph below.

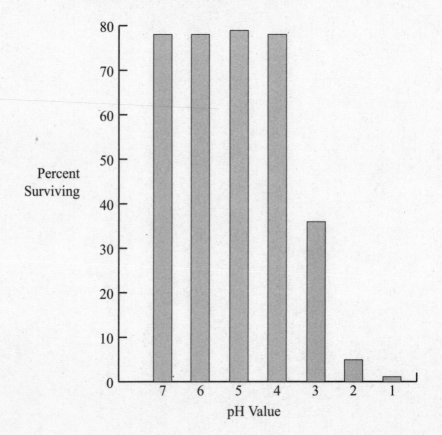

1. The LD50 is the value at which 50% of a population dies. Which of the values below represents the LD50 in this experiment?

   (1) 6.0
   (2) 4.0
   (3) 3.5
   (4) 3.0
   (5) 2.5

2. At what pH value do the fewest fish hatch?

   (1) 7.0
   (2) 6.0
   (3) 3.5
   (4) 2.0
   (5) 1.0

3. Which of the following best describes the goal of the experiment?

   (1) To test the hypothesis that the bigger the fish, the smaller the pH tolerance range.
   (2) To observe how many fish would hatch at different pH values.
   (3) To find out how many fish live in streams with different pH values.
   (4) To understand how acid rain affects life in streams.
   (5) To see what chemical is best at changing the pH of water.

4. An archaeologist examining the mask pictured above would NOT be able to prove that the object

    (1)   had a religious significance to its creator

    (2)   is 30 centimeters high

    (3)   resembles other objects found in South America

    (4)   was made with metal tools

    (5)   is constructed of tropical hardwood

Questions 5–6 refer to the following paragraph and chart.

The term *solubility* refers to the amount of a substance (solute) that will dissolve in a given amount of a liquid substance (solvent). The solubility of solids in water varies with temperature. The graph below displays the water solubility curves for six crystalline solids.

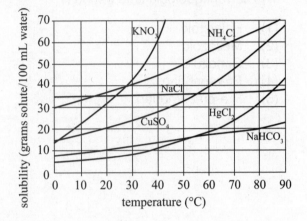

5. Based on the graph, as temperature increases, the solubility of KNO_3

  (1) increases.
  (2) decreases.
  (3) increases, then decreases.
  (4) decreases, then increases.
  (5) stays the same.

6. Which substance had the least change in solubility?

  (1) $HgCl_2$
  (2) NH_4Cl
  (3) KNO_3
  (4) $NaCl$
  (5) $CuSO_4$

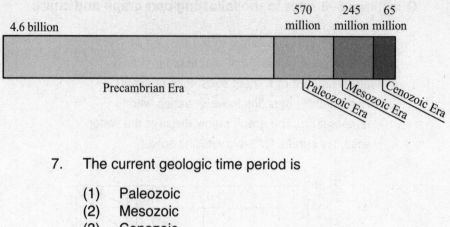

570 million   245 million   65 million

4.6 billion

Precambrian Era

Paleozoic Era

Mesozoic Era

Cenozoic Era

7. The current geologic time period is

    (1)   Paleozoic
    (2)   Mesozoic
    (3)   Cenozoic
    (4)   Precambrian
    (5)   Pre-precambrian

8. *Ethylene glycol* is the main ingredient in antifreeze and has the chemical structure shown below:

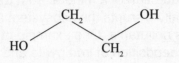

The figure below shows how the melting point (the temperature at which solid antifreeze would begin melting) of antifreeze varies with % EG.

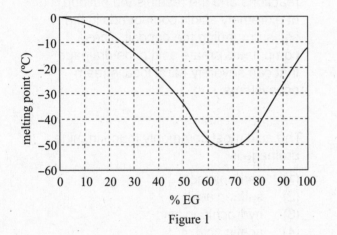

Figure 1

According to the figure above, the temperature at which solid antifreeze begins to melt in a 60% EG solution at 101.3 kPa is closest to which of the following?

(1)   0°C
(2)   −12°C
(3)   −24°C
(4)   −48°C
(5)   −60°C

9. Environmental concerns about mining revolve around the damage that is done during the extraction process. The extraction of a mineral from Earth generally disrupts the ecosystem and leaves pollutants. One example of this is the deposition of iron pyrite and sulfur in the mining of coal. The acid forms as water seeps through mines and carries off sulfur-containing compounds. The chemical conversion of sulfur-bearing minerals occurs through a combination of biological and inorganic chemical reactions and the result is the buildup of extremely acidic compounds in the soil surrounding the deposit. These compounds create acid mine drainage that can severely harm local stream ecosystems.

The acid most commonly found in mine drainage is

(1) carbonic acid
(2) sulfuric acid
(3) hydrochloric acid
(4) acetic acid
(5) citric acid

Atmospheric Composition	
Nitrogen (N_2)	78%
Oxygen (O_2)	20%
Argon (Ar)	< 1%
Water Vapor	variable
Other	< 1%

10. According to the chart above, the third-most abundant gas in Earth's atmosphere is:

    (1) Carbon
    (2) Nitrogen
    (3) Oxygen
    (4) Neon
    (5) Argon

Questions 11–12 refer to the following diagram.

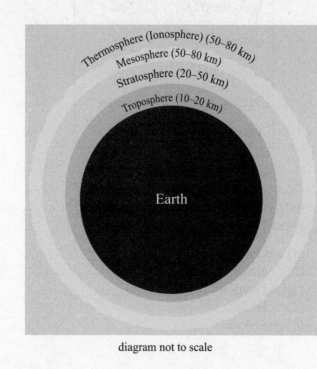

diagram not to scale

11. An object located 35 kilometers above the earth's surface is located in which region of the earth's atmosphere?

    (1)   Thermosphere
    (2)   Mesosphere
    (3)   Stratosphere
    (4)   Troposphere
    (5)   Earth

12. Which layer of the earth's atmosphere is the highest layer?

    (1)   Thermosphere
    (2)   Mesosphere
    (3)   Stratosphere
    (4)   Troposphere
    (5)   Earth

13. The Second Law of Thermodynamics says that entropy (disorder) of the universe is increasing. One corollary of this law is the concept that, in most energy transformations, a significant fraction of energy is lost to the universe as heat.

The Second Law of Thermodynamics is best described by which of the following?

(1) The amount of solar radiation going into an ecosystem is equal to the total amount of energy going out of that system.

(2) The amount of carbon in the atmosphere has increased due to the combustion of fossil fuels.

(3) As electricity is transmitted through wires, some of the power is lost to the environment as heat.

(4) Wind-generated electricity has more power than electricity generated at a hydropower plant.

(5) The amount of electricity used to light a light bulb is less than the amount of light that the bulb produces.

14. In an ecosystem, there are many living things that must get energy to survive. For example, in the forest, mice eat leaves, and snakes eat mice. The path that energy takes through an ecosystem can be shown with a food chain.

leaves → mice → snakes

A food web is another way to show how energy is passed from one living species to another in an ecosystem. The picture below shows a food web for an ocean ecosystem.

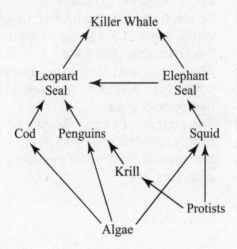

Which term describes the role of the leopard seal in this ecosystem?

(1) producer
(2) herbivore
(3) decomposer
(4) carnivore
(5) detritivore

Questions 15–17 refer to the flow chart below.

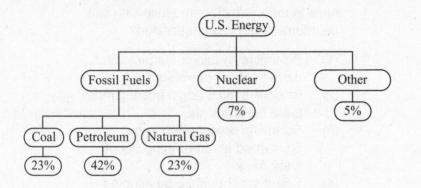

15. According to the chart, how much energy used in the U.S. comes from hydroelectric power?

    (1)   0%–5%
    (2)   7%
    (3)   23%
    (4)   42%
    (5)   88%

16. According to the chart, how much energy used in the U.S. comes from fossil fuels?

    (1)   0%–5%
    (2)   7%
    (3)   23%
    (4)   42%
    (5)   88%

17. Scientists suggest that the supply of fossil fuels on the earth is quickly being used up. It took millions of years for these types of fuels to form. Which of the following can be inferred from this information?

(1) Scientists should continue to find more uses for petroleum.
(2) Scientists must begin making more fossil fuels quickly.
(3) Scientists do not need to be concerned about running out of fossil fuels.
(4) Scientists should be developing alternative energy sources to fossil fuels.
(5) Scientists should use fossil fuels to run nuclear power plants.

18. Scientists measured the volume of a balloon when it was heated to different temperatures. Their results are shown in the graph below.

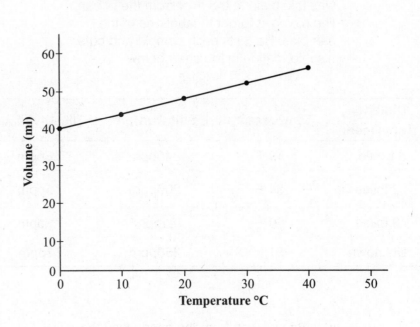

What can be concluded from looking at this graph?

(1) The balloon weighed more at higher temperatures.
(2) The balloon weighed less at higher temperatures.
(3) The volume of air in a balloon increases as the temperature increases.
(4) Air must be leaking out of the balloon as it is heated.
(5) The balloon could not hold more than 2,450 mL of air.

19. A marine biologist collected four water samples from different points along a river that flows out to the ocean. Each sample was labeled with the distance it was taken along the river from the ocean. The biologist forgot to label one of the samples. He tests each sample and puts his information in the chart below.

Distance from Ocean	Temperature	Salt Content	Dissolved as
1 mile	49°F	340ppm	7.8ppm
2 miles	54°F	200ppm	7.5ppm
3 miles	60°F	81ppm	7.2ppm
Unknown	51°F	250ppm	7.7ppm

At what distance from the ocean was the unknown sample most likely collected?

(1) 0.5 miles
(2) 1.5 miles
(3) 2.5 miles
(4) 3.5 miles
(5) 4.0 miles

20. Most people believe that forest fires are a bad thing despite the fact that they are part of the natural life of a forest. Some trees and plants need fire in order for their seeds to germinate. Surface fires typically burn only the forests' underbrush and do little damage to mature trees. These fires serve to protect the forest from more harmful fires by removing dry leaves, needles, wood and dead materials that would burn quickly and at high temperatures, escalating more severe fires. In addition, these fires help in the decomposition of organic matter and help to eliminate unfavorable plant species.

Smaller forest fires are beneficial to forests for all of the following reasons EXCEPT

(1) removal of competing plants
(2) combustion of dried leaves or needles, which reduces the threat of large fires
(3) burning the crowns of trees
(4) germinating seeds of certain plant species
(5) making burned matter available as a nutrient

21. The Clean Water Act of 1972 had a dramatic effect on the quality of water in the United States. It helped to pass laws which sharply reduced direct pollutant discharges into waterways and financed municipal wastewater treatment facilities. The act also helped to set federal health standards for drinking and surface water.

The Clean Water Act established all of the following guidelines EXCEPT

(1) implemented pollution control programs
(2) set water quality standards for all contaminants in surface waters
(3) made it unlawful for any person to discharge any pollutant from a point source into navigable waters
(4) demanded that an environmental impact statement be prepared for any major development
(5) funded the construction of sewage treatment plants

Questions 22 and 23 refer to the following graph which gives characteristics about amphibians and reptiles.

Characteristics	Amphibians	Reptiles		
		Lizards	Snakes	Turtles
Belly drags on ground when walking	Yes	No	Yes	No
Hearts have two chambers	Yes	No	No	No
Produce dry waste to conserve water	No	Yes	Yes	Yes
Cold-blooded (ectothermic)	Yes	Yes	Yes	Yes
Four legs	Most	Yes	No	Yes
Tough, dry skin	No	Yes	Yes	Yes
Are vertebrates	Yes	Yes	Yes	Yes
Lay watertight eggs	No	Yes	Yes	Yes

22. What characteristic could be used to tell that an unknown animal is an amphibian and not a reptile?

    (1) The animal has four legs
    (2) The animal has four legs and is cold-blooded
    (3) The animal has four legs and tough, dry skin
    (4) The animal has four legs and does not produce dry waste products
    (5) The animals are vertebrates

ANSWERS AND EXPLANATIONS

1. **(3)** If you read the graph, you can see that the LD50 falls closest to the solution with the pH of 3.5. As a side note, LD50 values are important because they help us understand the health risks of certain materials. As you might imagine, if a chemical is very toxic, it has a very low LD50.

2. **(5)** As you can see from the graph, in the solution that had a pH of 1, almost no fish eggs hatched, so (5) is the correct answer. This graph analysis question asks you to understand that the size of the bar represents the percent surviving. You will almost certainly be asked to answer questions on this exam that include bar graphs, so if you need to practice reading them, get it.

3. **(2)** The purpose of this test was to observe how many fish would hatch at different pH values, plain and simple. If you chose any other answer, then you might have been reading too much into the experiment. Remember not to make any inferences—you must answer the question only on the basis of the information you're given. In this experiment, the percent surviving is the dependent variable and the pH is the independent variable; the data collected relates to hatching survival rates.

4. **(1)** Each of the incorrect answers can be demonstrated through scientific measurement and observation. Choice (1), however, requires speculation regarding the use of the object. Assuming there are no descendants of the people who created this mask, there is no reliable way for an archaeologist to prove its purpose.

5. **(1)** As you can see from the graph, the solubility line of KNO_3 goes up as it moves to the right (when temperature increases). Thus the correct answer is (1).

6. **(4)** In this case, we are looking for the line that is the closest in resemblance to a straight line. The only one that fits in this case is NaCl, or choice (4).

7. **(3)** According to the figure, the Cenozoic era started about 65 million years ago and continues today.

8. **(4)** According to the passage, all readings are taken at atmospheric pressure 101.3 kPa, so you can disregard that part of the question. According to the figure, at 60% EG, the melting point is roughly −48°C, or choice (4).

24. The following graph shows the flow rate of a river at different times of the year. When a river's flow rate gets very high, the river can flood. The flow rates were taken from 1986 through 1988.

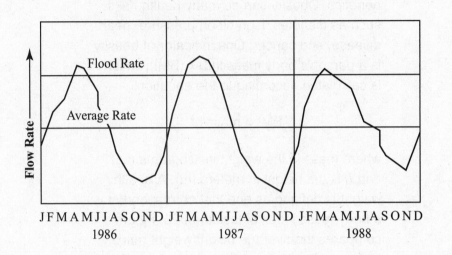

How long is the cycle of flooding in this river?

(1)   3 months
(2)   6 months
(3)   9 months
(4)   12 months
(5)   24 months

Questions 25–27 refer to the following information:

Many factors play a role in the development of obesity, including lack of physical exercise, excessive intake of calories (overeating), and genetics. Obesity carries many health risks such as diabetes, high blood pressure, heart disease, and cancer. One indicator of obesity is a person's body mass index (BMI), which is calculated according to the equation

$$BMI = mass/h^2$$

where mass is the weight in kilograms (kg) and h is the height in meters (m). A healthy weight is defined as one that corresponds to a body mass index of less than 25. Figure 1 compares the average height/weight ratios to the healthy BMI for different sectors of the U.S. population.

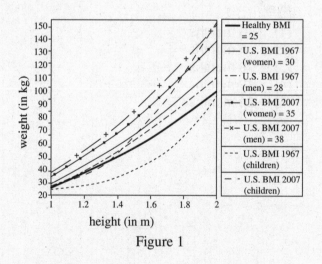

Figure 1

The health risks related to obesity increase significantly at BMI values greater than 25; these are displayed in Table 1.

Table 1										
Body Mass Index (BMI)										
	26	27	28	29	30	31	32	33	34	35
Death, all causes (versus BMI<19)			60%			110%			120%	
Death by cancer (versus BMI<19)					80%				110%	
Death by heart disease (versus BMI<19)			210%			360%			480%	
High blood pressure (versus BMI<23)		180%			260%				350%	
Degenerative arthritis (versus BMI<23)							400%			
Type II diabetes (versus BMI<22–23)			1,480%		2,660%			3,930%		5,300%

25. According to the data presented in Table 1, a person with a BMI of 32 is at greatest increased risk for which of the following?

(1) Death, all causes
(2) Death by cancer
(3) Type II diabetes
(4) Degenerative arthritis
(5) High blood pressure

26. According to Figure 1, which of the following best describes the relationship between the height of U.S. children in 2007 and their weight? As height increases, weight:

(1) increases only.
(2) decreases only.
(3) increases, then decreases.
(4) decreases, then increases.
(5) stays the same.

27. As a person becomes more obese, the risk of developing chronic diseases increases. The closer one can get to a healthy BMI of 25 or lower, the less risk one has of illness. Of the conditions listed in Table 1, a person who has a BMI of 34 has the smallest increased risk of:

(1) dying of cancer.
(2) dying of heart disease.
(3) developing type II diabetes.
(4) suffering from degenerative arthritis.
(5) having high blood pressure.

Questions 28–30 refer to the following article on animal behavior.

Some animals behave in a programmed way to specific experiences while others behave according to some type of learning. An instinct is an inborn, unlearned behavior. Sometimes, the instinctive behavior is triggered by environmental signals called releasers. The releaser is usually a small part of the environment that is released. For example, when a male European robin sees another male robin, the sight of a tuft of red feathers on the male is a releaser that triggers fighting behavior.

Imprinting is form of learning that occurs during a brief period of time, usually early in an animal's life. Animals undergo imprinting in order to recognize members of their own species. Think of a mother goose and her goslings. The first moving object that a newborn sees is the animal it will recognize as its mother. Once the newborn sees it mother, it will mimic her movements and song calls.

Classical conditioning involves learning through association. A classic example is the experiment that Russian scientist Ivan Pavlov conducted where every time he fed his dogs, he would ring a bell. Due to classical conditioning, his dogs would start to drool whenever they heard a bell, regardless of whether or not food was available.

In operant conditioning, an animal learns to perform an act in order to receive a reward. Psychologist B. F. Skinner performed an experiment where he put a rat in a cage with different levers to see if it would pull them. Through trial and error, the rat figured out that one of the levers would always produce food through a dispenser. Over time the rats associated pulling the lever with getting food and would hang out near the food-delivering lever.

Insight involves using reasoning or problem solving skills. Human beings tend to be great at reasoning as a form of learned behavior, but other animals use insight as well. For example if you wanted to remove a carrot from the ground, you could use a small shovel to dig it up.

28. A stickleback fish will not attack an intruder that lacks a red belly. This is an example of

    (1)   instinct
    (2)   operant conditioning
    (3)   imprinting
    (4)   classical conditioning
    (5)   insight

29. A blue jay avoids monarch butterflies after experiencing their distasteful poisoning. This is an example of:

    (1)   instinct
    (2)   operant conditioning
    (3)   imprinting
    (4)   classical conditioning
    (5)   insight

30. A chimpanzee uses several boxes on the floor to reach bananas hung from the ceiling. This is an example of

    (1)   instinct
    (2)   operant conditioning
    (3)   imprinting
    (4)   classical conditioning
    (5)   insight

Chapter 10
Science
Drill Answers

ANSWERS AND EXPLANATIONS

1. **(3)** If you read the graph, you can see that the LD50 falls closest to the solution with the pH of 3.5. As a side note, LD50 values are important because they help us understand the health risks of certain materials. As you might imagine, if a chemical is very toxic, it has a very low LD50.

2. **(5)** As you can see from the graph, in the solution that had a pH of 1, almost no fish eggs hatched, so (5) is the correct answer. This graph analysis question asks you to understand that the size of the bar represents the percent surviving. You will almost certainly be asked to answer questions on this exam that include bar graphs, so if you need to practice reading them, get it.

3. **(2)** The purpose of this test was to observe how many fish would hatch at different pH values, plain and simple. If you chose any other answer, then you might have been reading too much into the experiment. Remember not to make any inferences—you must answer the question only on the basis of the information you're given. In this experiment, the percent surviving is the dependent variable and the pH is the independent variable; the data collected relates to hatching survival rates.

4. **(1)** Each of the incorrect answers can be demonstrated through scientific measurement and observation. Choice (1), however, requires speculation regarding the use of the object. Assuming there are no descendants of the people who created this mask, there is no reliable way for an archaeologist to prove its purpose.

5. **(1)** As you can see from the graph, the solubility line of KNO_3 goes up as it moves to the right (when temperature increases). Thus the correct answer is (1).

6. **(4)** In this case, we are looking for the line that is the closest in resemblance to a straight line. The only one that fits in this case is NaCl, or choice (4).

7. **(3)** According to the figure, the Cenozoic era started about 65 million years ago and continues today.

8. **(4)** According to the passage, all readings are taken at atmospheric pressure 101.3 kPa, so you can disregard that part of the question. According to the figure, at 60% EG, the melting point is roughly −48°C, or choice (4).

9. **(2)** For this answer, double-check the paragraph. The word sulfur is mentioned twice so you now that any acid is going to be composed of sulfur. Indeed, sulfuric acid forms as water seeps through mines and carries off sulfur-containing compounds.

10. **(5)** Refer to the chart to find your answer. Nitrogen and oxygen can be immediately ruled out. Argon is the only other gas named and it takes up roughly one percent of the Earth's atmosphere so (5) is your best answer. Keep in mind that even if traces of carbon and neon exist in the Earth's atmosphere they would both fall under the other categories, which could be made up of hundreds of other particles.

11. **(3)** This question requires a little bit of math in addition to your ability to read the diagram. We know that 35 km would lie between the 20–50 km range. Using this information, you can see that the correct answer is the stratosphere, choice (3).

12. **(1)** For this question, you have to take a look at the diagram and determine which layer is the one farthest away from the earth. In this case, the correct answer is the thermosphere (or choice 1).

13. **(3)** Recall that the paragraph stated that a corollary of the Second Law of Thermodynamics is that energy will be lost due to heat. The statement in choice (3) also contains the same phrases. Choice (3) is the best answer.

14. **(4)** First, look for the leopard seal in the food web. Remember that the arrows show the flow of energy. So, leopard seals get energy from penguins, elephant seals, and cod. Leopards give energy to killer whales (in other words, killer whales eat them). So, in this food web, the leopard seal's role is to eat other animals. Carnivores are animals that eat other animals so the correct answer choice is (4). Don't be thrown off by choice (5); detritivores eat dead organisms.

15. **(1)** Hydroelectric power isn't mentioned in the flow chart, but don't get thrown off. It technically belongs in the "Other" category. As you can see from the chart, the "Other" types of energy make up 5% of the U.S. energy sources. That means that hydroelectric power is part of that 5%. It could be anywhere from 0 to 5%, but anything over 5% is not possible. The correct answer choice is (1).

16. **(5)** Fossil fuels is mentioned in the flowchart, but it is one level higher than coal, petroleum, and natural gas. To solve this problem, you have to add up the total energy usage for coal, petroleum, and natural gas. The total amount is 88%, or choice (5).

17. **(4)** This questions required a little bit of application of the information you've been given. First off, we are already using petroleum the most out of all the energy sources, and using more of it would not add to anything. Cross out choice (1). Next the question says that it takes millions of years to make fossil fuels, so scientists cannot make more quickly. Get rid of choice (2). Since we know that fossil fuels are used in a variety of ways (home heating, air conditioners, and cars to name a few), we definitely should be concerned about running out of fossil fuels. Get rid of choice (3). Since nuclear power plants use a different kind of fuel than fossil fuel, you can eliminate choice (5). Besides, if fossil fuels are running out, we couldn't use them for a nuclear power plant, anyway. The best option is choice (4).

18. **(3)** Look closely at the graph. It compares temperature and volume. As a quick reminder, volume is how much space something takes up. Answer choices (1) and (2) talk about how much the balloon weighed, which is not volume. Eliminate those two choices. Answer choice (4) doesn't make sense; the balloon's volume increased as it was heated so air could not have been leaking out. Cross out (4). Finally the graph tells us that the balloon did get larger than 2,450 mL at the end of the experiment. So answer choice (5) is incorrect. Answer choice (3) correctly describes the relationship between the balloon's volume and its temperature.

19. **(2)** This question asks you to read the chart carefully. You must figure out where the unknown sample fits in with the other samples. Use what you know about the sample to figure out how far from the ocean it was collected. It temperature is 51 degrees, which is higher than the sample taken at 1 mile, but lower that the sample taken at 2 miles. The unknown's salt content is 250 ppm, which is between the salt readings for the samples taken at 1 and 2 miles. Finally, the unknown's dissolved gases are 7.7, which is also between the readings for the samples taken at 1 and 2 miles. This all suggests that the unknown sample was taken between the 1-mile and the 2-mile sample. The only answer choice that best fits this is choice (2).

20. **(3)** For this you'll have to look back at the paragraph, as well as know a little bit of vocabulary. Recall that the paragraph says that fires are responsible for allowing the seeds of many plant species to germinate, burns away needles and leaves to eliminate fuels for future fires, and breaks down matter to provide nutrients to the trees. Crowns or the tops of the trees aren't mentioned at all in this article (as a side note, in large forest fires, the crowns of the the trees burns which weakens and/or outright kills many trees). The best choice here is (3).

21. **(4)** This question may be seem daunting, but if you refer to the paragraph, you will be able to easily eliminate choices. You can see that the program set federal health standards, so you can get rid of choices (1) and (2). Choice (5) can be eliminated because this is directly stated in the second sentence. Choice (3) may seem tough, but you can use synonyms to figure out what the answer is saying, which is that the act made it illegal for a person to dump pollutants into the water. The act takes care of that. The best choice is (4), which is not mentioned at all in the paragraph.

22. **(4)** Look carefully at the chart for this question. You need to find a characteristic that is true of amphibians, but not true of reptiles. Read each answer choice, and get rid of any that do not fall into this pattern. Choices (1), (2), and (5) are incorrect because amphibians and reptiles can be four-legged and cold-blooded. Choice (3) tells you how to be sure an animal is a reptile and not an amphibian. Choice (4) is the best answer in this case.

23. **(4)** Here, we can use the Process of Elimination to cross out answers that do not make sense. Just because a reptile has dry skin does not mean that it won't learn to swim, so cross out answer choice (1). Answer choice (2) is nonsensical; amphibians are indeed vertebrates. Choice (3) is incorrect because the question itself states that amphibians live in tropical climates, which are by definition hot. Be careful of choice (5); just because an animal has dry skin doesn't mean it doesn't want to live where it rains. Choice (4) is the best fit answer.

24. **(4)** For this answer, you'll have to look carefully at the graph and estimate the amount of months in between peaks of the graph, since the cycle runs form peak to peak. From the graph, we can see that the cycle runs from about June of one year to June of another year. Thus, 12 months is the best answer.

25. **(3)** For this problem, we need to look at Table 1 to locate the information that the question is asking. You want to go down the list and check to see which of all the choices shown has the highest percentage. If you check the bottom of the graph, type II diabetes has a 3,390% risk. Thus, the answer is (3).

26. **(1)** Look at Figure 1, and pay special attention to the dotted yellow line that signifies the BMI rate of U.S. children in 2007. As we can see the line rises, which means that the weight increases as the height increases. Choice (1) is the best answer.

27. **(1)** Once again, we will go back to Table 1 to find the answer to this question. Look for the column that says 34, and then look down to see which of the listed answers best answers the question. The row that says "Death by cancer" has the smallest increase (from 80% to 110%) out of all the other rows, so choice (1) is the best fit answer.

28. **(1)** A stickleback attacking an object if it has a red belly sounds very similar to the example of an instinct in the paragraph about male robins and their tufted feathers. Choice (1) is the answer that best fits this question.

29. **(2)** The key word in this case is "experiencing." The blue jay does not avoid the monarch naturally, so we can rule out instinct. We also know that the blue jay did not learn by observing the behavior but experiencing its bad taste. Thus we can cross off imprinting (3). The blue jay did not use any complex reasoning skills to figure out how to avoid the monarch, so choice (5) is out as well. This leaves (2) and (4). Since we know that the blue jay had eaten the monarch before and "knows" that it's bad, we know that the bird associated monarch butterflies with bad food. The clear answer is (2).

30. **(5)** For this question, let's figure out what is happening. The chimpanzee wants to eat the bananas and has devised a plan to reach the bananas (by stacking several boxes on the floor). In this case, the chimpanzee is using reasoning skills that are independent of association or reinforcement. This is the definition of insight; the correct answer here is (5).

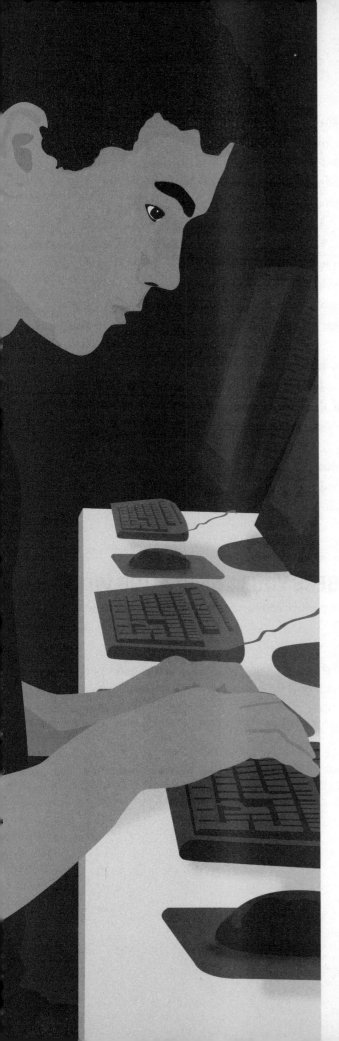

Chapter 11
Arithmetic

INTRODUCTION

The GED Math Test consists of 50 questions, and it focuses on the basics of arithmetic, geometry, statistics, and algebra. You won't see any of the really hard high school math stuff from pre-calculus or calculus. There are no formulas to remember, because they give you a full page of all the formulas you'll ever need and even some you'll never need. You'll never have to do a proof (remember those?) or use logarithms (no need to remember those).

The GED Math Test is split into two parts. Part I has more straight calculations, and Part II has more problems in which you may be interpreting graphs, using estimation, or simply explaining how you'd solve a problem (rather than getting into the actual calculations). You won't even miss having a calculator for most of the questions in Part II.

We're going to review things you may have learned as far back as elementary school but have probably forgotten about. In adult life, you aren't often asked to use a number line or reduce a fraction; however, these skills will be awfully handy on the GED. We'll help you get up to speed on the following topics:

I. Number operations
II. Measurement and geometry
III. Statistics and data analysis

THE KINDS OF NUMBERS YOU'LL BE DEALING WITH

You will do problems that involve positive numbers, negative numbers, fractions, decimals, and percents.

Positive numbers are all the numbers greater than zero. They're numbers that you probably use every day. If you say "pick a number," most people will pick a positive number. The chance of their picking –22.5, for example, is kind of small. Positive numbers include decimals and fractions, such as 16½ or 53.22.

Negative numbers are all the numbers less than zero. They include decimals and fractions as well.

THE NUMBER LINE

Positive numbers are all the numbers, up to infinity, to the right of zero on the number line.

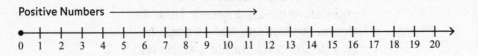

Negative numbers go on forever to the left of zero on the number line.

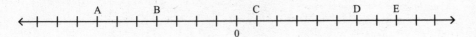

It's good to be familiar with the number line because the GED may ask you something like this:

Question 1 refers to the following number line.

Number line with labeled points:

```
        A         B              C          D    E
←─┼──┼──┼──┼──┼──┼──┼──┼──┼──┼──┼──┼──┼──┼──┼──┼──┼──→
                        0
```

1. Which letter on the number line above represents 6?

    (1) A
    (2) B
    (3) C
    (4) D
    (5) E

The correct answer here is D. Count six to the right of zero, and you end up at D. What numbers do the other letters represent?

$$A = -7$$

$$B = -4$$

$$C = 1$$

$$E = 8$$

It's helpful to think about the number line when working with negative numbers.

2. At the top of the mountain, the temperature is –23 degrees. Near the lodge at the bottom, it is –4 degrees. How many degrees warmer is it at the bottom?

(1) –27
(2) –19
(3)   4
(4)   19
(5)   27

Think about the number line. –23 is 23 units to the left of zero on the number line. To get from –23 to –4 we have to move 19 units to the right.

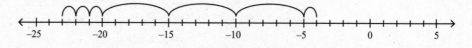

It is 19 degrees warmer at the bottom of the mountain.

3. When Jeanne woke up this morning, it was –2 degrees outside. By the time she got to work, the temperature had increased by 8 degrees. What was the temperature when Jeanne got to work?

(1) –10
(2)   –8
(3)   –2
(4)   6
(5)   8

Use the number line. –2 is two units to the left of zero. If the temperature increased by 8 degrees, we have to move 8 units to the right.

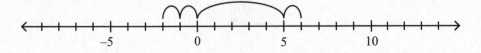

Moving 8 units to the right, we get to 6. So it was 6 degrees when Jeanne got to work.

Some GED questions show a number line, and some don't. Draw a quick number line with these types of questions to get a better idea of how the problem should be solved.

_____◯_____

ADDING AND SUBTRACTING

Some of the biggest challenges on the GED come from figuring out exactly what math you need to do. You will be given word problems, and you'll have to add, subtract, multiply, and divide, but first you need to figure out which operation to perform.

_____◯_____

1. Fiona's class is collecting cans for a food drive. On Monday the class collects 235 cans, on Tuesday it collects 210 cans, and on Wednesday it collects 198 cans. What is the total number of cans collected by Fiona's class?

    (1)   345
    (2)   408
    (3)   433
    (4)   533
    (5)   643

When a word problem asks you for a *total number*, you add.

Quick Note

"Total," "sum," or "all together" means you probably need to add.

In this case we add:

$$
\begin{array}{r}
235 \\
210 \\
+\ 198 \\
\end{array}
$$

When adding, start with the right-most, or ones, column. This column totals 13. The number 13 represents 3 ones plus 1 ten. So we put 3 in the ones column sum, and we carry, or regroup, the 1 (ten) to the tens column:

$$
\begin{array}{r}
{}^{1} \\
235 \\
210 \\
+\ 198 \\
\hline
3 \\
\end{array}
$$

Now we add the tens and hundreds column too. Remember to regroup the first digit of each sum with the next column to the left:

$$
\begin{array}{r}
{}^{1\ 1} \\
235 \\
210 \\
+\ 198 \\
\hline
643 \\
\end{array}
$$

Fiona's class collected a total of 643 cans, answer choice (5).

Solve these addition problems below without using your calculator. Then, use your calculator to check your answers. The answer key is on page 386.

1.
$$
\begin{array}{r}
275 \\
409 \\
+\ 128 \\
\end{array}
$$

2.
$$
\begin{array}{r}
145 \\
855 \\
+\ 1,450 \\
\end{array}
$$

3.
$$
\begin{array}{r}
650 \\
401 \\
+\ 399 \\
\end{array}
$$

4.
$$
\begin{array}{r}
1,009 \\
321 \\
+\ 480 \\
\end{array}
$$

5.
$$
\begin{array}{r}
877 \\
2,590 \\
+\ 553 \\
\end{array}
$$

2. Frank's Coffee needs to order a total of 100 pounds of coffee for the week. Frank orders 18 pounds on Sunday, 23 pounds on Monday, 17 pounds on Tuesday, and 25 pounds on Wednesday. How many more pounds does Frank need to order to get to the total of 100 pounds?

(1) 100
(2) 83
(3) 42
(4) 17
(5) 0

Quick Note

"More" or "fewer" means you probably need to subtract.

Notice that the question asks how many *more* pounds Frank needs to order. When a question asks for *how many more* or *fewer,* you need to subtract. But, first, we have to figure out how many total pounds Frank has already ordered. Remember that when a question asks for a total, you add. In this case, we need to perform two operations.

Let's add up the number of pounds. Remember to regroup the digits if you get two-digit answers when you add each column.

$$\begin{array}{r} {\scriptstyle 2} \\ 18 \\ 23 \\ 17 \\ +\ 25 \\ \hline 83 \end{array}$$

This is how many pounds of coffee Frank has already ordered. To find out how many *more* he should order to get 100 pounds, we subtract what we *already have* from the total that we *need:*

$$\begin{array}{r} Need:\qquad 100 \\ Already\ have:\ -\ 83 \\ \hline \end{array}$$

We subtract the same way we add, starting with the right-most ones column. To subtract 3 from 0, we have to "borrow" from the number before it. If we can't borrow from that number, we borrow from the one before that.

We have to borrow from the 1 in 100. That means we take one 100 from the 100's column. That makes the 1 a 0 and adds the 1 to the next column to the right, making it a 10.

$$
\begin{array}{r}
\overset{0\ \ 10}{1\,0\,0} \\
-\ \ 8\,3 \\
\end{array}
$$

Then, we borrow 1 from that 10 and make it a 9 and add the one to the next column to the right:

$$
\begin{array}{r}
\overset{0\ \ \overset{9}{\cancel{10}}\ \ 1}{1\cancel{0}\,0} \\
-\ \ 8\,3 \\
\end{array}
$$

Now we can subtract 3 from 10 to get 7 and then subtract 8 from 9 to get 1. The answer is 17.

$$
\begin{array}{r}
\overset{0\ \ \overset{9}{\cancel{10}}\ \ 1}{1\cancel{0}\,0} \\
-\ \ 8\,3 \\
\hline
1\,7 \\
\end{array}
$$

Frank needs to order 17 more pounds of coffee to get to a total of 100 pounds.

———————○———————

Solve these subtraction problems below without using your calculator. Then, use your calculator to check your answers. The answer key is on page 386.

1. 128 – 17 =

2. $\begin{array}{r} 456 \\ -\ 299 \\ \hline \end{array}$

3. $\begin{array}{r} 770 \\ -\ 319 \\ \hline \end{array}$

4. 382 – 45 – 209 =

5. $\begin{array}{r} 1,422 \\ -\ 1,010 \\ \hline \end{array}$

6. $\begin{array}{r} 500 \\ -\ 127 \\ \hline \end{array}$

7. $1,200 - 798 =$

8. $2,350 - 1,555 =$

———————⊙———————

4. Farmer Ted is putting a fence around his rectangular garden. He wants to leave a 4-foot opening so he can get in. The total distance around the garden is 108 feet. Which is the correct expression to find out how much fencing Ted needs?

    (1) 108×4
    (2) $108 \div 4$
    (3) $108 - 4$
    (4) $108 + 4$
    (5) $108 + 4 + 4$

If Farmer Ted were putting a fence around his entire garden, he'd need 108 feet, but we know that he wants to leave a 4-foot opening, so he doesn't need any fencing for that. That means we should subtract 4 feet from the total of 108 feet. Answer (3) correctly shows this expression.

———————⊙———————

ANSWER KEY

Addition Problem Solutions

1. 812

2. 2,450

3. 1,450

4. 1,810

5. 4,020

Subtraction Problem Solutions

1. 111

2. 157

3. 451

4. 128

5. 412

WHOLE NUMBER PRACTICE

1. Rob has a bank account that allows for a negative balance. This month Rob starts with a balance of $1,250. He writes a $453 check for supplies, a $150 check for electricity, and a $900 check for advertising and marketing. What is Rob's balance in dollars at the end of the month?

    (1) −1,250
    (2) −253
    (3) 0
    (4) 253
    (5) 1,503

This is similar to Frank's Coffee ordering problem. First, we have to figure out how much Rob spent this month, so we add all his expenses in dollars. Don't forget to carry if necessary.

$$
\begin{array}{r}
\overset{1}{4}53 \\
150 \\
+\ \ 900 \\
\hline
\end{array}
$$

Rob spent $1,503 this month. Now we have to subtract that from his beginning balance of $1,250 to figure out what the balance is. We know that it will be a negative balance, so we will have a negative answer.

How do we subtract a big number from a smaller number? First, we find the positive difference between 1,503 and 1,250. That means that we put the smaller number under the larger number to find the difference. Then, we add a negative sign to the answer to make it negative.

We start at the right. We subtract 0 from 3

$$
\begin{array}{r}
1503 \\
-\ \ 1250 \\
\hline
3
\end{array}
$$

Now we have to subtract 5 from 0, but since you can't take 5 from 0, we have to regroup.

$$\begin{array}{r} \overset{4\ \ 1}{1\cancel{5}03} \\ -\ 1250 \\ \hline 3 \end{array}$$

Now we can subtract 5 from 10 and subtract 2 from 4.

$$\begin{array}{r} \overset{4\ \ 1}{1\cancel{5}03} \\ -\ 1250 \\ \hline 253 \end{array}$$

Since 1 subtracted from 1 gives us 0, the answer is just 253. We know it is *negative*, so the answer is that Rob has a balance of negative $253, or $–253, in his account.

2. Julianna is at the Swiss Alps ski resort. The temperature is 13 degrees near the base of the mountain and –5 degrees at the top. How much warmer is it near the base of the mountain?

(1)   0 degrees
(2)   5 degrees
(3)   8 degrees
(4)   13 degrees
(5)   18 degrees

Use the number line. To get from –5 to zero, we move 5 units, and then we have to move another 13 units to get to 13 degrees. We moved a total of 5 + 13 = 18 units. It is 18 degrees warmer at the base of the mountain.

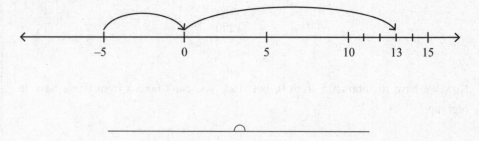

3. Carla needs $1,820 for a laptop. She already has $984 in the bank and just deposited her $346 paycheck. How much more does Carla need for the laptop?

    (1) $490
    (2) $836
    (3) $1,474
    (4) $2,804
    (5) $3,150

Carla has $984 plus $346 so far:

$$\begin{array}{r} 984 \\ +346 \\ \hline 1330 \end{array}$$

She has a total of $1,330. To figure out how much *more* she needs, subtract:

$$\begin{array}{r} 1,820 \\ -1,330 \\ \hline 490 \end{array}$$

Carla needs $490 more to have enough money for the laptop.

In some cases, the GED may give you extra information. This information is there only to distract you from what's important. Concentrate only on the information that is necessary to solve the problem.

4. Syd delivered 45 newspapers Sunday morning and then 25 more that evening. Kayla delivered 52 newspapers Sunday morning and then 22 more that afternoon. Which is the correct expression to find the total number of newspapers Syd delivered?

    (1)   45 + 52
    (2)   45 + 25
    (3)   45 + 22
    (4)   52 + 22
    (5)   52 + 25

Kayla's information isn't important because the question asks only about *Syd*. Disregard all the information about Kayla. Syd delivered 45 + 25 newspapers. Answer (2) is correct.

Some questions will have "Not enough information is given" as answer choice (5).

5. The sporting goods store had a sale on tennis rackets. At the end of the first day, the store had sold 78 tennis rackets. At the end of the second day, the store had sold another 123 tennis rackets. How many tennis rackets were left at the beginning of the third day?

    (1)   45
    (2)   78
    (3)   123
    (4)   201
    (5)   Not enough information is given.

Don't rush into selecting "not enough information given" when you see it as a choice
Try to solve first.

When a question asks "how many are left," we have to subtract. We know the store sold
78 + 123 tennis rackets. Add:

$$\begin{array}{r} \overset{1}{78} \\ + 123 \\ \hline 201 \end{array}$$

They sold a total of 201 rackets, but the question asks how many *are left*. So we subtract 201 from the total they had before the sale. That information, however, is missing.
So we cannot solve the problem, and we select (5).

Quick Note

Try to solve all the
problems—do not rush
to select "Not enough
information is given."

WHOLE NUMBER DRILL

1. When Susan woke up this morning, the temperature was –3 degrees. By the time she got to work, the temperature had risen 10 degrees. What was the temperature in degrees when Susan got to work?

   (1) –3
   (2) 0
   (3) 7
   (4) 10
   (5) Not enough information given

2. Since the beginning of the month, Karla has written a check for $150 and then made a deposit of $80. What is Karla's checking account balance?

   (1) $70
   (2) $80
   (3) $150
   (4) $230
   (5) Not enough information is given.

3. Phineas is collecting cans for a charity drive. He collects 45 cans on Sunday morning and 28 cans Sunday evening. On Tuesday he collects 53 cans and on Wednesday morning he collects 17 cans. Which is the correct expression to find the total number of cans Phineas collected on Sunday?

   (1) 17 + 53
   (2) 17 + 45
   (3) 28 + 45
   (4) 28 + 53
   (5) 45 + 53

4. Caroline has 90 flowers and has to make bunches with 15 flowers each. How many bunches can she make?

    (1) 90
    (2) 45
    (3) 15
    (4)   6
    (5) Not enough information is given.

5. Ferguson has 36 CDs in his collection. Andrew has 18 more CDs than Ferguson has. How many CDs does Andrew have?

    (1) 18
    (2) 36
    (3) 44
    (4) 54
    (5) Not enough information given.

MULTIPLICATION AND DIVISION

Multiplication

Multiplication can be represented in a few different ways. You need to review your basic multiplication facts to get through these types of problems with ease.

$$4 \times 5$$
$$(4)(5)$$
$$4 \cdot 5$$

Quick Note

When you see words such as "per" or "each," you may need to multiply.

Let's work through a sample multiplication problem. Fancy Foods catered a wedding for 95 people. The cost of food and drinks for each person was $45. How much did the food and drinks cost for the entire wedding party?

If the problem has the words "per" or "each", that means it is likely a multiplication problem. If there was a total of 95 people and the food and drinks for *each* person cost $45, we need to multiply to find out the total cost.

$$
\begin{array}{r}
95 \\
\times\ \ 45 \\
\hline
\end{array}
$$

Multiplying is similar to addition in that you work from right to left, first multiplying the 5 ones in 45 by the 5 ones in 95. As in addition, you put the ones value in the ones column and regroup the tens value to the tens column.

$$
\begin{array}{r}
\overset{2}{9}5 \\
\times\ \ 45 \\
\hline
5 \\
\end{array}
$$

Then multiply the 5 ones by the 9 tens in 95. That gives you 45. Then add the 2 tens that were regrouped to get 47. Put this under the total bar next to the 5 to get 475.

$$
\begin{array}{r}
\overset{2}{9}5 \\
\times\ \ 45 \\
\hline
475 \\
\end{array}
$$

Then you start the same process with the 4 tens in 45. First, write a 0 in the rightmost column. This 0 indicates that we are now multiplying by *tens*.

Now do the same thing with the 4 tens in 45. First multiply 4 by the 5 ones in 95. That's 20, so we put 0 to the left of the 0 already in place and regroup the 2.

$$
\begin{array}{r}
\overset{2}{9}5 \\
\times 45 \\
\hline
475 \\
00
\end{array}
$$

Now we multiply the 4 by 9, to get 36, and add the 2 that is regrouped to get 38. Add 475 plus 3800.

$$
\begin{array}{r}
\overset{2}{9}5 \\
\times 45 \\
\hline
475 \\
3800 \\
\hline
4275
\end{array}
$$

Food and drinks at the wedding cost $4,275.

---

1. **Singh sews costumes for the theatre. For one production, he uses 12 yards of fabric for each costume. Singh makes 35 costumes on Monday and 32 costumes on Tuesday. How many total yards of fabric does Singh use?**

We have a lot going on here. First let's figure out how many yards Singh uses on Monday. The key word here is *each*, which means we multiply. On Monday Singh makes 35 costumes and for each costume he uses 12 yards of fabric. To figure out how many yards of fabric he uses on Monday, multiply.

Starting at the right, multiply the 2 in 12 by the 5 in 35. Don't forget to regroup if needed.

$$
\begin{array}{r}
\overset{1}{3}5 \\
\times 12 \\
\hline
0
\end{array}
$$

Quick Note

When you see words such as "per" or "each," you may need to multiply.

Now multiply the 2 by the 3 in 35, and add the regrouped 1.

$$\begin{array}{r} \overset{1}{}35 \\ \times12 \\ \hline 70 \end{array}$$

Before multiplying by the 1 ten in 12, don't forget to insert a 0.

$$\begin{array}{r} \overset{1}{}35 \\ \times12 \\ \hline 70 \\ \overset{1}{3}50 \\ \hline 420 \end{array}$$

On Monday Singh uses 420 yards of fabric. But we're not done! Now we have to do the multiplication to figure out how many yards he used on Tuesday.

$$\begin{array}{r} 32 \\ \times12 \\ \hline 64 \\ 320 \\ \hline 384 \end{array}$$

We're still not done. The question asks how many *total* yards of fabric Singh uses. That means we add 420 and 384.

$$\begin{array}{r} \overset{1}{}420 \\ +384 \\ \hline 804 \end{array}$$

Singh uses a total of 804 yards of fabric on Monday and Tuesday.

Try these. Do the calculations by hand and then check your work on your calculator. It is important to practice multiplication by hand so you can more easily catch any calculator mistakes. Refer back to the Fancy Food and Singh problems for a reminder of how to perform the multiplication correctly.

MULTIPLICATION DRILL

1. At Joe's Pet Grooming, they use 48 gallons of water for each pet bath. If Joe's gave 132 pets baths last week, how many gallons of water did they use?

    (1)   48
    (2)   180
    (3) 6,336
    (4) 6,600
    (5) Not enough information given.

2. Pete's Canning can ship 45 cans of snow peas or 70 cans of corn in 1 carton. On Friday they shipped out 19 cartons of snow peas and 28 cartons of corn. What was the total number of cans they shipped out on Friday?

    (1)   47
    (2)   115
    (3)   855
    (4) 1,960
    (5) 2,815

3. A truck travels an average of 65 miles per hour on a certain trip and a car travels an average of 58 miles per hour on the same trip. How many hours will it take the truck to complete the trip?

    (1)   3
    (2)   7
    (3)   8
    (4) 10
    (5) Not enough information is given.

4. Marla plans to cycle 70 miles per week for the next 12 weeks to train for a triathlon. She will also run 30 miles per week and swim 5 miles per week. How many miles will Marla cycle, run and swim over the next 12 weeks?

(1)   840
(2)   1,260
(3)   4,200
(4) 25,200
(5)   Not enough information is given.

5. Janine bought a new computer system and set up a payment plan. She pays $145.70 every month for 16 months. What is the total cost of the computer?

(1) $2,331.20
(2) $2,768.30
(3) $8,742.00
(4) $23,312.00
(5)   Not enough information is given.

DIVISION

Division can be represented in a few different ways:

$$\frac{48}{6} = \qquad 6\overline{)48} \qquad 48 \div 6 =$$

These all ask, "How many times does 6 go into 48?" The answer is 8. You need to review basic division facts to get through these problems with ease. Let's try a division problem like one that you might see on the GED.

───────────────

1. Kelly earned $684 last week at her position as a physician's assistant. If Kelly worked 38 hours, at what hourly rate is she paid?

The giveaway here is the word *rate*. Words such as *rate, per, each* and *average* often indicate division. This is often true of multiplication as well. That is because multiplication and division are closely related.

Ask yourself, am I looking for a *per item* or *per hour rate*? If you are, you probably need to divide.

The total amount in a division problem is what you need to divide *into*. We know that Kelly earned a total of $684, so we divide 38 hours *into* $684. Here's what that looks like:

$$38\overline{)684}$$

In a division problem, you work from left to right. First, try to divide 38 into 6. 6 is too small, so we add the next digit. That means we try to divide 38 into 68.

We find that 38 goes into 68 one time. So we put a 1 on top and we subtract 38 from the 68. There is 30 left over.

$$
\begin{array}{r}
1 \\
38\overline{)684} \\
\underline{38} \\
30
\end{array}
$$

Quick Note

When you see words such as "per," "rate," or "each," you may need to divide.

Now we bring the next number "down" next to what we have left over, changing 30 into 304.

$$
\begin{array}{r}
1 \\
38\overline{)684} \\
38 \\
\hline
304
\end{array}
$$

Now we divide 38 into 304. Take a guess of how many times 38 goes into 304. We know that 38×10 is 380, and that's too much, so 10 is too high. How about 9?

$$
\begin{array}{r}
\overset{7}{3}8 \\
\times\ \ 9 \\
\hline
342
\end{array}
$$

Still too big. How about 8?

$$
\begin{array}{r}
38 \\
\times\ \ 8 \\
\hline
304
\end{array}
$$

That's it. The more you multiply and divide, the easier this "guessing" will become.

38 goes into 304 exactly 8 times, so put 8 up next to the 1. That makes 18, so 38 goes into 684 18 times.

$$
\begin{array}{r}
18 \\
38\overline{)684} \\
38 \\
\hline
304
\end{array}
$$

Now go back to the problem. What does our answer mean? It means that Kelly makes $18 per hour as a physician's assistant.

———————◯———————

2. Franco can type 70 words per minute. He has a report to type with 4,760 words in it. How long will it take him to type the report?

The word *per* helps us know that this is a division problem. The total number is 4,760 words and the rate is 70 words per minute.

We divide 70 into 4,760:

$$70\overline{)4760}$$

First we try to divide 70 into 47, but 47 is too small, so we try to divide 70 into 476. 70 times 10 is 700, and that's almost twice as big as 476, so let's try 5.

$$\begin{array}{r} 70 \\ \times\ \ 5 \\ \hline 350 \end{array}$$

Not big enough. Let's try 6.

$$\begin{array}{r} 70 \\ \times\ \ 6 \\ \hline 420 \end{array}$$

That's closer. Let's see if 7 works.

$$\begin{array}{r} 70 \\ \times\ \ 7 \\ \hline 490 \end{array}$$

That's bigger than 476, so we should use 6.

We put the 6 on top. 70 times 6 is 420, so we put that under 476 and subtract. We have 56 left over.

$$\begin{array}{r} 6 \\ 70\overline{)4,760} \\ 4\ 20 \\ \hline 56 \end{array}$$

Quick Note

Even if you don't see the word rate in a problem, if it gives a rate, think about division.

Then we bring the 0 down and turn 56 into 560. How many times does 70 go into 560? Looking at our previous work, we see that $70 \times 7 = 490$. Let's see about 70×8:

$$\begin{array}{r} 70 \\ \times\ \ 8 \\ \hline 560 \end{array}$$

We put the 8 on top. 70 goes into 4,760 68 times. Go back to the problem to understand what that means. That means that it will take Franco 68 minutes to type his report.

$$\begin{array}{r} 68 \\ 70\overline{)4,760} \\ \underline{4\ 20} \\ 560 \end{array}$$

What if the answers were written in terms of hours? In order to go from minutes to hours, divide by 60:

$$60\overline{)68}$$

This is not a very complicated problem. 60 goes into 68 one time.

$$\begin{array}{r} 1 \\ 60\overline{)68} \\ \underline{60} \\ 8 \end{array}$$

But what do we do with the 8 left over? There are no more numbers to bring down. 8 is the **remainder** in this calculation. **Remainders** are what's left over when there are no more numbers to bring down. It will take Franco 1 hour and 8 minutes to type the report. (That's equivalent to 68 minutes.)

---

1. Maria is making fruit salad at her restaurant. She puts 12 grapes into each fruit salad. If she has 940 grapes, how many complete fruit salads can she make?

    (1)   78
    (2)   80
    (3)   94
    (4)   100
    (5)   928

We see the word *each*, so we divide:

$$
\begin{array}{r}
78 \\
12\overline{)940} \\
84 \\
\hline
100 \\
96 \\
\hline
4
\end{array}
$$

Maria can make 78 complete fruit salads, but she has 4 grapes left over. There is nothing to do with the 4 grapes because the question asks how many *complete* fruit salads Maria can make. The extra grapes don't matter. She can make 78 *complete* fruit salads.

DIVISION DRILL

Do the calculations by hand and then check your work on your calculator. It is important to practice division by hand so you can more easily catch any calculator mistakes.

1. Corrina and her friends are on a 1,235 mile road trip. They drive 95 miles per day. How many days will it take them to complete the trip?

   (1)   10
   (2)   12
   (3)   13
   (4)   117,235
   (5)   Not enough information is given.

2. Simon is a traveling salesperson. Last month he flew a total of 5,673 miles. About how many miles per day is this if the month had 31 days?

   (1)   183
   (2)   189
   (3)   17,019
   (4)   170,190
   (5)   175,863

3. Felicia made $70,616 in salary last year. Given that a year has 52 weeks, about how much did Felicia earn per week in dollars last year? Round your answer to the nearest dollar.

   (1)   128
   (2)   135
   (3)   1,358
   (4)   1,445
   (5)   19,904

4. The stadium seats 30,240 people. The seats are arranged in rows of 12, 18, and 28. How many rows of 28 seats are in the stadium?

    (1) 1,008
    (2) 1,080
    (3) 1,680
    (4) 2,520
    (5) Not enough information is given.

5. The maple tree in Katrina's yard has grown 3.4 inches diameter in the last 17 years. About how many inches per year has the tree grown?

    (1) 20.4
    (2)   6.8
    (3)   3.4
    (4)   0.2
    (5) Not enough information is given.

AVERAGE, MEDIAN, AND MEAN

First of all, "average" and "mean" are the same thing. You will often see a GED question that has "mean" and then "average" in parentheses after:

_____ ⌣ _____

1.   Serena's class loves chocolate donuts. On Monday they ate 43, on Tuesday they ate 50, on Wednesday they had 35, on Thursday they had 30, and on Friday they had 52. What was the mean (average) number of donuts they ate per day?

(1)   42
(2)   45
(3)   50
(4)   55
(5)   Not enough information given.

Quick Note

"Mean" or "average" is a combination of addition and division.

In order to calculate the average, you add all the numbers in a problem and divide the sum by how many items (numbers) you added.

First we add:

$$\begin{array}{r} {}^{1} \\ 43 \\ 50 \\ 35 \\ 30 \\ +\ 52 \\ \hline 210 \end{array}$$ ←*Don't forget to regroup/carry the 1.*

Now we divide the sum by the number of items/numbers. There were 5 numbers, one for each weekday, so we divide by 5:

$$5\overline{)210}^{42}$$

42 is the average of the 5 numbers. Serena's class ate an average of 42 donuts per day.

You may also be asked for the median of a set of numbers. Let's use Serena's class and their donut addiction. To find the median of a set of numbers, write the numbers out in ascending order, from least to greatest:

30, 35, 43, 50, 52

The median is simply the number in the middle. In this case, it is 43.

If you have an even amount of numbers, you take the average of the two numbers in the middle.

1. Jacques did a survey of the cost of popcorn at 6 different movie theaters. His results are listed below.

Theater 1 $2.95
Theater 2 $3.25
Theater 3 $2.50
Theater 4 $2.25
Theater 5 $3.50
Theater 6 $3.50

What is the median price of popcorn?

First, write the numbers in ascending order:

2.25; 2.50; 2.95; 3.25; 3.50; 3.50

We dropped the dollar sign to make it easier to see the numbers. The two middle numbers are 2.95 and 3.25. To get the median, we need to take the average of these two numbers. That means we add them and divide the sum by 2:

$$
\begin{array}{r}
\overset{1\ \ 1}{2.95} \\
+\ \ 3.25 \\
\hline
6.20
\end{array}
$$

The sum is 6.20. Now we divide that by 2:

$$
\begin{array}{r}
3.10 \\
2\overline{)6.20}
\end{array}
$$

The median price of popcorn is $3.10.

2. Fred took photos every day of his 4-day vacation. Day 1 he took 23 photos, Day 2 he took 38 photos, Day 3 he took 38 photos, and Day 4 he took 49 photos. What is the mean number of photos Fred took per day?

(1) 37
(2) 38
(3) 45
(4) 49
(5) 148

To get the mean or the average, add the numbers and divide by the number of items.

First we add:

$$
\begin{array}{r}
\overset{2}{2}3 \quad \leftarrow Carry\ the\ 2 \\
38 \\
38 \\
+\ \ 49 \\
\hline
148
\end{array}
$$

Quick Note

$$mean = \frac{sum}{\#items}$$

Now we divide the sum, 148, by the number of items, which in this case is 4:

$$
\begin{array}{r}
37 \\
4\overline{)148}
\end{array}
$$

The mean number of photos Fred took was 37.

What is the median number of photos he took?

Put the numbers in order:

$$23;\ 38;\ 38;\ 49$$

There is an even number of items, so we take the average of the middle two numbers. We add 38 and 38:

$$
\begin{array}{r}
\overset{1}{3}8 \\
+\ \ 38 \\
\hline
76
\end{array}
$$

Divide by 2:

$$2\overline{)76}^{\,38}$$

The median number of photos Fred took was 38. You may have noticed that the average of two numbers that are the same is equal to those numbers. You don't have to remember that, but it will always happen that way if you have all the same numbers.

AVERAGE, MEAN, AND MEDIAN DRILL

1. Donna does sit-ups every day and keeps track in the table below.

Sunday	28
Monday	27
Tuesday	30
Wednesday	30
Thursday	31
Friday	32
Saturday	25

   What is the average number of sit-ups Donna does every day?

   (1) 20
   (2) 25
   (3) 29
   (4) 35
   (5) 39

2. The running times for members of the track team to run the 100-yard dash are recorded in the table below.

Runner	Time
Andra	12.2
Kim	11.1
Kyle	10.9
Marnie	11.5
Rob	12.1
Daryl	11.2
Stephan	11.5

   What is the median running time for the team?

   (1) 11.2
   (2) 11.35
   (3) 11.5
   (4) 12.0
   (5) 13.4

3. Sy's Shoes kept track of the number of customers in the store every hour for 9 hours: 20, 23, 48, 55, 63, 58, 32, 30, 40. What is the average number of customers per hour?

    (1) 40
    (2) 41
    (3) 45
    (4) 48
    (5) 51

4. Michelle's bowling scores for the past 5 weeks were: 220, 255, 190, 240, 300. What is Michelle's mean score?

    (1) 230
    (2) 231
    (3) 240
    (4) 241
    (5) Not enough information is given.

5. The basketball team's scores at the last 8 games were: 38, 21, 68, 71, 62, 43, 27, 54. What was the median score?

    (1) 40.5
    (2) 43
    (3) 48.5
    (4) 64
    (5) Not enough information is given.

EXPONENTS AND SQUARE ROOTS

Exponents are just numbers that tell you how many times to multiply a number by itself. The exponent is the small number on the upper right-hand side. See the expression below:

$$4^2$$

In this case, the small number 2 tells us to multiply 4 by itself. The 2 tells us that we write the number 4 two times:

$$4^2 = 4 \times 4 = 16$$

In this expression: 2^3 the small number 3 tells us to multiply 2 three times:

$$2^3 = 2 \times 2 \times 2$$

To calculate this, multiply the first part first:

$$2 \times 2 = 4$$

Then multiply:

$$4 \times 2 = 8.$$

So: $2^3 = 8$

The exponent tells us how many times to write the number:

$$5^2 = 5 \times 5 = 25$$
$$5^3 = 5 \times 5 \times 5 = 125$$
$$3^2 = 3 \times 3 = 9$$
$$3^3 = 3 \times 3 \times 3 = 27$$

When the exponent is 3, it's easier to multiply the first two numbers first and then take that product and multiply by the last number. In the example seen below:

$$4^3 = 4 \times 4 \times 4$$

First multiply $4 \times 4 = 16$. Then multiply 16 by 4: $16 \times 4 = 64$.

$$
\begin{array}{c}
\underbrace{4 \times 4} \times 4 \\
16 \quad \times 4 = 64
\end{array}
$$

The square root of a number is kind of like the reverse of the exponent. The square root of some number, *x*, is the number you multiply by itself to produce *x*.

For example, the square root of 9 is 3, because when you multiply 3 by itself, you get 9: $3 \times 3 = 9$ *and* $\sqrt{9} = 3$.

It's easier to see if you look at a table of some exponential and square root expressions.

$1^2 = 1$	$\sqrt{1} = 1$
$2^2 = 4$	$\sqrt{4} = 2$
$3^2 = 9$	$\sqrt{9} = 3$
$4^2 = 16$	$\sqrt{16} = 4$
$5^2 = 25$	$\sqrt{25} = 5$
$6^2 = 36$	$\sqrt{36} = 6$
$7^2 = 49$	$\sqrt{49} = 7$
$8^2 = 64$	$\sqrt{64} = 8$
$9^2 = 81$	$\sqrt{81} = 9$
$10^2 = 100$	$\sqrt{100} = 10$

Make sure you look carefully at the exponent when you see an exponential problem so you know how many times to write the number.

For larger numbers, you'll probably need to use your calculator.

EXPONENTS AND SQUARE ROOTS DRILL

1. $3^3 =$

2. $\sqrt{25}$

3. $\sqrt{81}$

4. $9^3 =$

5. $\sqrt{225}$

6. $23^2 =$

7. $19^3 =$

8. $\sqrt{2,025}$

9. $\sqrt{4,624}$

10. $33^2 =$

FRACTIONS, PERCENTS, AND DECIMALS

Fractions are the numbers in between integers, such as:

$$\frac{1}{8}; -\frac{2}{3}; 8\frac{1}{2}; \frac{25}{7}$$

Fractions on the number line lie between the integers:

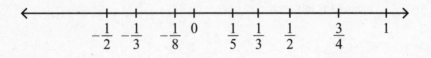

There are a couple of different ways to write fractions. The most common way is with a smaller number over a larger number. The top number in a fraction is called the *numerator* and the bottom number is called the *denominator*.

A *mixed number* is one that has and integer plus a fractional part: $8\frac{1}{2}$

It is called a *mixed number,* because it has two kinds of numbers, the integer part and the fractional part.

An *improper fraction* has a numerator that is bigger than the denominator: $\frac{25}{7}$

Any improper fraction can be written as a mixed number, and vice versa. For example,

$8\frac{1}{2}$ can be written as an improper fraction. To convert, use the following three steps:

Step 1 Multiply the integer (8) by the denominator of the fraction (2):
$8 \times 2 = 16$.

Step 2 Take this number, 16, and add the numerator (top number) of the fraction: $16 + 1 = 17$. This is the top number of your final answer.

Step 3 Put your new top number, 17, over the old bottom number, 2: $\frac{17}{2}$.

Quick Note

In a fraction the top number is the *numerator*; the bottom number is the *denominator*.

$$\frac{numerator}{denominator}$$

$\dfrac{25}{7}$ may also be written as a mixed number. To go from an improper fraction to a mixed

number, use three steps:

 Divide the numerator by the denominator: $7\overline{)25}^{\ 3r\,4}$.
When you divide 25 by 7, it goes in 3 times with a *remainder* of 4. That means 4 is left over.

 The integer part of the mixed number is how many times it goes in: 3.

The fraction part is the remainder, 4, over the denominator, 7: $\dfrac{4}{7}$ The new

mixed number is $3\dfrac{4}{7}$.

You can check to be sure you've correctly converted an improper fraction into a mixed number by converting it back to an improper fraction:

1. Multiply the integer, 3, by the denominator of the fraction, 7: $3 \times 7 = 21$
2. Add the numerator, 4, to this number: $21 + 4 = 25$
3. Put this number over the denominator of the fraction: $\dfrac{25}{7}$

This is what we started with, so the conversion is correct.

You may see a question like this one:

2. On the number line below, which letter most closely represents the number $-\dfrac{5}{4}$?

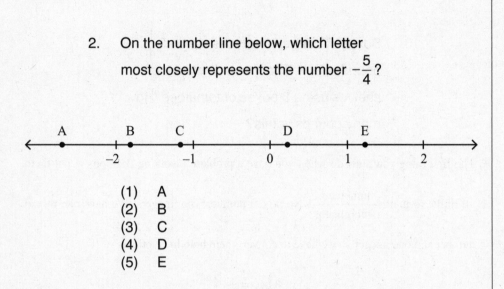

(1) A
(2) B
(3) C
(4) D
(5) E

It's negative, so you can eliminate D and E as possible answer choices because they are both positive (to the right of zero on the number line).

It may be easier if you think of $-\dfrac{5}{4}$ as $-1\dfrac{1}{4}$. This number is actually a little *less* than –1, which means it is a little to the *left* of –1 on the number line. Point C is just to the left of –1 on the number line, so (3) is the best answer.

You will have to add and subtract integers and fractions. It makes it easier if you write the integer as a fraction.

All integers can be written as fractions. To write 10 as a fraction, simply put it over 1: $\dfrac{10}{1}$

Just put any integer over 1, and you have a fraction.

$$\dfrac{5}{1} = 5$$

$$\dfrac{13}{1} = 13$$

Take a look at problem 10 below.

---

10.   Boxes of canned tomatoes weigh $3\frac{1}{4}$ pounds each. The grocer is stocking his shelves using 8 boxes of tomatoes. How many pounds is this?

The first thing you must do when you have a problem involving fractions is put them all in the format: $\dfrac{numerator}{denominator}$. No mixed numbers, no integers. We have one mixed number and one integer so we have to convert them both to fractions.

$$8 \text{ becomes } \frac{8}{1}$$

$$3\frac{1}{4} \text{ becomes } \frac{13}{4}$$

So if this tomato-stocking grocer has 8 boxes weighing $3\frac{1}{4}$ pounds each, how do we figure out how many pounds this is in all? We multiply.

MULTIPLYING FRACTIONS

Multiplying fractions is easy. You just multiply the numerators straight across and the denominators straight across:

$$\frac{8}{1} \times \frac{13}{4} = \frac{8 \times 13}{1 \times 4} = \frac{104}{4}$$

You will probably not see the answer written as $\frac{104}{4}$. You have to reduce this fraction.

To go from an improper fraction to a proper fraction, divide: be written as

$$4\overline{)104}^{\,26} \text{ so } \frac{104}{4} = 26 \text{ (no remainder)}$$

That means that there are 26 pounds in all.

DIVIDING FRACTIONS

What if you have to divide fractions?

What if someone wanted to divide 10 pounds of coleslaw into $\frac{1}{3}$ pound containers? How many containers of coleslaw would they get?

First put 10 in $\dfrac{\text{numerator}}{\text{denominator}}$ format: $\dfrac{10}{1}$.

The problem is now: $\dfrac{10}{1} \div \dfrac{1}{3}$

When you divide fractions, you invert the second fraction, meaning you switch the numerator and the denominator: $\dfrac{1}{3}$ becomes $\dfrac{3}{1}$.

The problem is now: $\dfrac{10}{1} \times \dfrac{3}{1}$ and you just multiply across:

$$\frac{10}{1} \times \frac{3}{1} = \frac{10 \times 3}{1 \times 1} = \frac{30}{1} = 30$$

The answer is that they'd get 30 containers of coleslaw from the original 10 pounds.

ADDING AND SUBTRACTING FRACTIONS

When adding and subtracting fractions, the first thing you have to do is get the fractions into the $\dfrac{\text{numerator}}{\text{denominator}}$ format.

Let's take a look at an example:

$$6\frac{1}{3}+\frac{3}{4}=$$

First we convert the first fraction into $\dfrac{\text{numerator}}{\text{denominator}}$ format:

$$6\frac{1}{3}=\frac{(6\times3)+1}{3}=\frac{19}{3}$$

Now the problem is:

$$\frac{19}{3}+\frac{3}{4}=$$

However, we cannot add or subtract fractions that have different denominators. So we have to find a *common denominator*. That means we have to find the lowest number that both of the denominators divide into evenly.

In this case we need a number that 3 and 4 divide into evenly. An easy way to find a common denominator is to multiply the two numbers together: $3 \times 4 = 12$. We can use 12 as our common denominator. That means we want to make each fraction have a denominator of 12.

We can't just change the denominator into 12; we have to have it make sense mathematically.

Quick Note

Fractions can only be added and subtracted if they have the same denominator.

Here's how that goes. Let's take one fraction at a time. We'll start with $\dfrac{19}{3}$.

We $\dfrac{19}{3}$ want to be some amount of twelfths. That looks like this:

$$\frac{19}{3}=\frac{?}{12}$$

We have to think, how do we turn 3 into 12? The answer is we multiply it by some number. What number do we multiply 3 by to get 12? The answer is 4. To change the 3 into 12 we multiply it by 4. If we multiply the 3 by 4, we have to multiply the 19 in the numerator by 4 as well:

$$\frac{19\times4}{3\times4}=\frac{76}{12}$$

The fraction $\frac{19}{3}$ is equivalent to the fraction $\frac{76}{12}$. As long as we multiply the numerator and denominator of a fraction by the same number, we keep the same fraction.

In simpler terms, it might be easier for you to think that if you got 5 out of 10 questions correct on a test, you got $\frac{1}{2}$ of the questions right. However, what your brain is really doing is converting from the fraction $\frac{5}{10}$ to the fraction $\frac{1}{2}$. Look: $\frac{1\times5}{2\times5}=\frac{5}{10}$. The fractions are the same; it's just that the numerator and denominator of one fraction are multiplied by some number (5 in this case) to get the other fraction.

Let's get back to our problem. We know now that $\frac{19}{3}=\frac{76}{12}$.

Now the problem is: $\frac{76}{12}+\frac{3}{4}=$ …and we have to convert $\frac{3}{4}$ to a fraction with twelfths in the denominator:

$$\frac{3}{4}=\frac{?}{12}$$

To turn 4 into 12, we multiply by 3. So we do the same thing to the numerator:

$$\frac{3\times3}{4\times3}=\frac{9}{12}$$

Now the problem is: $\frac{76}{12}+\frac{9}{12}=$

Once you have the denominators equal to each other, you can just add across:

$$\frac{76}{12}+\frac{9}{12}=\frac{85}{12}$$

To check if you can simplify this further, try dividing 12 into 85: $12\overline{)85}^{\,7r1}$. This fraction could also be written as a mixed numeral: $7\frac{1}{12}$

PUTTING FRACTIONS IN THEIR SIMPLEST FORM

Fractional answers on the GED will most likely be in their simplest form. You will not see an answer such as $\frac{12}{24}$ because this fraction can be reduced to $\frac{1}{2}$. For some fractions, it will be easy to see the simplest form. For others, you have to work a little bit.

To find the simplest form of a fraction, think about the *factors* of the numerator and the denominator. Remember those? Factors are numbers that divide evenly into another number. For example, the factors of 12 are: 1, 2, 3, 4, 6, and 12. The factors of 24 are: 1, 2, 3, 4, 6, 8, 12, and 24.

The way to simplify a fraction is to divide the numerator and denominator by a common factor. Both 12 and 24 have a factor of 6, so let's see how that works.

First, we divide the numerator and the denominator by 6:

$$\frac{12 \div 6}{24 \div 6} = \frac{2}{4}$$

$\frac{2}{4}$ is equivalent to $\frac{12}{24}$. We have simplified $\frac{12}{24}$.

But have we simplified it to its *simplest* form? Nope. Because there is still a number that divides evenly into 2 and 4:

$$\frac{2 \div 2}{4 \div 2} = \frac{1}{2}$$

Now the fraction is in its simplest form. Any time the numerator is 1, the fraction is in its simplest form. It does not *have* to be 1, but it's a sure thing if it is 1.

When you are trying to reduce, or simplify, a fraction, use the *greatest common factor* of the numerator and the denominator.

Let's look at the factors of 12 and 24 again:

Factors of 12: 1, 2, 3, 4, 6, and 12.
Factors of 24: 1, 2, 3, 4, 6, 8, 12, and 24.

What is the *greatest common factor*? 12 is the greatest number on both lists. It is the greatest common factor. If we divide the numerator and the denominator of a fraction by their greatest common factor, we get the simplest form of the fraction:

$$\frac{12 \div 12}{24 \div 12} = \frac{1}{2}$$

That's the quick way to get right to the simplest form.

Try to simplify these fractions. (Some are already in their simplest form.)

1. $\dfrac{2}{8} =$

2. $\dfrac{4}{12} =$

3. $\dfrac{1}{32} =$

4. $\dfrac{7}{8} =$

5. $\dfrac{12}{3} =$

To summarize adding and subtracting fractions:

1. Find a common denominator
2. Convert each fraction into a new fraction with the common denominator.
3. Add or subtract the numerators from left to right.

POSITIVE AND NEGATIVE FRACTION DRILL

Try these positive and negative fraction problems. Try to reduce your answers to their simplest form. Remember: To do that, see if you can divide the numerator and the denominator by the same number. The answers are at the very bottom of the page.

1. $\left(\dfrac{3}{8}\right)\left(-\dfrac{5}{3}\right) =$

2. $24 \div \dfrac{2}{3} =$

3. $\dfrac{4}{17} - \dfrac{1}{2} =$

4. $18 \div \dfrac{1}{2} =$

5. $120 \times \left(-\dfrac{3}{4}\right) =$

6. $\dfrac{3}{5} + \dfrac{2}{3} =$

7. $2\dfrac{3}{4} - \dfrac{5}{8} =$

8. $6\dfrac{1}{2} \div 26 =$

1. $\dfrac{5}{8}$; 2. 36; 3. $-\dfrac{9}{34}$; 4. 36; 5. –90; 6. $\dfrac{19}{15}$; 7. $\dfrac{17}{8}$; 8. $\dfrac{1}{4}$

FRACTIONS DRILL

1. Karim is driving $10\frac{3}{4}$ miles to his job. He stops after $3\frac{1}{3}$ miles to pick up a sandwich. How many more miles must he drive to get to his job?

   (1) $7\frac{1}{6}$

   (2) $7\frac{1}{4}$

   (3) $7\frac{1}{3}$

   (4) $7\frac{5}{12}$

   (5) $7\frac{1}{2}$

2. Mallory worked $36\frac{3}{4}$ hours one week and $40\frac{1}{4}$ hours the following week. How many more hours did she work the second week than the first week?

   (1) $3\frac{1}{4}$

   (2) $3\frac{1}{2}$

   (3) 4

   (4) $4\frac{1}{2}$

   (5) Not enough information is given.

3. A recipe calls for $3\frac{1}{3}$ cups of water, $1\frac{2}{5}$ cups of oil, and $\frac{7}{15}$ cup of cooking sherry. How many cups of liquid are in the recipe?

(1) $4\frac{1}{2}$

(2) 5

(3) $5\frac{1}{5}$

(4) 6

(5) Not enough information is given.

4. Natalie's gerbil gets $\frac{2}{5}$ cup of food at mealtime. She feeds her gerbil twice a day. How many cups of food does she use in 9 days?

(1) $\frac{4}{5}$

(2) $1\frac{4}{5}$

(3) $3\frac{3}{5}$

(4) $7\frac{1}{5}$

(5) $9\frac{2}{5}$

5. Ken has to divide $38\frac{1}{2}$ pounds of feed evenly among the elephants at the zoo. Each elephant eats 5 times per day. How many pounds of feed does each elephant get?

(1) 5
(2) 7.7
(3) 8
(4) 12.5
(5) Not enough information is given.

PERCENTS

Percents are just fractions with a denominator of 100. For example, 50% is the same

as $\dfrac{55}{100}$. Any percent is just that number over 100:

$$18\% = \frac{18}{100}$$

$$78\% = \frac{78}{100}$$

$$23\% = \frac{23}{100}$$

To find a certain percent of any amount, multiply the amount by the fractional equivalent of the percent.

---

1.   What is 55% of 250?

First, find the fractional equivalent of 55%: $\dfrac{55}{100}$. Next multiply the fraction by the amount: $\dfrac{55}{100} \times 250$. It is easier if you put 250 in fractional form:

$$\frac{55}{100} \times 250 = \frac{55}{100} \times \frac{250}{1}$$

Now we can multiply straight across:

$$\frac{55}{100} \times \frac{250}{1} = \frac{13,750}{100}$$

Now what do we do with that?

We divided 13,750 by 100: $100\overline{)13,750}^{\,137r50}$

The problem here is that 137 remainder 50 is not really a number that makes sense to most people. We always think in terms of fractions or decimals, even if we don't realize it. If you told your friend you saved 137 remainder 50 dollars, would that make sense to her?

When you have an answer like this, you put it in decimal format. That means that you take the remainder and put it over the divisor, or the number that you're dividing *into* another number. Here, we are dividing 100 into 13,750, so we put 50 over 100, which equals $137\frac{50}{100}$, and then that reduces to: $137\frac{1}{2}$. $137\frac{1}{2}$ is 55% of 250.

If you told your friend you saved dollars, that would probably make more sense. However, you would probably say you saved $137.50. You'd use the decimal format.

———○———

You will probably see questions on the GED in which you are given a graph. Let's take a look at this high school enrollment graph. It shows the number of juniors and seniors in each year from 2000 through 2004.

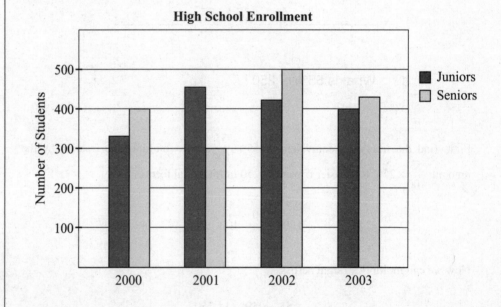

High School Enrollment

The height of each bar indicates how many juniors or seniors were enrolled in each year. The striped bar represents juniors and the plain white bar represents seniors, as indicated in the key on the right side.

For example, if you look at the year 2000, about 330 juniors and 400 seniors were enrolled. In 2001 about 450 juniors and 300 seniors were enrolled.

A percent question about a graph may ask: What was the percent increase in the number of seniors enrolled from 2001 to 2002?

A percent increase or decrease problem is solved by creating a fraction. The top number is how much the thing increased or decreased. The bottom number is the original, beginning number. In this case, the number of seniors in 2001 was 300. That is our original beginning number, so that goes on the bottom:

$$\frac{?}{300}$$

The amount that this number changes, whether it increases or decreases, is the top number. In 2001 there were 300 seniors. In 2002 there were 500 seniors, so there was an increase of 200 students. 200 is our top number:

$$\frac{200}{300}$$

Now we have to change this into a percent. In order to convert a fraction into a percent,

you set it equal to some number over 100:

$$\frac{200}{300} = \frac{x}{100}$$

To solve, you cross-multiply. That means you multiply the top number of the first fraction, which is 200 here, by the bottom number of the second fraction, which is 100. Then you multiply the bottom number of the first fraction, 300, by the top number of the second fraction, x. We have to find x.

Set up the cross-multiplication:

$$200 \times 100 = 300 \times x$$

Multiply, using your calculator:

$$20,000 = 300x$$

Divide both sides by 300:

$$x = \frac{20,000}{300}$$

$$x \cong 66$$

This is the answer in percent terms. The percent increase from 2001 to 2002 in the number of enrolled seniors is 66% (rounded a little).

2. Sam and Karen collected 540 pieces of candy during trick-or-treating for Halloween last year. This year they collected 486 pieces of candy. What is the percent decrease from last year to this year?

First, we find the difference from last year to this year. $540 - 486 = 54$.

They collected 54 pieces less. Now we put the difference over the original number, which is 540 in this problem:

$$\frac{54}{540} = 0.10$$

To convert 0.10 to percent format, multiply by 100: $0.10 \times 100 = 10$

Sam and Karen collected 10% less candy this year than last year.

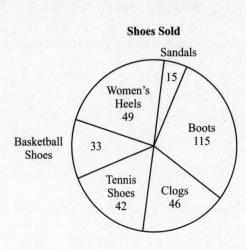

Shoes Sold

Sandals 15

Women's Heels 49

Boots 115

Basketball Shoes 33

Tennis Shoes 42

Clogs 46

10.   What percent of the shoes sold were tennis shoes?

Mark your answer in the circles in the grid on your answer sheet.

You're probably thinking "Wait a minute—where are the answer choices?" You may get a couple of questions where you will need to fill in bubbles on the answer sheet that represent numbers. The strategy is the same—just use your appropriate number operations and you'll be fine.

To find the percent of tennis shoes sold, we need to create fraction, with the number of tennis shoes sold, which is given as 45, over the total number of shoes sold. So, we have to add up all the shoes sold first.

$$
\begin{array}{r}
\textit{Regroup the 2 and the 3} \rightarrow \quad {}^{3}_{2}15 \\
115 \\
46 \\
42 \\
33 \\
+\ 49 \\
\hline
300
\end{array}
$$

So we create our fraction: $\dfrac{42}{300}$ and divide using the calculator: 0.14. To convert from decimal to percent, we *multiply* by 100: $0.14 \times 100 = 14$. The percent of tennis shoes sold is 14%.

DECIMALS

Decimals are another way of writing a fraction or a percent. It's helpful to think in terms of dollars, as we did in the previous problem. $137.50 is a decimal, as are all numbers with the decimal point that represent numbers in between whole number.

All fractions and percents can be written as decimals:

Fraction	Percent	Decimal
$\frac{1}{2}$	50%	0.50
$\frac{1}{4}$	25%	0.25
$\frac{1}{8}$	12.5%	0.125
$\frac{1}{3}$	33%	0.33
$\frac{1}{5}$	20%	0.20
$\frac{1}{10}$	10%	0.10

Adding and subtracting decimals works in the same way as adding and subtracting whole numbers. The important thing is to line up the decimal points.

1. Three beakers in a lab are mixed together.
   The first beaker has 0.14 liters of liquid,
   the second has 1.23 liters of liquid and the
   third has 0.005 liters of liquid.

   How many total liters of liquid is this?

The golden rule of decimal addition and subtraction is line up the decimal points.

$$
\begin{array}{r}
0.14 \\
1.23 \\
+ 0.005 \\
\hline
1.375
\end{array}
$$

There is a total of 1.375 liters.

2. Mark's term paper will take him 8.25
   hours to write. He works on it for 1.75
   hours on Monday and then 3.6 hours
   on Wednesday. How many more hours
   should it take Mark to finish his term
   paper?

The question asks how many *more*, so we will need to subtract. First, however, we find out how much time Mark has spent so far by adding:

$$
\begin{array}{r}
\overset{1}{1}.75 \\
+ 3.6 \\
\hline
5.35
\end{array}
$$

Quick Note

Line up the decimal point when adding or subtracting decimals.

He has done 5.35 hours of work so far. He needs to work for a total of 8.25, so we subtract to find out how many *more* hours he has to work.

$$\begin{array}{r} \overset{7}{\cancel{8}}.\overset{1}{2}5 \\ -\ \ 5.35 \\ \hline 2.90 \end{array}$$

Mark has to work 2.9 more hours.

INTEREST

It is common to see a problem on the GED in which you calculate interest, like on money a bank account.

---

1. Gianni took out a $10,400 loan with an annual interest rate of 5.4%. What is the total amount of interest Gianni will pay in 4 years?

The formula for interest is $i = prt$, where i is the interest, p is the principal, r is the interest rate, and t is the amount of time.

In this problem:

$$p = \$10.400$$
$$r = 5.4\%$$
$$t = 4$$

To multiply by a percent such as 5.4%, we must write it as a decimal.

To convert from percent to decimal, we divide the percent by 100. To divide a number by 100, we move the decimal point two spaces to the left:

$$\frac{5.4}{100} = 0.054$$

We have to insert 0s as place holders in order to move the decimal point to the left. So

5.4% is equal to 0.054. Let's put this into the formula.

This is a good place to use your calculator.

$$i = 10,400 \times 0.054 \times 4 = 2,246.40$$

Gianni will pay $2,246.40 in interest in 4 years.

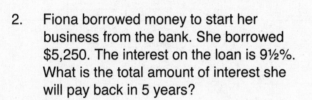

2.   Fiona borrowed money to start her business from the bank. She borrowed $5,250. The interest on the loan is 9½%. What is the total amount of interest she will pay back in 5 years?

(1) $831.25
(2) $1,662.50
(3) $2,493.75
(4) $5,748.75
(5) $49,875.00

Use the interest formula $i = prt$. In this problem:

$$p = \$5,250$$
$$r = 9\tfrac{1}{2}\%$$
$$t = 5$$

We want to divide 9½ by 100 to get the decimal equivalent. First convert 9½ to 9.5 to make the division easier:

$$\frac{9.5}{100} = 0.095$$

Let's put this into the formula: $i = \$5,250 \times 0.095 \times = \$2,493.75$.

Answer (3) is the best answer.

DECIMAL AND PERCENT DRILL

Questions 1 and 2 refer to the following graph.

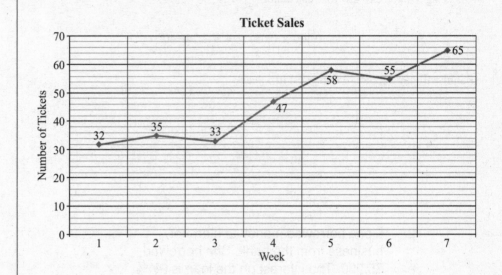

1. What was the percent increase in ticket sales from Week 6 to Week 7?

    (1)   10
    (2)   18
    (3)   30
    (4)   52
    (5)   65

2. What percent of the total number of tickets sold was sold in Week 7?

    (1)   65
    (2)   50
    (3)   25
    (4)   20
    (5)   2

3. At the school store, notebooks are $2.99 each, pens are $1.45 per box and paper is $4.50 per ream. What is the cost, before tax, to buy 3 notebooks, 2 boxes of pens, and 2 reams of paper?

(1) $2.08
(2) $2.90
(3) $8.97
(4) $19.00
(5) $20.87

4. A recipe calls for $2\frac{3}{4}$ cup of flour, 2.25 cups of chocolate chips, $1\frac{2}{5}$ cups of sugar and 0.6 cups of butter.

What is the total volume, in cups, of all the ingredients listed above?

(1)   5.4 cups

(2) $6\frac{2}{5}$ cups

(3)   7 cups

(4) $7\frac{2}{5}$ cups

(5)   7.4 cups

Questions 5 and 6 refer to the following graph.

Home States of Theatergoers

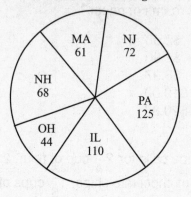

5. What percentage of theatergoers is from New Jersey (NJ)?

6. The number of theatergoers from Illinois (IL) is what percent less than the number of theatergoers from Pennsylvania (PA)?

PROPORTIONS AND RATIOS

Proportions are used to compare ratios. Ratios are numbers used in comparisons. For example, for a certain recipe you use 1 cup of water and 3 cups of sugar. The ratio of water to sugar is 1 to 3 or 1:3 or $\frac{1}{3}$. You could write a ratio in any of these three ways.

If you have a cement mixture with 2 parts aggregate and 3 parts water the ratio of aggregate to water is 2:3.

If you spend 3 hours studying math and 4 hours studying grammar, the ratio of time spent studying math to time spent studying grammar is $\frac{3}{4}$.

If your car can go 54 miles on 2 gallons of gas, the ratio of miles to gallons of gas is

$\frac{54 miles}{2 gallons}$. This reduces to $\frac{27 miles}{1 gallon}$.

Proportions come in when you compare ratios.

---

1. Felicia can bake 340 cookies in 17 hours. How long would it take her to bake 100 cookies?

To answer this question, you set up a proportion. Write each ratio in the form of a fraction. In this case, our first ratio is 300 cookies to 17 hours and our second ratio is 100 cookies to some number, x, hours.

$$\frac{340}{17} = \frac{100}{x}$$

Cross-multiply to solve:

$$\frac{340}{17} = \frac{100}{x}$$

$$1,700 = 340x$$

$$\frac{1,700}{340} = x$$

$$x = 5$$

Felicia can bake 100 cookies in 5 hours.

---

2. Maura works 48 hours per week and gets paid $540. How much does Maura get paid in a week when she works 40 hours?

Set up a proportion with what you know, using a variable (let's go with h for hours) for the unknown number.

$$\frac{48}{540} = \frac{40}{h}$$

$$48h = 21,600$$

$$h = \frac{21,600}{48}$$

$$h = 450$$

Maura earns $450 for working 40 hours. How much does she get per hour?

Set up another proportion:

$$\frac{450}{40} = \frac{x}{1}$$

$$450 = 40x$$

$$x = 11.25$$

Maura earns $11.25 per hour.

Make sure to put the same unit on top and bottom of your fractions. In other words, make sure that if you pout dollars on top in the first fraction you put dollars on top in the second fraction.

---

3. Sara walks 7 miles in 2 hours. How many miles does she walk in 15 minutes?

Be careful when you have to convert from one kind of unit to another. Here, you have to convert from hours to minutes. First, convert the ratio you are given into the ratio you want.

There are 60 minutes in 1 hour, so there are 120 minutes in 2 hours. So Sara walks 7 miles in 120 minutes. Set up a proportion now using minutes:

$$\frac{7\,miles}{120\,min} = \frac{x\,miles}{15\,min}$$

Cross multiply:

$$105 = 120x$$
$$x = \frac{105}{120} = \frac{7}{8}$$

Sara walks $\frac{7}{8}$ of a mile in 15 minutes.

PROPORTIONS DRILL

1. Selena uses 7.5 feet of ribbon for every 3 wreaths she makes. How many feet of ribbon does she use for 100 wreaths?

    (1)   2.5
    (2)   35
    (3)   75
    (4)   100
    (5)   250

2. Mike bikes 16.8 miles per hour. How far can he go in 3.2 hours?

    (1)   5.25 miles
    (2)   13.6 miles
    (3)   20 miles
    (4)   53.76 miles
    (5)   Not enough information is given.

3. Sally earns $14.50 per hour and her brother Sam earns $14.75 per hour. How much more does Sally earn in one day of work?

    (1) $0.25
    (2) $28.25
    (3) $29.25
    (4) $57.50
    (5)   Not enough information is given.

4. Ed swims 40 laps in 25 minutes. How many laps does he swim in 1 hour?

    (1)   30
    (2)   42
    (3)   80
    (4)   96
    (5)   Not enough information is given.

5. Two inches on a map represent 150 miles. If two cities on a map are 8.5 inches apart, how many miles is that?

    (1)   158.5
    (2)   300
    (3)   637.5
    (4)   800
    (5)   Not enough information is given.

MEASUREMENT AND GEOMETRY

The good news is that you do not have to remember any formulas for the GED since you are given all the formulas you will need to solve any geometry problem. However, you do have to know a few geometry facts, such as how many degrees are in a triangle (180, by the way), but with practice you'll start to recall all that information. All you really have to do for questions on measurement and geometry is remember a few basic facts and use your number operations skills (adding, subtracting, multiplying and dividing whole numbers, fractions, decimals, and percents) to solve the problem.

The more you practice geometry and refer to the formulas supplied by the GED, the more you will start to remember some of the formulas without even looking. Remember that practice makes perfect!

Another piece of good news about measurement and geometry is that you are often given a picture or diagram. That makes it much easier to understand what operations you need to perform.

Area

The formula for the area of a square or any rectangle is simply: *Area = length × width*

---

1. What is the area of the square below?

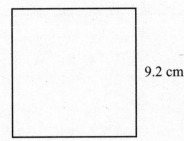

9.2 cm

All four sides of a square are equal in length. So even though the picture only labels one side of the square as being 9.2 centimeter, we know that all the sides are 9.2 centimeters. That means that the length and width = 9.2. We put this value into the formula:

$$area = \ length \times width$$
$$area = \ 9.2 \times 9.2 = 84.64$$

The area of the square is 84.64 square centimeters.

2. Karl wants to know how many square feet of carpet he needs for his room. The length of his room is 14 feet and the width is 9 feet. How many square feet of carpet does Karl need?

(1)   23
(2)   90
(3)   126
(4)   140
(5) 1,260

Use the formula:

$$area = length \times width$$
$$area = 14 \times 9 = 126$$

Choice (3) is the best answer.

The formula for the area of a triangle is $area = \frac{1}{2}bh$, where b is the length of the base of the triangle and h is the height. Remember, these formulas will be available to you. (Don't forget: The more you practice, the less you'll need to keep flipping back to the formula page.)

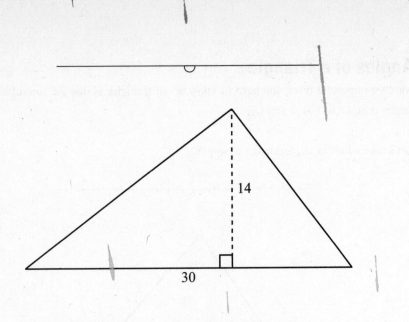

3. Felicia is painting a triangular piece of wood. The base measures 30 inches and the height is 14 inches. What is the area, in square inches, of the piece of wood?

(1) 420
(2) 300
(3) 210
(4) 150
(5) 44

As soon as you see area of a triangle, use the formula:

$$area = \frac{1}{2}bh$$

$$area = \frac{1}{2} \times 30 \times 14 = 210$$

Answer choice (3) is the best answer.

Angles of a Triangle

Another important thing you have to know about triangles is that the sum of all three angles is equal to 180 degrees.

Let's take a look at the following example:

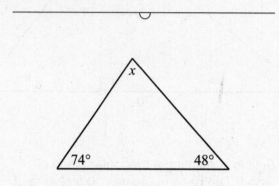

Quick Note

The sum of the three angles of a triangle is 180°.

4. One of the three internal angles of the triangle above measures 48°. Another measures 74°. What is the degree measure of the third interior angle of the triangle?

    (1) 26°
    (2) 58°
    (3) 122°
    (4) 238°
    (5) Not enough information is given.

All 3 angles must add up to 180 degrees. We know what two of the angles are, so we have to calculate the sum of those two angles to see how many degrees we already have:

$$\begin{array}{r} {\scriptstyle 1} \\ 48 \\ +\ 74 \\ \hline 122 \end{array}$$

← *Don't forget to regroup/carry the 1.*

We have 122 degrees so far and we need to get to a total of 180 degrees. Now we need to figure out how many *more* degrees we need to get to 180 degrees.

If we need to find how many *more* are needed, we need to subtract the total that we have so far, 122, from the total that we want, 180:

$$\begin{array}{r} 180 \\ - \ 122 \\ \hline 58 \end{array}$$ ← *Remember to borrow.*

Since we need 58 more degrees to get to 180, the third angle must be 58 degrees.

———————○———————

Perimeter

The formula for perimeter is given to you in the first pages of the test. The perimeter of a shape is the distance around it.

Check out the following example:

———————○———————

5.   One side of square *S* measures 12.7 centimeters. What is the perimeter of square *S* ?

To get the perimeter of square *S*, you add up the lengths of the four sides. Since all the sides of a square are equal, so you simply multiply the length of one side by 4:

$$12.7 \times 4 = 50.8$$

The perimeter of the square is 50.8 centimeters.

———————○———————

6. Gayle has at triangular garden. One side measures 15 feet, another side measures 17.8 feet, and the third side measures $20\frac{4}{5}$ feet. What is the total distance around the garden?

This is a perimeter question. We have fractions and decimals so we have to convert them all into either fractions or decimals to add. Let's do decimals:

$$15 = 15.0$$
$$17.8 = 17.8$$
$$20\frac{4}{5} = 20.8$$

Now add, using your calculator.

$$15 + 17.8 + 20.8 = 53.6$$

The distance around the whole garden is 53.6 feet.

7. Oscar is making a frame for the picture
    shown below.

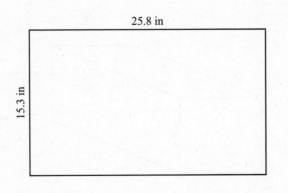

25.8 in

15.3 in

How many inches of wood does he need
for the frame?

This is also a perimeter question, but two sides aren't labeled. In a rectangle, opposite
sides are equal. The two long sides, in this case those that measure 25.8 inches, are
equal. The two short sides, that measure 15.3 inches, are also equal.

We add the lengths of all the sides together:

$$
\begin{array}{r}
25.8 \\
25.8 \\
15.3 \\
+ \quad 15.3 \\
\hline
82.2
\end{array}
$$

The total distance around the picture is 82.2 inches, so Oscar needs 82.2 inches of
wood.

Volume

Volume is how much space a three-dimensional object takes up. Imagine you are trying to fit crates into a big container. You need to figure out the *volume* of each crate, and the total volume of the container, to determine how many crates you can fit.

Say you have a big shipping crate that measures 8 feet by 9 feet by 15 feet.

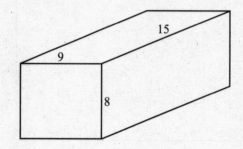

The volume of the crate is $8 \times 9 \times 15 = 1,080$ cubic feet. You simply multiply all the dimensions of an object to get its volume.

A GED question may ask how many smaller boxes you can fit in the crate. Each smaller box measures 2 feet by 3 feet by 6 feet. The volume is $2 \times 3 \times 6 = 36$ cubic feet.

How many smaller boxes can fit into the big crate? This sounds like a division problem! We divide the total cubic feet of the big crate, 1,080, by the cubic feet of each smaller box, 36:

$$36 \overline{)1,080} \quad \begin{array}{c} 30 \end{array}$$

We can put 30 smaller boxes into the big shipping crate.

8. Carrie is filling the town pool for the season. If the pool is 50 meters long, 25 meters wide, and 2 meters deep, approximately how many cubic meters of water are needed to fill the pool?

    (1)   2,500
    (2)   1,250
    (3)   1,000
    (4)   500
    (5)   100

When a problem asks for cubic meters or cubic feet or inches or anything cubic, it's a volume problem. Just multiply the dimensions: $50 \times 25 \times 2 = 2,500$. Make sure you take a moment after you use your calculator to make sure that your answer makes sense. In other words, you know that $50 \times 2 = 100$ and $50 \times 10 = 500$ and that you're multiplying 50 by numbers that are bigger than 10 and 2, so answers (4) and (5) don't make any sense. Taking that extra few moments after you answer a question to confirm that yes, that's the best answer, can save you from making mistakes.

Quick Note

When you see the word "cubic," you are looking for the volume.

Triangle Angles and Sides

There are special triangles the GED may ask you about. One is the isosceles triangle. Isosceles just means that two of the sides are equal.

This triangle is isosceles because two of its sides measure 8:

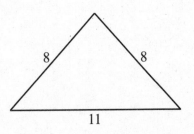

This one isn't because all three sides are different:

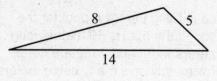

That's all there is to it—two sides are equal. When two sides of a triangle are equal, the angles *opposite* those sides are also equal.

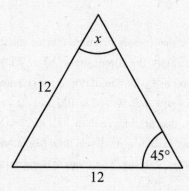

In the triangle above, since the angle opposite one of the sides that measures 12 is 45°, the angle opposite the other side that measures 12 is also 45°. In this triangle, $x = 45°$.

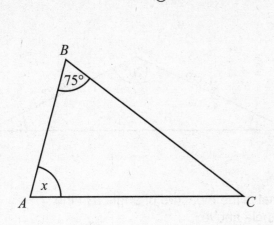

9. In the triangle above, if *AC = BC*, then what is the measure, in degrees of angle *A*?

(1) 45°
(2) 75°
(3) 90°
(4) 105°
(5) 180°

First of all, we know that answer can't be (5), because all of the angles in a triangle add up to 180°. They tell us that side *AC* is equal to side *BC*, so that means we have an isosceles triangle and the angles opposite these sides are equal. The angle opposite *AC* is 75°, so the angle opposite *BC* is also 75°. The best answer is (2).

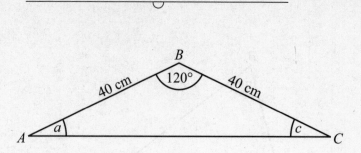

10. What is the measure of angle *a* in the triangle above?

    (1)   30°
    (2)   80°
    (3)   120°
    (4)   140°
    (5)   150°

Because $AB = BC$, angle *a* = angle *c*. All three angles of a triangle add up to 180°. If we subtract 120° from 180°, there are only 60 left, so angle a plus angle *c* must equal 60°. They are equal, so we divide 60° by 2 to get each angle measuring 30°, answer choice (1).

GEOMETRY DRILL

Questions 1 and 2 refer to the following diagram.

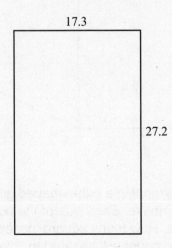

17.3

27.2

1. A carpenter is refinishing a wood floor, shown in the diagram above. She needs to know how many square meters the room is in order to buy enough varnish. What is the area, in square meters, of the room?

   (1)   459
   (2)   470.56
   (3)   544
   (4)   4,705.6
   (5)   47,056

2. The carpenter is also putting a border all around the edges of the floor and needs to know how many meters of molding she needs. What is the perimeter of the floor, in meters?

   (1)   89
   (2)   54
   (3)   44.5
   (4)   35
   (5)   34.6

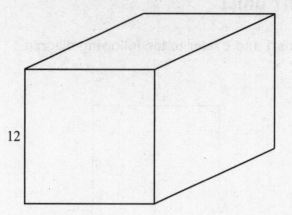

12

3. Artie is wrapping a cube-shaped gift box, pictured above. Each side of the box is a square. How many square inches of wrapping paper will he need to cover the box?

(1)   72
(2)   144
(3)   576
(4)   1,728
(5)   20,736

4. The dimensions of a rectangular box are 8 inches long by 6 inches wide by 10 inches deep. Which of the following expressions represents the volume (in cubic inches) of the box?

(1)   8 + 6 + 10
(2)   (8 + 6) × 10
(3)   8 × 6 × 10
(4)   (8 × 6) + (10 × 6)
(5)   8 × (6 + 10)

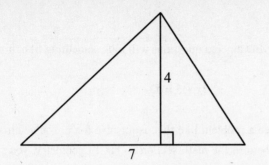

5. The triangle above has a base of 7 and a height of 4. Which of the following expressions gives the area of the triangle?

(1) $7 \times 4 \times 2$

(2) $\frac{1}{2}(7)(4)$

(3) $7 + 4 + 2$

(4) $7 + 4 + \frac{1}{2}$

(5) $\frac{1}{2}(7 + 4)$

ALGEBRA

One of the basic types of GED algebra questions will look something like this:

$$2x + 5 = 53$$

Your mission, when you see a problem like this, is to solve for x. You've already been solving for unknown numbers in the math section so far. In geometry, you solved for angles a or x. Any non-algebra math question can be turned into an algebra question just by inserting a variable (a letter that represents some unknown number).

For example, here's a problem from earlier in the section, just changed around a little:

1. Michelle's bowling scores for the past 5 weeks were: 220; 255; 190; 240; and x. If Michelle's mean score is 241, what is the value of x?

Just take what you know about how to figure out the mean (average) of a set of numbers.

First, you add them all up. Then you divide by the number of items you have.

$$mean = \frac{total}{\#\,items}$$

Plug in the values that we know. In this problem, we already know the mean, 241, and we know the number of items, 5:

$$241 = \frac{total}{5}$$

We can't figure out the total by adding all the items because one of the items is the unknown, x. But we can solve for the total using the equation above. First, we multiply both sides by 5:

$$241 \times 5 = total$$
$$1{,}205 = total$$

Now we know that all the numbers have to add up to 1,205. Let's set that up:

$$
\begin{array}{r}
220 \\
255 \\
190 \\
240 \\
+\ \ \ x \\
\hline
1{,}205
\end{array}
$$

We add what we have to simplify:

$$
\begin{array}{r}
905 \\
+ \quad x \\
\hline
1{,}205
\end{array}
$$

$$x = 300$$

The missing score is 300.

———————◯———————
———————◯———————

2. Helena takes 7 tests throughout the semester, with a mean score of *m*. The sum of all the scores on her test is 651. What is the value of *m* ?

$$mean = \frac{total}{\#\,items}$$

Just plug in what you know:

$$mean = \frac{651}{9} = 93$$

Helena's mean score, or average score, is 93, so *m* = 93.

———————◯———————
———————◯———————

3. The average snowfall in a certain town, in inches, is 3.6 inches. Eight different measurements were taken: 4.2; 1.4; 2.5; 4.4; 6.2; 4.2; 2.4; and *i*. What is the value of *i* ?

Use the formula:

$$mean = \frac{total}{\#\,items}$$

$$3.6 = \frac{total}{8}$$
$$3.6 \times 8 = 28.8$$

A total of 28.8 inches of snow fell. Now we add the numbers that we know:

$$4.2 + 1.4 + 2.5 + 4.4 + 6.2 + 4.2 + 2.4 = 25.3$$

We have a total of 28.8, so we subtract 25.3 to figure out what i is:

$$28.8 - 25.3 = 3.5$$
$$i = 3.5$$

4. $x + 12 = 10^3$

First simplify the exponent: $10^3 = 1,000$

So the problem becomes:

$$x + 12 = 1,000$$
$$x = 1,000 - 12 = 988$$
$$x = 988$$

5. Katrina mows y square feet of the lawn before breakfast. The total square footage of the lawn is 4,725 feet. She still has $\frac{2}{5}$ of the lawn left to mow after breakfast. What is the value of y?

Let's figure out how much Katrina has left to mow. She has $\frac{2}{5}$ of 4,725 square feet of lawn left. "Of" in word problems means multiply. To find $\frac{2}{5}$ of 4,725, we multiply:

$$\frac{2}{5} \times 4,725 = \frac{2}{5} \times \frac{4,725}{1} = \frac{9,450}{5} = 1,890$$

Katrina has 1,890 *left* to mow. How much did she mow already? We subtract to find that out: $4,725 - 1,890 = 2,835$. Katrina still has 2,835 square feet of lawn to mow. Hope she had a hearty breakfast.

Quick Note

"Of" in a word problem means multiply.

You may also be given equations or formulas with variables in them and asked to solve:

6. Given the formula $ab^2 + 7 = c - 10$, find c if $a = 2$ and $b = 3$.

This looks a lot harder than it is. All you do is plug the values in that you're given and solve.

$a = 2$ and $b = 3$, so put those values in:

$$2(3)^2 + 7 = c - 10$$

Now carefully perform all the mathematical operations:

$$2(9) + 7 = c - 10$$
$$18 + 7 = c - 10$$
$$28 + 7 = c$$
$$35 = c$$

Try this one:

7. If $2.5x - 2(y) = 20$, what is the value of y when $x = 8$?

Just plug in the values you are given:

$$2.5(8) - 2y = 17$$
$$20 - 2y = 17$$
$$-2y = 17 - 20$$
$$-2y = -3$$
$$y = \frac{-3}{-2} = \frac{3}{2}$$

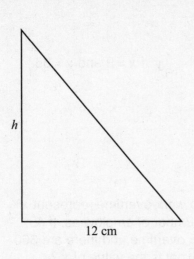

h

12 cm

8. The area of the triangle above is 36 square centimeters. What is the value of the height, *h* ?

(1)   3
(2)   4
(3)   6
(4)   8
(5)   12

You know how to figure out the area of the triangle, so write the formula for that down:

$$a = \frac{1}{2}bh$$

What values are given to us? The base, *b*, is 12 centimeters and the area, *a*, is 36 square centimeters. Plug those values in:

$$36 = \frac{1}{2}(12)h$$

Now we want to isolate *h* (get it by itself):

$$36 = \frac{1}{2}(12)h$$

$$36 = 6h$$

$$\frac{36}{6} = h$$

$$6 = h$$

Answer choice (3) is correct.

ALGEBRA DRILL

1. Evaluate $4x^3 - \dfrac{2}{5}y$ if $x = 3$ and $y = 35$.

   (1)   14
   (2)   27
   (3)   94
   (4)   108
   (5)   122

2. Workers who work overtime represent $x\%$ of the total number of employees. If 45 workers work overtime and there are 360 employees, what is the value of x?

   (1)   10
   (2)   12.5
   (3)   15
   (4)   15.75
   (5)   Not enough information is given.

3. The area of a square is 361 square centimeters. What is the length of a side, s?

   (1)   60
   (2)   45
   (3)   40.5
   (4)   24.6
   (5)   19

4. Solve for x: $25 + x^2 = 100 - 11$

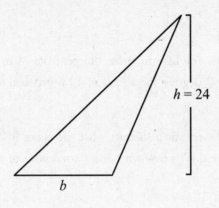

$h = 24$

b

5. The area of the triangle above is 108 square centimeters. What is the value of b?

(1) 216
(2) 54
(3) 24
(4) 9
(5) Not enough information is given.

ANSWERS AND EXPLANATIONS

Whole Number Drill

1. **(3)** Draw a number line. You have to move 3 to get from –3 to 0 and then another 7 to get to 7 degrees for a total of 10 degrees in temperature change.

2. **(5)** To find Karla's balance, you'd subtract what she spent from what she started with, but we don't know what she started with so there is not enough information.

3. **(3)** Disregard the information about Tuesday and Wednesday—this is extra info and you don't need it! We only care about the 45 + 28 cans he collected Sunday.

4. **(4)** Divide: $15\overline{)90}$ with quotient 6

5. **(4)** Add 36 + 18 = 54. Don't forget to carry the 1.

Multiplication Drill

1. **(3)** Multiply: $132 \times 48 = 6{,}336$

2. **(5)** Multiply the number of cartons of snow peas times the number of cans of snow peas in each carton: $45 \times 19 = 855$. Then multiply the number of cartons of corn times the number of cans of corn in each carton: $28 \times 70 = 1{,}960$. Add: $855 + 1{,}960 = 2{,}815$

3. **(5)** We need to know how many hours the truck travels, and this information is not given.

4. **(2)** First, multiply $70 \times 12 = 840$ cycling, $30 \times 12 = 360$ running, and $5 \times 12 = 60$ swimming. Then, add $840 + 360 + 60 = 1{,}260$.

5. **(1)** Multiply $\$145.70 \times 16 = \$2{,}331.20$.

Division Drill

1. **(3)** Divide total miles by miles per day (rate): $95\overline{)1{,}235}$, quotient 13.

2. **(1)** Divide total miles by number of days: $31\overline{)5{,}673}$, quotient 183.

3. **(3)** Divide salary by number of weeks: $52\overline{)70{,}616}$, quotient $1{,}358$.

4. **(5)** Since we need to know how many rows of 12 and 18 seats there are in the stadium, we cannot figure out how many rows of 28 seats there are in the stadium.

5. **(4)** Divide total inches grown by number of years: $17\overline{)3.4}$, quotient 0.2.

Average, Mean, and Median Drill

1. **(3)** First, add the number of sit-ups: $28 + 27 + 30 + 30 + 31 + 32 + 25 = 203$. Then, divide the total by 7 days: $7\overline{)203}$, quotient 29.

2. **(3)** Write the running times in order from least to greatest: 10.9; 11.1; 11.2; 11.5; 11.5; 12.1; 12.2. The number in the middle, 11.5, is the median.

3. **(2)** Add the number of customers: $20 + 23 + 48 + 55 + 63 + 58 + 32 + 30 + 40 = 369$.

   Divide by the number of hours, 9: $9\overline{)369}$, quotient 41.

4. **(4)** Add the scores: $220 + 255 + 190 + 240 + 300 = 1{,}205$. Divide by 5 weeks: $5\overline{)1{,}205}$, quotient 241.

5. **(3)** Write the scores in order from greatest to least: 21; 27; 38; 43; 54; 62; 68; 71. Average the two middle scores: $\dfrac{43 + 54}{2} = \dfrac{97}{2} = 48.5$

Exponents and Square Roots Drill

1. $3^3 = 27$

2. $\sqrt{25} = 5$

3. $\sqrt{81} = 9$

4. $9^3 = 729$

5. $\sqrt{225} = 15$

6. $23^2 = 529$

7. $19^3 = 6{,}859$

8. $\sqrt{2{,}025} = 45$

9. $\sqrt{4{,}624} = 68$

10. $33^2 = 1{,}089$

Fractions Drill

1. **(4)** First, convert each mixed number into an improper fraction:

   $$10\frac{3}{4} = \frac{43}{4} \qquad 3\frac{1}{3} = \frac{10}{3}$$

   Then, convert each fraction so it has a common denominator (for this case we'll use 12):

   $$\frac{43}{4} = \frac{129}{12} \qquad \frac{10}{3} = \frac{40}{12}$$

   Finally, subtract: $\dfrac{129}{12} - \dfrac{40}{12} = \dfrac{89}{12} = 7\dfrac{5}{12}$

2. **(2)** Convert each mixed number to an improper fraction:

   $$36\frac{3}{4} = \frac{147}{4} \qquad 40\frac{1}{4} = \frac{161}{4}$$

   Then subtract: $\dfrac{161}{4} - \dfrac{147}{4} = \dfrac{14}{4} = 3\dfrac{2}{4} = 3\dfrac{1}{2}$

3. **(3)** Convert each mixed number to an improper fraction. Use 15 as the common denominator:

   $$3\frac{1}{3} = \frac{10}{3} = \frac{50}{15} \qquad\qquad 1\frac{2}{5} = \frac{7}{5} = \frac{21}{15} \qquad \frac{7}{15}$$

   Add: $\dfrac{50}{15} + \dfrac{21}{15} + \dfrac{7}{15} = \dfrac{78}{15} = 5\dfrac{3}{15} = 5\dfrac{1}{5}$

4. **(4)** Multiply: $\dfrac{2}{5} \times 2 \times 9 = \dfrac{2}{5} \times \dfrac{2}{1} \times \dfrac{9}{1} = \dfrac{36}{5} = 7\dfrac{1}{5}$

5. **(5)** We don't know how many elephants there are so we can't figure out how much each elephant gets.

Decimal and Percent Drill

Questions 1 and 2 refer to the following graph.

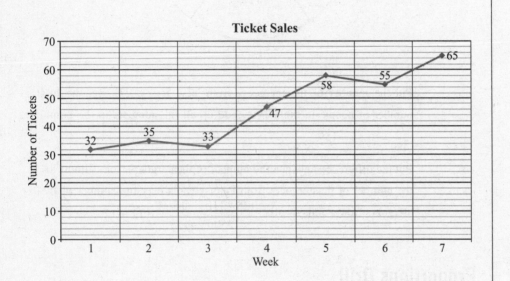

1. **(2)** Put the change over the original number: $\dfrac{10}{55} \cong 0.18 = 18\%$

2. **(4)** Put the number sold in week 7 over the total number of tickets sold:

   $\dfrac{65}{325} = 0.2 = 20\%$

3. **(5)** Multiply $2.99 \times 3 = \$8.97$, $\$1.45 \times 2 = \$2.90$ and $\$4.50 \times 2 = \$9.00$

   Add: $\$8.97 + \$2.90 + \$9.00 = \$20.87$

4. **(3)** Convert $2\dfrac{3}{4}$ to 2.75 and $1\dfrac{2}{5}$ to 1.4 and then add:
   $2.75 + 2.25 + 1.4 + 0.6 = 7$

Questions 5 and 6 refer to the following graph.

Home States of Theatergoers

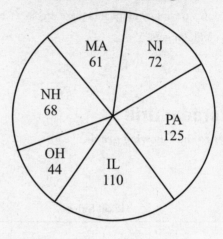

5.   Put the number of theater goers from New Jersey, 72, over the total number of people in the survey (add up all the numbers in the graph): $\frac{72}{480} = 0.15 = 15\%$

6.   Put the difference between the number of theatergoers from Illinois and the number of theatergoers from Pennsylvania over the number of theatergoers from Pennsylvania: $\frac{125 - 110}{125} = \frac{15}{125} = 0.12 = 12\%$

Proportions Drill

1. **(5)** Set up a proportion: $\frac{7.5}{3} = \frac{x}{100}$. Cross multiply to solve:

$750 = 3x$
$x = 250$

2. **(4)** Set up a proportion: $\frac{16.8}{1} = \frac{x}{3.2}$. Cross multiply to solve:

$16.8 \times 3.2 = 1x$
$x = 53.76$

3. **(5)** We don't know how many hours Sally or Sam works in one day so we don't have enough information.

4. **(4)** First, convert 1 hour to 60 minutes. Then, set up a proportion: $\dfrac{40}{25} = \dfrac{x}{60}$

Cross multiply to solve:

$40 \times 60 = 25x$

$2{,}400 = 25x$

$x = 96$

5. **(3)** Set up a proportion: $\dfrac{2}{150} = \dfrac{8.5}{x}$

Cross multiply to solve:

$2x = 8.5 \times 150$

$2x = 1{,}275$

$x = 637.5$

Geometry Drill

1. **(2)** Multiply the length by the width: $17.3 \times 27.2 = 470.56$.

2. **(1)** Add up the lengths of all 4 sides: $17.3 + 17.3 + 27.2 + 27.2 = 89$.

3. **(4)** Multiply the length by the width by the height: $12 \times 12 \times 12 = 1{,}728$.

4. **(3)** Multiply the length by the width by the height: $8 \times 6 \times 10$

5. **(2)** Multiply one-half the base times the height: $\dfrac{1}{2}(7)(4)$

Algebra Drill

1. **(3)** Plug in the values given:

$$4x^3 - \frac{2}{5}y$$

$$4(3^3) - \frac{2}{5}(35)$$

$$4(27) - \frac{2}{5}\left(\frac{35}{1}\right)$$

$$108 - \frac{70}{5} = 108 - 14 = 94$$

2. **(2)** Put the number of workers who work overtime over the total number of workers: $\dfrac{45}{360} = 0.125 = 12.5\%$

3. **(5)** Recall that the area of a square is the side, s, multiplied by the side or s^2. Set s^2 equal to 361 and solve:

$$s^2 = 361$$
$$s = \sqrt{361} = 19$$

4. Isolate x:

$$25 + x^2 = 100 - 11$$
$$x^2 = 100 - 11 - 25$$
$$x^2 = 64$$
$$x = \sqrt{64} = 8$$

5. **(4)** Use the formula for area of a triangle: $area = \dfrac{1}{2}bh$

The area is given as 108 and the height is given as 24. Plug in these values and solve for b:

$$108 = \frac{1}{2}b(24)$$
$$216 = b(24)$$
$$\frac{216}{24} = b$$
$$9 = b$$

ARITHMETIC DRILL

Part I

1. Fiona is making a frame for the square
    photo shown below

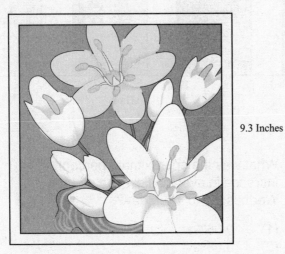

9.3 Inches

How many inches of molding does she
need?

(1)   9.3
(2)   18.6
(3)   27.9
(4)   37.2
(5)   Not enough information is given.

Question 2 refers to the following graph.

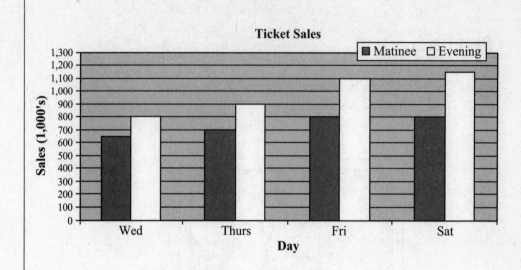

2. What was the approximate percent increase in evening ticket sales from Wednesday to Thursday?

    (1)   0.05%
    (2)   0.08%
    (3)   12.5%
    (4)   22%
    (5)   25%

3. On a map, $1\frac{1}{2}$ inches represent 80 miles. Fulton City is 9 inches from Dalton on the map. What is the actual distance from Fulton City to Dalton in miles?

   (1)   90
   (2)   160
   (3)   480
   (4)   720
   (5) 1,080

4. Corrine took out a loan of $1,200 for 2 years at a rate of 8% annual interest. How much total interest will Corrine owe?

   (1) $8.00
   (2) $16.00
   (3) $24.00
   (4) $96.00
   (5) $192.00

Questions 5 and 6 refer to the graph below.

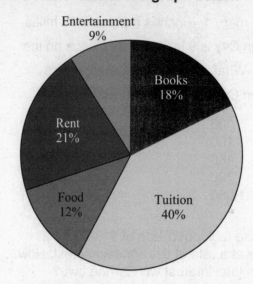

5. Yvonne has a total budget of $6,800 per semester. The percentage of her total budget spent on different expenses is shown in the graph above. How much does Yvonne spend on rent per semester?

   (1) $1,428.00
   (2) $1,360.00
   (3) $1,224.00
   (4) $816.00
   (5)   Not enough information is given.

6. How much does Yvonne spend on food and entertainment?

   (1) $612.00
   (2) $816.00
   (3) $1,428.00
   (4) $2,856.00
   (5) $6,936.00

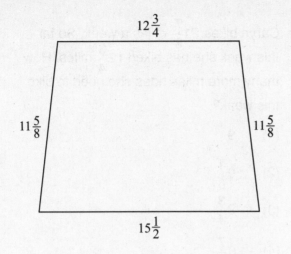

$12\frac{3}{4}$

$11\frac{5}{8}$ $11\frac{5}{8}$

$15\frac{1}{2}$

7. Terrence is building a fence to put around his flower garden, shown in the diagram above. What is the total distance around the garden in feet?

(1) $48\frac{3}{4}$

(2) 49

(3) $51\frac{1}{2}$

(4) 53

(5) $54\frac{1}{4}$

8. When Carlos left for school, the thermometer read −2.7 degrees. When he got back, it read 11.5 degrees. How many degrees warmer was it when Carlos got back from school?

(1) 8.8
(2) 11.5
(3) 13.5
(4) 14.2
(5) 15

9. Caryn bikes $21\frac{7}{8}$ miles a week. So far this week she has biked $12\frac{3}{4}$ miles. How many more miles does she need to bike this week?

(1) 9

(2) $9\frac{1}{8}$

(3) $9\frac{3}{4}$

(4) $9\frac{7}{8}$

(5) $10\frac{1}{8}$

10. The square root of 28 is between which of the following?

(1) 2.8 and 3.0
(2) 3 and 4
(3) 4.5 and 5.0
(4) 5 and 6
(5) 13 and 15

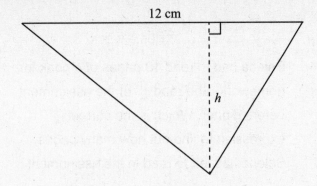

11. The area of the triangle above is 48 square centimeters. What is the value of the height, h?

    (1)   4
    (2)   8
    (3)   12
    (4)   24
    (5)   Not enough information is given.

12. Tasteful Tees sold 124 t-shirts on Tuesday and 214 t-shirts on Wednesday. It received a shipment of 250 t-shirts Wednesday night and sold another 196 t-shirts Thursday. How many t-shirts were left in stock at the end of the day Thursday?

    (1)   588
    (2)   338
    (3)   142
    (4)   54
    (5)   Not enough information is given.

13. Given the formula $2x^3 \div 8 = \frac{1}{2}yz$, find x if $y = 8$ and $z = 4$.

Part II

14. Selena had to read 18 pages of a book for homework. She read $\frac{1}{3}$ of the assignment before dinner. Which is the correct expression to find out how many pages Selena has left to read in the assignment?

   (1) $18 \times \frac{1}{3}$

   (2) $\frac{1}{3} + 18$

   (3) $18 - \frac{1}{3}$

   (4) $18 \div \left(\frac{1}{3} \times 18\right)$

   (5) $18 - \left(\frac{1}{3} \times 18\right)$

15. A delivery truck has 480 square feet of capacity. A company needs to put boxes in the truck measuring $4'' \times 1'' \times 3''$ feet. Which of the following expressions can be used to find out how many boxes the company can fit in the truck?

   (1) $480 \times 4 \times 1 \times 3$
   (2) $480 \div (4 + 1 + 3)$
   (3) $480 \div (4 \times 1 \times 3)$
   (4) $480 + 4 + 1 + 3$
   (5) $(480 \times 4) + (480 \times 1) + (480 \times 3)$

Question 16 refers to the following graph.

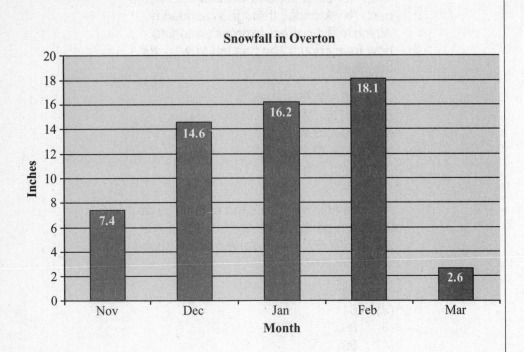

Snowfall in Overton

16. How many more inches of snow did Overton get in January than in December?

   (1) 1.4
   (2) 1.6
   (3) 1.9
   (4) 2.4
   (5) 2.6

17. A rectangular sign is 18 inches long and 10 inches wide. Which is the correct expression to find the area of the sign in square inches?

   (1) 18×10
   (2) $18 \times 10 \times 18 \times 10$
   (3) $18 + 10 + 18 + 10$
   (4) $18^2 + 10^2$
   (5) $18^2 + (10 \times 2)$

18. Nancy has to work 30 hours per week to keep her benefits. She worked 3.75 hours each day Monday through Wednesday. Which is the correct expression to find how many hours she has left to work for the week?

(1) $30 - 3.75$
(2) 3.75×3
(3) $30 - (3.75 \times 3)$
(4) $30 + (3.75 \times 3)$
(5) $3.75 \times 5 + 30$

19. A police officer records the speeds of cars that pass on the highway: 58, 63, 65, 59, 56, 66, 70, 67. What is the median speed of these cars?

(1) 63
(2) 64
(3) 65
(4) 66
(5) 67

20. Which of the following expressions can be used to find how many $\frac{1}{8}$-pound baggies of candy can be filled using $8\frac{1}{2}$ pounds of candy?

(1) $8\frac{1}{2} + \frac{1}{8}$

(2) $8\frac{1}{2} \div \frac{1}{8}$

(3) $8\frac{1}{2} \times \frac{1}{8}$

(4) $8\frac{1}{2} \div 8$

(5) $8\frac{1}{2} + \frac{1}{8}$

Question 21 is based on the following figure.

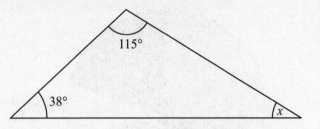

21. One of the three internal angles of the triangle above measures 115° and another measures 38°. What is the degree measure of the third angle, *x* ?

(1) 27°
(2) 38°
(3) 50°
(4) 153°
(5) 180°

22. Katie has an average test score of 89 so far on the first five math tests. Her scores on the first five tests were: 79, 95, 90, 88, and *x*. What is the value of *x* ?

(1) 82
(2) 88
(3) 90
(4) 93
(5) Not enough information is given.

23. Yanique and Akil collected $225 for the benefit on Sunday. Monday they collected $175. What was the approximate percent decrease in the amount of money they collected from Sunday to Monday?

(1) 50
(2) 30
(3) 28
(4) 22
(5) 15

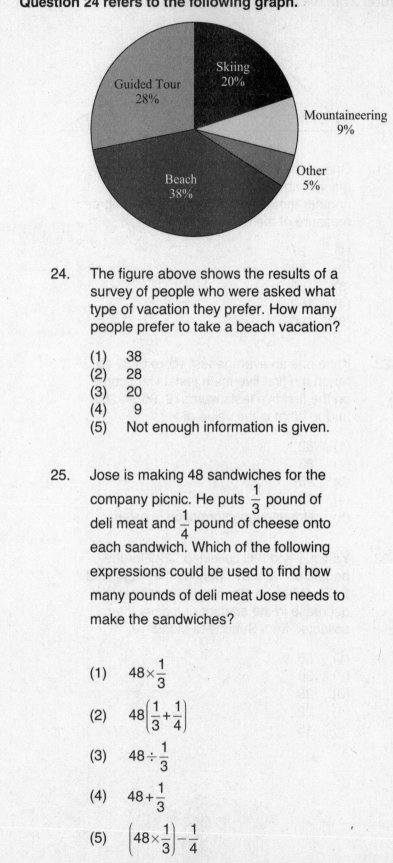

24. The figure above shows the results of a survey of people who were asked what type of vacation they prefer. How many people prefer to take a beach vacation?

(1)   38
(2)   28
(3)   20
(4)   9
(5)   Not enough information is given.

25. Jose is making 48 sandwiches for the company picnic. He puts $\frac{1}{3}$ pound of deli meat and $\frac{1}{4}$ pound of cheese onto each sandwich. Which of the following expressions could be used to find how many pounds of deli meat Jose needs to make the sandwiches?

(1) $48 \times \frac{1}{3}$

(2) $48\left(\frac{1}{3} + \frac{1}{4}\right)$

(3) $48 \div \frac{1}{3}$

(4) $48 + \frac{1}{3}$

(5) $\left(48 \times \frac{1}{3}\right) - \frac{1}{4}$

Chapter 12
Arithmetic
Drill Answers

ANSWERS AND EXPLANATIONS

Drill Part I

1. **(4)**   Because the photo is square, all sides are equal so they are all 9.3 inches. Multiply $9.3 \times 4 = 37.2$.

2. **(3)**   For percent increase you put the difference, 100, over the original number, 800: $\dfrac{100}{800} = 0.125 = 12.5\%$.

3. **(3)**   Set up a proportion, changing $1\dfrac{1}{2}$ to 1.5: $\dfrac{1.5 inches}{80 miles} = \dfrac{9 inches}{x miles}$. Cross multiply to solve:

    $$1.5x = 720$$

    $$x = \frac{720}{1.5} = 480$$

4. **(5)**   Use the formula $i = prt$, where $p = 1{,}200$, $r = 0.08$ and $t = 2$.

    $i = 1{,}200 \times 0.08 \times 2 = 192$.

5. **(1)**   Multiply the total budget, 6,800, by the percent spent on rent in fractional form, $\dfrac{21}{100}$: $6{,}800 \times \dfrac{21}{100} = \dfrac{6{,}800}{1} \times \dfrac{21}{100} = \dfrac{142{,}800}{100} = 1{,}428$.

6. **(3)**   First, add the percentages: $9\% + 12\% = 21\%$. Then, multiply the total budget by the fractional form of the percent. You may notice that this is the same percent spent on rent alone, so you get the same number, 1,428.

7. **(3)**   Convert the fractions into improper fractions with the common denominator, 8: $12\dfrac{3}{4} = \dfrac{51}{4} = \dfrac{102}{8}$, $15\dfrac{1}{2} = \dfrac{31}{2} = \dfrac{124}{8}$, $11\dfrac{5}{8} = \dfrac{93}{8}$.

    Don't forget that we have 2 sides that are $11\dfrac{5}{8}$ or $\dfrac{93}{8}$.

    Add: $\dfrac{102}{8} + \dfrac{124}{8} + \dfrac{93}{8} + \dfrac{93}{8} = \dfrac{412}{8} = 51\dfrac{4}{8} = 51\dfrac{1}{2}$

8. **(4)**   Draw a number line. You have to move 2.7 degrees to get to 0 and then another 11.5 degrees to get to 11.5 so you add: $2.7 + 11.5 = 14.2$.

9. **(2)**   Convert both fractions to improper fractions with denominators of 8: $21\dfrac{7}{8} = \dfrac{175}{8}$, $12\dfrac{3}{4} = 12\dfrac{6}{8} = \dfrac{102}{8}$. Subtract: $\dfrac{175}{8} - \dfrac{102}{8} = \dfrac{73}{8} = 9\dfrac{1}{8}$.

10. **(4)** Think about the perfect square number that is closest to 28, which is 25. The square root of 25 is 5, so the square root of 28 is a little more than 25, between 5 and 6.

11. **(2)** Use the formula for area of a triangle and fill in what's given:

$$area = \frac{1}{2}bh$$

$$48 = \frac{1}{2}(12)h$$

$$48 = 6h$$

$$\frac{48}{6} = h = 8$$

12. **(5)** We don't know how many t-shirts Tasteful Tees had before Tuesday, so we cannot figure out how many were left on Thursday.

13. Plug the values in and solve:

$$2x^3 \div 8 = \frac{1}{2}(8)(4)$$

$$2x^3 \div 8 = 16$$

$$2x^3 = 128$$

$$x^3 = \frac{128}{2} = 64$$

$$x^3 = 64$$

$$x = 4$$

Drill Part II

14. **(5)** You have to calculate $\frac{1}{3}$ of 18 to see how much Selena read so far: $18 \times \frac{1}{3} = \frac{18}{1} \times \frac{1}{3} = \frac{18}{3} = 6$ and then subtract from 18.

15. **(3)** You have to divide the capacity of the truck, 480, by the volume of each box, which is $4 \times 1 \times 3$.

16. **(2)** Subtract the number of inches of snow in December, 14.6, from the amount in January, 16.2: $16.2 - 14.6 = 1.6$

17. **(1)** Area of a rectangle = *length* $\times$ *width*. Plug in the values 18×10.

18. **(3)** Subtract the number of hours Nancy worked on the 3 days from Monday to Wednesday: 3.75×3, from 30.

19. **(2)** Write the numbers in order from least to greatest: 56, 58, 59, 63, 65, 66, 67, 70. Average the two middle numbers: $\dfrac{63+65}{2} = \dfrac{128}{2} = 64$.

20. **(2)** To find how many bags, divide the total number of pounds, $8\dfrac{1}{2}$, by how much goes in each bag, $\dfrac{1}{8}$.

21. **(1)** The three angles of a triangle add up to 180. Subtract (115 + 38) = 153 from 180: 180 − 153 = 27.

22. **(4)** To find the average, you add all the numbers and divide by the number of items:

$$\frac{79+95+90+88+x}{5} = 89$$
$$\frac{352+x}{5} = 89$$
$$352 + x = 89 \times 5 = 445$$
$$352 + x = 445$$
$$x = 445 - 352 = 93$$

23. **(4)** Percent decrease is the amount of the change over the original number: $\dfrac{50}{225} = 0.22 = 22\%$

24. **(5)** To find a percent of a number, you must know what the total is. We are not given any actual total or numbers, so we cannot figure out how many people prefer the beach.

25. **(1)** Jose is putting $\dfrac{1}{3}$ pound in 48 sandwiches, so we multiply. The fact that he puts $\dfrac{1}{4}$ pound of cheese in the sandwiches is extra information that we don't need.

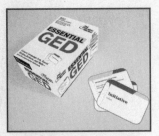